Ministering to Youth

A Strategy for the 80's

edited by
David
Roadcup

STANDARD PUBLISHING
Cincinnati, Ohio   88582

Textbooks by Standard Publishing:

The Christian Minister
Sam E. Stone
Introduction to Christian Education
Eleanor Daniel, John W. Wade, Charles Gresham
Ministering to Youth
David Roadcup, editor

Commentary on Acts
J. W. McGarvey
The Equipping Ministry
Paul Benjamin
Essays on New Testament Christianity
C. Robert Wetzel, editor
The Fourfold Gospel
J. W. McGarvey and P. Y. Pendleton
The Jesus Years
Thomas D. Thurman
How to Understand the Bible
Knofel Staton
Teach With Success
Guy P. Leavitt, revised by Eleanor Daniel

Library of Congress Cataloging in Publication Data

Ministering to youth.

Bibliography: p. 213
Includes index.
1. Church work with youth—addresses, essays, lectures. 2. Church work with young adults—addresses, essays, lectures. I. Roadcup, David.
BV4447.M53   259'.2   79-92586
ISBN   0-87239-395-X

to the glory of God
and to the trustees,
            administration,
            faculty,
            staff,
      and sons and daughters
of Ozark Bible College
in Joplin, Missouri
—a school with vision.

Contents

Introduction

Ralph Waldo Emerson said, "What the tender and poetic youth dreams today, is tomorrow public opinion, and the day after is the character of nations."

The young people of today's church are the church of tomorrow. The youth who are lurking in our youth groups and Sunday-school classes are the ministers, leaders, evangelists, elders, teachers, and visionaries for the rest of this century and the first half of the next. How important for us, then, to devote much love, prayer, man-hours, and finances to the development of the young people in our homes and churches!

The field of youth ministry has dramatically come to the fore in the decades of the 60's and 70's. The emergence of youth consciousness in our culture has spilled over into the church. On many fronts, this awareness is good. More Bible teaching opportunities, retreats, social events, camps, youth choirs, drama troupes, and youth workers are available than ever before.

Because of this growth of interest in youth work in the church, and because of the comparatively small amount of literature written on the subject, this volume has been assembled. It is a useful tool for those professional ministers already serving in churches, for those who are preparing in the formal classroom, and for the volunteer adult workers of the church.

The first chapters of this book deal with the development of the youth culture, the personal life of the youth worker, and the main goals of youth ministry.

The chapter entitled "Practical Structures for Reaching the Goal" deals with the vital experiences that lead young people to a mature relationship with Christ. Each of these experiences should be carefully prepared and executed for maximum growth and effect in the lives of the young people with whom you are working.

Additional sections of the book deal with practical areas such as the development of a functioning adult volunteer staff, ministry management, leadership development, age group characteristics, activity suggestions, and resources.

On behalf of the authors, it is our collective prayer that this book will strengthen and enhance your ministry to the greatest natural resource of the church today—the young people.

David Roadcup
Joplin, Missouri

Contributors

Dick Alexander is Associate Minister with First Christian Church, Anaheim, California; he also lectures in Christian Education at Pacific Christian College, Fullerton, California.

Les Christie is Youth Minister at Eastside Christian Church in Fullerton, California; he also lectures in Christian Education at Pacific Christian College.

Ed Fine is Minister of Education with Central Christian Church, St. Petersburg, Florida, and administrator for the Central Christian Church Day School.

Andy Hansen is Associate Minister with Kentwood Christian Church, Grand Rapids, Michigan.

Richard Hargrove is Associate Professor of Music at Kentucky Christian College, Grayson, Kentucky.

Richard Hicks is Minister of Children's Education with Chapel Rock Christian Church, Indianapolis, Indiana.

Don Hinkle is Associate Minister at Central Christian Church, San Jose, California. He also teaches Old Testament at San Jose Bible College.

Randy Kirk is Youth Minister and Minister of Education at First Christian Church, Elizabethton, Tennessee.

Dan Lawson is Associate Minister with First Christian Church, Dodge City, Kansas.

Ron Mobley is Minister with First Christian Church of Boca Raton, Florida.

Roy Reiswig is Associate Minister at Eastview Christian Church, Bloomington, Illinois.

Wayne Rice is Minister with Milford Christian Church, Milford, Kentucky.

David Roadcup taught Youth Ministry at Ozark Bible College, Joplin, Missouri. He has since been appointed Dean of Students at Cincinnati Bible College, Cincinnati, Ohio.

Paul Schlieker is Youth Minister at First Christian Church, Longmont, Colorado.

Gene Shepherd is Youth Minister with Lincoln Christian Church, Lincoln, Illinois.

Gerald Tiffin is Associate Professor of Social Science at Pacific Christian College, Fullerton, California.

David Wheeler is Youth Minister with the Church of Christ in Converse, Indiana.

Part One

YOUTH MINISTRY
TODAY

Section Outline

1. Youth Culture Today: Backgrounds and Prospects
   A. From Agrarian to Post-Industrial Society
   B. The Role of Change
   C. American Youth
   D. Into the 70's
   E. An Analysis of Contemporary Youth
   F. Into the Future
   G. Christian Responses and Reactions

2. The Person of the Youth Minister
   A. His Relationship With God
   B. His Relationship With His Family
   C. Time for Himself

3. The Goal of Youth Ministry
   A. Seeing the Goal
   B. Characteristics of Implementation

4. Practical Structures for Reaching the Goal
   A. Discipling for Depth
      1. Principles of Discipling
      2. Getting Started
   B. A Creative Approach to Effective Bible Study
      1. Bible Study and Exposure to Bible Content
      2. Types of Bible Learning Activities
   C. *Koinonia* (Fellowship) in Process
      1. Bibical Precedent
      2. Practical Application
   D. Authentic Service by the Youth Group
      1. Some Possible Service Projects

1

Youth Culture Today: Backgrounds and Prospects

by Gerald C. Tiffin

As you read, think about these questions:
—How are today's young people like the youth in classical times, and how are they different?
—What historical changes have created and altered the period we now call adolescence?
—How do contemporary subcultures form, and how do they function?
—How can a youth leader *most effectively* respond to the situation in which Christian young people find themselves?

I see no hope for the future of our people today if they are dependent on the frivolous youth of today, for certainly all youth are reckless beyond words. . . . When I was a boy, we were taught to be discreet and respectful of elders, but the present youth are exceedingly wise and impatient of restraint.   —attributed to Hesiod

Young men have strong passions and tend to gratify them indiscriminately. . . . They are changeable and fickle in their desires, which are violent while they last, but quickly over. . . . They think they know everything, and are always quite sure about it; this, in fact, is why they overdo everything.[1]   —Aristotle

These ancient quotations probably strike us as very modern. They certainly remind us that contemporary adult complaints about youth are hardly new. Ours is not the first and undoubtedly not the last generation to complain about youth. Generational differences and conflicts have been historically understood as typical and normal, something to be expected and endured.

The situation in which youth find themselves today is exactly the same as youthful generations past, and yet exactly different. Today's youth share with their historical predecessors the need to distance themselves from the parental and adult generation as a means of self-definition and the establishment of personal and separate identity. Thus, it is appropriate to speak of "generation gap" and "intergenerational conflict" as a normal part of life, and something out of which the young grow as they take on the responsibilities of an occupation, a marriage, and a mortgage. Therefore, youth culture can be viewed, correctly, as the means by which youth achieve reinforcement and temporary identity as they travel the harrowing trip from childhood to adulthood.

If this scenario was as simple and closed as so far explained, this chapter would need occupy only a short moment of the reader's time. Youth leaders would need only to understand and endure the temporary tantrums and rebellion of the young as they separate from home and establish themselves as full-fledged adults.

The understanding that youth have always, and will always, need to distance themselves from adults, even though only temporarily, does not totally explain modern youth culture. In the last 200 years, Western industrialized societies have witnessed the development of adolescence, a stage of life unknown before modern times. Youth now form what sociologists term a *subculture*, rather than just moving directly from childhood to adulthood as the young used to do. The term "generation gap" has been used often in recent years to describe tensions and conflicts between parents and teenagers. Growing numbers of youth postpone occupational choices—sometimes into their late twenties. Many young people claim that they don't know who they are. While youth today find themselves in exactly the same situation as did the youth of ancient Greece, that predicament is true only in certain dimensions of life. In fact, youth today find the challenges of life exactly different from those in Greece so long ago.

Nothing is as practical as good theory. Effective ministry

to youth must begin with an adequate understanding of youth and a concept of how historical time has affected individual time. When we understand how youth culture has changed in response to changing history, we come to appreciate the new as well as the old dilemmas of youth.

From Agrarian to Post-Industrial Society

Youth in Agrarian-Preindustrial Societies

Adolescence is a very recent phenomenon in history, dating back only to the nineteenth century and the maturing of industrialism in Europe and America. Prior to the development of industrialism, most families raised their children in agricultural settings. In such environments, the cycle of life moved relatively undisturbed from childhood to adulthood. That cycle included a vague few years when the person was not really a child, but certainly not quite adult. Society even then recognized that for a time a period of youth existed, but such a period from age ten to fifteen or sixteen was rarely considered a problem, and did not usually include the kind of storm and stress so often associated with modern adolescence.[2]

In some non-Western tribal agrarian societies, a rite of passage conferred the status of adulthood upon a youth with accompanying public acceptance and recognition of that attainment. Such a new status included privileges such as well-defined work roles, sexual rights, and territorial claims. In many Western societies, early marriage, the ability to work physically, the assumption of economic independence, or the early death of parents served as an informal but functional rite of passage. The movement from childhood into adult status was less complicated, more clearly defined, and more easily achieved than in the twentieth century.

More often than not, the movement of the youth into adult status was determined by the family economic and social situation, birth order, or social demand. This well-defined and predictable life cycle prevented anxiety over "What will I be when I grow up?" That was usually determined for the young person long before such a decision became necessary. Work roles were clearly defined and easily achieved, and, in general, the culture offered a harmonious message and instruction to the growing child. Youth viewed parents as appropriate models of their future, since youth expected to inherit a similar world, land, and life, relatively unchanged. Parents raised children anticipating that their children (and grandchildren) would live in a world basically the same as theirs, creating continuity between generations.

There was no need for excessive anxiety over life roles or expectations in a world that changed very slowly, and in which religious and political leaders viewed life in static and unchanging terms. Such a world neither fostered nor needed adolescents. By the eighteenth century, however, life was changing.

Youth in Industrial Societies

As factories replaced home cottage industries, as the steam engine replaced horsepower, and as tenement housing replaced the family farm, youth were deeply affected, first in England and continental Europe, then in America. Often children and teenagers worked long hours to help make ends meet. Even at that, youth felt uneasy. Girls would still grow to marry and bake bread, their destiny tied to marriage, but boys would grow to manhood unsure of their future. In this world, families no longer could guarantee a work role.

Interestingly, industrialism often forced youth to spend excessive idle time at home—usually until marriage. This extended time, coupled with frustration regarding work and economic security, tended to heighten generational distance and conflict because intimate daily interactions with parents led to arguments and conflict over freedom, money, and leisure—issues that normally didn't emerge in rural societies—as roles and life situations developed more naturally and earlier in the life cycle. The time of steady and rhythmic movement from childhood to adulthood thus ended with the coming of industrial society.

Industrialism breeds adolescence because it delays adult status. Work roles become more refined and specialized, often requiring extended education. Physical strength doesn't always suffice to secure a job—required education delays marriage, job entry, and adult status. This problem is referred to as the *discontinuity of statuses*. It constitutes one important origin of modern adolescence. Additionally, industrial societies foster adolescence because they do not provide consistent cultural instruction concerning values and beliefs—a necessary prerequisite to adult identity. Parents in industrial societies compete directly with schools, media, civic leaders, youth peers, and even other families, all or any of which may promote different or contradictory values. These forces confuse the teenager in regard to morality, standards, and values.

The inability to easily achieve a role in the work force, and mixed messages from the larger culture, conspire to induce uncertainty and confusion as to a youth's identity. Adulthood seems distant and difficult to achieve. Since industrial societies do not provide rites of passage apart from marriage and permanent work roles, youth find themselves rebuffed in their attempts to quickly fit into adult society. At best, they face delays. These delays with their accompanying frustrations are part of adolescence.

When youth cannot move easily or with precision into adulthood, they create a world (subculture) of their own that provides them with a temporary sense of identity, companionship, and meaning. What the adult or "parent" culture cannot deliver, youth find in their peers. Adolescence comes to be the time of turning to other teens for mutual reinforcement, when parents, adults, and society are unable to completely meet these very real needs. Youth subcultures have taken many forms, from urban lower class "gang" groupings to upper middle class drug and counter cultures. Each has served to meet age-specific needs of youth.

Post-Industrial Society

The United States moved to a post-industrial situation earlier and more fully than any other nation. Most of its labor force no longer manufactures and processes essential goods, since fewer persons are needed to produce these goods. As incomes and standards of living escalated, consumers demanded more services. Most of the labor force is now employed in service fields such as health, education, entertainment, sports, scientific research, finance, and recreation.

If industrial societies produce adolescents, then post-industrial societies intensify the conflicts and confusion experienced by adolescents in industrial societies.[3] Post-industrial societies feature a highly refined and specialized socioeconomic structure, which changes rapidly, thereby appearing vague in the eyes of adolescents. This complex economic structure demands a high degree of education and sophistication for work roles, which leads to a longer period of education before entering the work force, which in turn further delays youthful entry into adulthood. Education is extended, marriage is delayed, and youth wonder when and where they will fit in. Parents wonder when, and if, their children will ever "settle down."

The social structure isn't prepared to receive adolescents into the job market, particularly without a college education. High school and college serve not only as preparatory institutions for adult work roles, but also as waiting (custodial) stations for adolescents not ready for adult roles.

In post-industrial societies, identity is not achieved without considerable struggle in the face of conflicting messages from media, church, family, and school. Mass media, public schools, national entertainment and sports celebrities, and peers transmit values that contradict parental and family values. This mixture of cultural messages creates intense confusion and prevents development of a strong identity and feeling of purpose.[4] Personal identity is more likely to be linked to a specific occupation or social position, rather than the broad culture.

To further complicate matters, youth mature physically earlier today than ever in the past.[5] This is due to improved and advanced medical, nutritional, and technological developments. These factors have combined to increase the rate of physical maturation by six months per decade since 1880. A fifteen-and-one-half-year-old today is as physically developed as a nineteen-year-old in 1900. While youth are physically maturing earlier, suggesting ability to move into adulthood earlier, the specialized social and economic structure requires more education and forces youth to wait longer at the other end of adolescence. These two factors combine to lengthen the period of stress, uncertainty, and discontinuity characteristic of industrial societies.

Children rarely follow parental footsteps in occupation in our era. It is not unusual for children to adopt values quite different from those of parents. This rejection, though, should not lead us to conclude that parents are unneeded. They may not be able to provide specific cues to the future, but they are able to provide love, hearing, acceptance, and trust, which greatly aid the uncertain journey into adulthood.

The above mentioned characteristics of post-industrialism have led to the development of a counterculture. Subcultures (like youth) create patterns of living that in part differ from the larger culture, but are still dependent upon that parent culture. Counctercultures seek to replace and displace the larger culture. According to Theodore Roszak, youth who form countercultures are in effect refusing to enter adulthood, based upon available models.[6] Instead, they seek to establish new styles and patterns of adulthood, whether through communes, drugs, or some other form of alternative lifestyle. Youthful opposition in recent times has been most often directed at the materialistic, impersonal, manipulative, or scientific and technological values of post-industrial society.

Such conditions have led Kenneth Keniston, a foremost scholar of youth, to propose an additional stage between adolescence and adulthood which he calls "youth." He notes that growing numbers of adolescents are not able, willing, or ready to move into permanent adult roles. At some point, they cease to be adolescents even though they are not yet adults. This leads to the possibility of an additional five to fifteen years of exploration, searching, and struggle before final adoption of adult roles. Even then, the conflict between self and society is very deep in such "youth." While few in number, these "youth" were highly visible in the 60's and continue to exercise disproportionate influence upon current young people.[7]

In contrast to youthful countercultures, the larger post-industrial youth subculture in America does not seek to revise adulthood (anti-adult) as much as it seeks to temporarily separate from adults (non-adult). This stance serves well the need of adolescents to create a pattern of life that makes up for that which is lacking in the adult culture. The youth subculture thus operates with the permission of the adult culture, precisely because the parent culture doesn't provide for all the needs of the young, especially the need for acceptance and status achievement.

The Role of Change

The process of growing up has changed significantly. The twentieth century has seen more change than the previous nineteen centuries combined, largely powered by the fuel of technological change. More important for modern youth culture, the *rate* of change is accelerating. As the rate of change increases, it becomes more difficult for successive generations to adjust to each other.[8]

Rapid change more quickly widens the gap between youth and parents. Most persons make decisions about personal identity, values, lifetime commitments, and world view during late adolescence—age eighteen to twenty-five. We then tend to live out our adult years in terms of the resolutions of identity, values, and world view we decided upon at that time. Most adults tend to stop there, living out their lives as an extension of those conclusions.[9] But many of these conclusions are made in the light of our cultural-historical environment, *which does change*. The context in which parents made important life decisions passes on, creating more distance between the generations. All of this serves to illustrate one aspect of a "gap" between generations that did not exist in slower moving pre-industrial societies. Youth do not expect to live in a world exactly like that of their parents. They question the kind of guidance parents are capable of giving for the future. But such change does not render parents irrelevant; it merely modifies their function.

Sociologists and historians who theorize about the word "generation," recognize that the term is more than biological. For example, a birth generation may be measured at fifteen- or twenty-year intervals. If generations are formed out of changing historical crises and experiences, however, generations are created more quickly than in the past. In preindustrial societies, a generation might span several decades, while two or three generations have passed since the late 1950's.

While the term *generation gap* is applicable to our discussion, it makes more sense to think about factors of continuity and discontinuity between the generations. No generation is that different from the preceding or succeeding generation. Yet rapid change does create certain discontinuities. Historian of youth John Janeway Conger has put it this way:

> Thus, to the extent that today's parents look only to their own experience as adolescents for expectations about their children's probable adolescent behavior, or for guidance in understanding their needs, outlooks, and goals, they are almost bound to encounter frustration, bewilderment, or disappointment.[10]

Thus, modern parents cannot lay out blueprints for tomorrow, but can provide models of problem solving, coping, love, trust, and acceptance, all absolutely necessary ingredients for successful adulthood in any historical circumstance. Conger puts it succinctly when he comments that "In the world of tomorrow, adolescents will have to grow beyond the models their parents can provide, but they still need their parents' love and active concern."[11] The same can be said for the models provided by youth leaders in the church.

Intergenerational relations must be understood not only in terms of the age-old truth that the child eventually grows up and rebels against his parents, but also in the sense that rapid change diminishes the ability of the parent to fully identify with and understand the world of the adolescent. For example, as we move into the 80's, youth face issues on medical ethics, information processing, new housing patterns, and international relations never before faced by another generation. This is why the adolescent often turns to teachers, peers, or cultural heroes for answers, guidance, and models, because those people are supposedly more in touch with life as experienced by the young.

Life for today's youth holds many of the problems and potentials experienced by the young in the nineteenth century and even in ancient Greece. Yet life is quite different today. Our world continues to change. Herein lies the context and challenge of today's youth work in the church.

American Youth

Comparisons

While American youth still tend to set the pace for youth around the world, the differences between American youth and non-American youth are fast diminishing. By the 1960's, an international youth culture had developed based upon music, fashions (blue jeans), drugs, and common experiences in education. Youth in Western Europe, Japan, Canada, Australia, and in some regions of Latin America identified with one another largely by means of media and travel. That identification was partially symbolized by the introduction of the eighteen-year-old vote in England (1969), West Germany (1970), and America (1971).

Nevertheless, American youth remain unique among the world's youth, particularly in terms of their cultural heritage and background. Unlike European, Asian, Latin American, and African youth, American youth grow up in a society that has a tradition of rootlessness. From the transatlantic migrations to

America in the eighteenth and nineteenth centuries, through the westward movement in the late nineteenth century across the plains to the western United States, and to the twentieth-century migrations from rural America to the cities, American youth have grown up in a culture that lacks deep roots and a rigid social structure. In America, traditions rarely take hold, giving way to constant change. This had tended to foster a "cult of the present" that emphasizes immediate gratification.

American culture has also fostered in parents a deep emotional attachment to their children. In a land of opportunity, mobility, and equality—where a child can supposedly become almost anything—children are doted over, groomed for greatness, and become the object of considerable parental attention. Such was apparent to British travelers in the past century, who were horrified at what they considered the American tendency to spoil their children.[12] American parents do tend to judge themselves on the basis of the accomplishments of their children, because American society continues to offer significant opportunity for the very able and talented person. Consequently, American youth are pampered and made the object of extensive parental emotional investment as parents seek to guarantee their offspring's chances for success.

The final point to be made with reference to unique American youth traits relates to the cultural emphasis upon independence and individualism. This emphasis has been historically fostered in America, because the land of equal opportunity is also the land of personal success. American youth grow up in a very competitive environment. They can never "let up."

American youth are trained to believe they have the right to participate in the working out of the destiny of their own lives, a destiny without deep historical tradition or roots, nurtured by parents who believe their young could become most anything. American individualism teaches American youth that this is a lonely journey—a lesson only partially muted by the comforting knowledge that other youth share the same journey.

American Youth in the Twentieth Century

As with European industrialism, American industrial development in the late nineteenth century led to the emergence of adolescents in American society. By the turn of the century, more and more American youth were attending high school, increasing from 202,963 in 1890 to 519,251 in 1900.[13] Extended education was necessary to prepare youth for work roles in the developing industrial economy of America. By World War I, compulsory education laws, child labor laws, and new legal definitions of juvenile delinquency combined to keep youth out of the labor force and in school longer than ever before. Youth were becoming adolescents.[14] By the 1920's, after most youth had gladly fought to help "make the world safe for democracy," most American youth pursued a high school education (although this was more true for urban than rural youth).[15] When the depression of the 1930's struck, youth as well as parents were deeply affected. Raised in an era of apparent prosperity in the 1920's, many of these youth expected to move into early adulthood in the 1930's without interruption. The depression not only disrupted the continuity of the life cycle, but it deeply scarred these youth. Their economic deprivation would affect later youth generations, as the youth of the 30's became parents in the 40's and 50's.

The depression also spawned radical youth movements in America, largely based upon the ideology of capitalistic breakdown. Such positions quickly evaporated as America entered World War II. Most American youth became involved in the war in one way or another. Since the issues of right and wrong were sufficiently clear in this war, few disputed national policy after Pearl Harbor. This attitude further illustrates generational differences, because these same youth who knew who, what, and why they were fighting in that war found it difficult to cope with their sons' unwillingness to take up arms in Vietnam.

When World War II ended, millions of American youth married, resumed their education on the G.I. Bill, and sought peace of mind in American consumerism. The war had been won, and for the moment, problems at home seemed inconsequential compared to the one just solved. High schools filled up with ten million students by 1950, compared to 1.8 million in 1920. Returning servicemen found that advancing technology had reduced the number of unskilled jobs available, through mechanization and automation. More and more white collar jobs required a high school diploma.[16]

Youth in the 50's moved through those "happy days" in a mood later to be termed "silent"—referring to the absence of social concern and consciousness, compared to the 1960's. Yet the 1950's witnessed the beginnings of modern youth culture with the emergence of Elvis Presley and rock 'n roll in 1956, the car as a teenage status symbol and love machine, the increased homogeneity of teen culture, and the beginning of turmoil over civil rights for blacks. And this whole life cycle was surrounded by the increased impact of television. By the end of the 1950's, a growing majority of American youth were looking to college as a necessary means of improving their status and chances for success as adults, particularly spurred by the Russian launching of Sputnik I in 1957, which jolted America to emphasize science and engineering in education. America was fast becoming a post-industrial society.

The Decade of Turbulence: The 60's

The full force of youthful alienation and opposition hit America in the 60's. Post-industrial societies are characterized in part by varied countercultures, but in the 60's it seemed as if all youth joined to form one large counterculture. Relatively few American youth actually participated in overt acts of disobedience and violence in the 60's, but the overall pattern of youthful opposition, both overt and covert, was significant then and affected the next youth generations.

Youthful opposition and upheaval in the 60's can be traced in part to the civil rights confrontations in the early part of the decade. Also, the 1964 Free Speech Movement at Berkeley coincided with the escalation of American military involvement in Vietnam, both of which would become points of contention for youth in that decade. By the middle of the 60's, more than seven million late adolescents on university campuses formed a significant and visible segment of the youth culture. Mass higher education coupled with universal high school education was supposed to guarantee the American dream of success, prosperity, and security. This was a generation that had enjoyed the fruit of American prosperity, provided by parents who had suffered the agony of the depression.

Some of the affluent young found the reality of material possessions, status, and privilege to be meaningless. The majority of youth who joined the New Left, got high on LSD, or joined a commune came from upper middle and upper class families. Such families had enjoyed the benefits of American prosperity, yet something was still missing in the eyes of their children.

Oppositional youth constituted less than ten percent of American youth in the 60's. The activist and alienated youth gained the attention of the press, claiming they knew what was wrong with American society and how to change it. The extensive media attention they received helped them create images that in turn influenced other youth. Through youthful protest on college campuses against ROTC, the Vietnam War, militarism, and ecological devastation, these students claimed (sometimes through violence) that they had experienced the American dream and had found it empty. Another ten to fifteen percent of youth in the 60's were minority youth, some of whom were also oppositional, especially on college campuses. The other seventy-five to eighty percent of American youth remained "silent," but many were sympathetic with the causes of oppositional youth, especially after force was used against those activists. When a small minority of youth took stands against the larger culture over the war, marijuana, the draft, drugs, or radical politics, other youth sometimes gave tacit support. Adult responses varied from sympathy to accusations of treason.

As the youth culture heated up in the 60's, it took on a number of interesting and sometimes controversial symbols. Blue jeans, the Beatles, slang, and long hair on males aided youth in identifying with the youth culture in specifically non-adult ways. Some oppositional youth operated in anti-adult ways through confrontations, protests, and sit-ins. The violence of the period demonstrated the extent of alienation among some segments of youth. Some oppositional youth chose not to express their alienation through political activism, but retreated into vagrancy, meditation, or the fantasy world of drugs. Reacting, they said, to the impersonal forces of advanced technology, these children of technocracy refused to be bent, folded, spindled, or mutilated by American society.[17, 18]

Some observers viewed this youthful opposition as the herald of a new consciousness and new age for America,[19] but most Americans believed the upheaval (the intensity of which peaked between the 1968 Chicago Democratic Convention violence and the 1970 Kent State killings over the Cambodian invasion, with Woodstock in between) would pass. John W. Aldridge echoed the beliefs of the average American when he asserted that most of the oppositional youth were parasites on America, rather than contributors to solutions of America's problems. Aldridge also said that they lacked responsibility and were more hypocritical than their parents.[20] In any case, the violence and confrontations did begin to wind down in the early 70's. The waning of youthful opposition, the splintering of the New Left, and the decline of the drug counterculture coincided with American withdrawal from Vietnam. The many configurations of American youth culture in that decade had deeply affected American life, including the military, music, cultural activities, and education. To illustrate, higher education institutions allowed more student participation in governance. The doctrine of *in loco parentis* had been successfully challenged, so that students no longer lived under the parental authority of the university. Beyond the campus, youthful influence was felt as the voting age was lowered to eighteen; casual dress became more acceptable; the "natural" became fashionable; sexuality within commitment, but outside of marriage was more widely accepted; the rights of youth (including children) and minorities were gaining broad acceptance; and universal draft was ended. Even if Aldridge was correct in alleging that the oppositional youth were the real hypocrites of the decade, there is no denying that youth in the 60's brought change in America as no generation had before. The article titled, "The Youth Revolution: It Is Over and It Has Won"[21] overstates the case, but it is, on the other hand, foolish to dismiss the 60's as merely a cyclical convulsion.

The Jesus People
General acceptance of the religious dimension of life is another legacy of the 60's among today's youth. Transcendental Meditation, Eastern mysticism, astrology and the occult, Maoism, the cult of ecology, and the Jesus People emerged as expressions of this toleration of diversity in religion. That toleration continues to this day; most people don't act surprised or bothered if told that another person is taking Jesus seriously. The usual response expresses satisfaction that the follower of Jesus has found something meaningful for himself. The Jesus People of the 60's represent an important case study for leaders of Christian youth today.

The Jesus People combined literal devotion to Scripture with a sense of alienation from modern culture. Organized into autonomous groups scattered in urban areas around the country, the Jesus People represented extreme fundamentalism in religion and deep cultural reactionism.

Many of the Jesus People had traversed routes through radical politics, drugs, counterculture, and Oriental mysticism. Finding these youthful forms of protest inadequate to deal with and express their sense of dislocation and alienation, they tried Jesus. It "took" for some, but many moved on after a few months or years, disillusioned with authoritarian adult leaders, continued calls for total self-denial, and, at times, attempted brainwashing. While God can and does work through revivals among any and all age groups, the Jesus People movement was created as much by the media as by evangelism; it was as much the result of the cultural dislocation felt by youth in the 60's as the Spirit of God.[22] The Jesus People, whether defined as a group, or viewed in terms of the individual youth's response to Jesus (often within the context of a local congregation), constituted a youthful judgment upon the rigidity and human traditions of many congregations. As such, the larger revival among Christian youth that accompanied the Jesus People movement was a positive and powerful stimulant to the American church.

Hypocrisy and the 60's

Having already mentioned that John W. Aldridge has claimed that youth were the real hypocrites of the 60's, a review of Kenneth Keniston's provocative essay, "Youth, Change, and Violence"[23] will serve to give fuller discussion to that issue. Keniston claims that while youth have always asserted that their parents are hypocrites, that charge took on new definition and meaning in the 60's. He outlines a three-generational pattern of relationships never before possible in history, created by rapid change. The grandparents of 60's youth were probably born in the decade of the 1890's. They were raised with Victorian values of moderation, restraint, propriety, and delayed gratification. Those values were ingrained in their children born in the World War I era (who became parents of 60's youth). But this parent generation that was raised with Victorian values could have switched to a new set of values in young adulthood in the areas of race relations, child rearing, and service to humankind. Having made that conversion, they doggedly reared their children (60's youth), who were born in the 40's and 50's, with systematic inculcation of the new set of values.

In times of rapid change, parents often are struggling, coping, and experimenting with their own new values and beliefs and do not have the time or experience to teach the exceptions of newly adopted ideals to their children. So they mouth the ideas, children believe and adopt them—and the children yell "hypocrite" if parents back off from those ideas even occasionally. So parents of 60's youth who believed, as adults, in the equality of the races, were still influenced by their racist upbringing and reverted to that upbringing when faced with a son or daughter who dated a person of another race. At no time in history have three generations undergone such rapid social and cultural change, that a youth generation could move so far from the values and positions held by the grandparents' generation.

Such a pattern of generations resulting in this situation as described would only occur in certain families, mainly those most deeply affected by social-cultural change in the 20's and 30's. Such families have also been identified by several researchers as the types of families out of which many oppositional youth came in the 60's. We see in this illustration one example of just how unique the 60's were in the history of American youth culture.

Christian parents also sometimes leave themselves open to the charge of hypocrisy. For example, they may stress or at least mouth the need to evangelize the world, witness to the community, or preach the gospel, yet they balk when a daughter or son announces plans to go to a Bible college and study for missionary service or a preaching/teaching ministry. They want to see their child pursue an education that will provide economic security before studying for the worthwhile endeavor of preaching or teaching. Understandably, the son or daughter may yell "hypocrite." The parents are trapped because they have taught their child evangelism, but have not succeeded in teaching the exceptions or qualifications to his obeying the Great Commission ("You don't have to take this literally, or evangelize to *that* extent").

Into the 70's

The protests of the 60's have given way to the "lull" in youthful activity in the 70's, we are told. While simplistic, there is some truth in this assertion. External indicators point to the reappearance of a more stable and even traditional youth culture in America. The counterculture is basically gone, alcohol and marijuana have replaced hard drugs, hard rock has given way to the Bee Gees and a host of successors to the

Beatles. ROTC and fraternities/sororities are back on campus again, and the traditional campus prank occurs more frequently. The entire country has turned in a conservative direction.

As early as 1973, research indicated that youth were taking a more traditional bent in comparison to the 60's, but at the same time, they had institutionalized the changes of the 60's. The *Chronicle of Higher Education* published a detailed survey in early 1973 offering evidence that college freshmen (Fall, 1972) were moving to more conservative positions on personal values, American life, and cultural attitudes.[24] Yet in that same year, Daniel Yankelovich, a leading youth pollster, confirmed that while youth might have moderated in some areas since the 60's, shifts toward what he styled a "new morality" had indeed occurred in youth culture.[25]

Louis Seagull documented (1977) an increase in political nonpartisanship among youth. Most of those who voted (more likely college educated than not) did not register as Democrats or Republicans anymore, but as Independents. By 1972, 50.9% of registered voters between ages eighteen and twenty-four registered as Independent.[26] Whether this suggests apathy toward traditional American politics or discriminating political participation is not clear.

Youth embraced more traditional stances toward their education. High school and college students seemed more determined than ever to move into a career through their education. So occupational guidance and guarantees of future jobs were increasingly demanded of study programs.

A recently published study of teenagers in a modern planned city in Maryland indicates that high school teenagers may operate in traditional ways in relation to their high school careers, but are somewhat permissive and liberal in attitudes and values.[27] Roger Karsk shows in this study of eight teenagers of the middle 70's that attitudes toward drugs, sex, and abortion match the change in values of the 60's. At the same time, attitudes toward work, money, friends, and status would fit well with the 50's. A 1975 study of 250 former Haight-Ashbury hippies states that forty percent reentered society, ostensibly having adopted regular social values, but thirty percent continued to grope for life outside of conventional society.[28]

While a more homogenous youth culture developed in the late 70's, the dawn of the 80's saw an amalgam of traditional youth concerns (jobs) combined with several 60's attitude changes (sex, marijuana). American youth culture was quite diverse, as is easily seen in the popularity of such diverse groups as the Village People, KISS, the Bee Gees, and the Carpenters during the 70's.

To use Margaret Mead's terms after World War II, Americans moved from a "post-figurative" society (children learn from parents) through a moment of "pre-figurative" trauma (in the 60's, when children taught parents—or tried to) to the present "co-figurative" society (adults and youth learn from each other).

An Analysis of Contemporary Youth

Youth Subculture

Subcultures arise when the larger culture fails to meet some needs of particular groups of persons. They offer different patterns of living, values, and behavior norms that meet the specialized needs of those disaffected from the larger culture. Subcultures still depend on that larger culture for general goals and direction. Unlike countercultures, subcultures do not seek to destroy or even alter the larger culture, but rather to compensate for the failure of that larger culture to provide adequate status, acceptance, and identity. Consequently, youth subcultures should generally be viewed in a positive and constructive light. They provide a kind of way station in which youth find age-related needs met through peer interactions.

Hans Sebald has outlined eight common elements of subculture, each of which help us understand current youth subculture:

1. Relatively unique values and norms.
2. A special slang not shared with larger society.
3. Channels of communication separate from other groups (youth newspapers).
4. Unique styles and fads.
5. A sense of primary group belonging, characterized by a sense of "we" and "they."
6. Existence of a hierarchy of social patterns that clarify the criteria for prestige and leadership.
7. Receptivity to the charisma of leaders.
8. Gratification of specific needs the larger social structure fails to meet.[29]

Youth are particularly annoyed when adults (pursuing the cult of youth) copy, imitate, or attempt to co-opt the identifying elements of their subculture. For example, youth deeply resent adults who use youthful slang or adopt youthful clothing styles or fads. Adults must respect the need of youth to identify with the subculture as an expression of common need and solidarity.

No Rite of Passage
Youth subculture exists partly because no certain path to adulthood is provided for them. Because of this, identity formation is either delayed or at best sidetracked into the temporary reinforcements offered by youth subculture. While some youth move into adulthood with little difficulty and few complications, this absence of a rite of passage continues to plague many youth.

Custodial Education
Because the American social-economic structure has become so refined and specialized, it does not simply or easily receive semi-skilled or even B.A. level college youth. In one sense, our society shuffles the young into educational tracks, sometimes lasting through several years of college, because the job market cannot absorb them. Federally based student aid programs in effect encourage this. Such custody has its values, but also lengthens the period between childhood and adulthood, further aggravating an already frustrating span of time for the youth.

Affluence
Affluence has become a major means of expressing subcultural values for youth. Some twenty-five million teenagers today have around fifteen billion spending dollars per year at their disposal. Youth norms, values, and conformity are extensively expressed through what money buys, particularly items such as electronic gadgets, cosmetics, records, recreational equipment, and specialized equipment for cars.

Privatism: The New Narcissism
Youth have not escaped what Francis Schaeffer calls the desire for "personal peace and affluence"[30] so characteristic of the larger adult culture in America. As the 70's "settled down,"

youth apparently have turned to self-interest and away from the more socially minded concerns of the 60's.

The self-righteousness of the 60's turned to self-indulgence in the 70's. The 50's were also privatistic, but with an orientation around family concerns. Youth in the 70's and early 80's have become privatistic again, but with focus upon self-fulfillment. For many youth, the past has been made antiquated and the future unpredictable by rapid change. Therefore, the present is the only reality with which to be concerned. The desire for personal peace, affluence, and instant gratification evidently appeals to many young people more than social activism. In that respect, they are hardly different from many of their elders and parents. Such a constellation of attitudes has been termed the new narcissism, reminiscent of Narcissus, who fell in love with his own reflection in a pool of water. While this tendency varies from person to person, it constitutes an important dimension of youth subculture.

The Class of Inferiority Complexes[31]

As parents struggle with a changing world, the passing of their life cycle, and the values of the cult of youth in America, they tend to feel inferior. That inferiority breeds a feeling of declining importance in the lives of their children. This feeling is intensified as other adults, such as teachers, are viewed by youth as more expert than their parents. Youth, on the other hand, feel inferior because they are groping through adolescence without experience or proven competency in social skills. They often respond to this deficiency by acting cocky, aggressive, and confident. Youthful confidence and assertiveness threatens parents, who respond with rigidity and authority, fearing their authority will not be upheld. This power play reinforces youth's feeling of inferiority as one plays into the inferiority of the other. Such situations call for an extraordinary measure of Christian grace.

Into the Future

Youth have always "bugged" parents and adults. If rapid change continues unabated, we can expect continuing and significant generational differences. This expectation results largely from the fact that each generation's world view is shaped by its immediate historical circumstances, which change quickly. The parents' historical formative circumstances become mere history for their children. In the foreseeable future, the young will probably continue to experience the discontinuity of statuses that has fostered adolescence and youth subculture. This situation doesn't reduce or minimize the role of the family or the church for youth, but intensifies the obligations of each to provide nurture, acceptance, loving understanding, and practice in problem solving for youth. While parents cannot lead their children to where they have not been themselves, they can lead as to *how* they got where they are. We can safely predict a continued overlapping of values between parents and youth, providing sufficient continuity between the generations to help offset the discontinuity of statuses. Youth subculture will continue to create its own music, entertainment, clothing styles, slang, and peer interactions, but that will not prevent youth from enjoying the company of adults and parents. Communication may be difficult and strained in moments of disagreement, partly because adolescence will extend deeper into the twenties for some, causing parental alarm over whether their children will ever emerge from their adolescence and settle down.

The unstructuredness and uncertainty that characterize modern society can be met successfully with the help of the family, even with the limitations outlined in earlier discussion of families in industrial and post-industrial societies. The church also has a significant role to play.

Christian Responses and Reactions

Too often well-meaning Christian teachers, parents, and leaders have ministered to youth by introducing them to Jesus, assuming the task ended there. Certainly, Jesus is the answer to the needs of youth, but Jesus does not deliver youth from their anxiety, problems and dilemmas. Jesus does help us put it all in perspective—in relation to the purposes of God. Jesus, alone, will not save youth from the problems of passing into adulthood or the perils of adolescence. Jesus will help youth live, minister, and cope in any culture. In that light, it is appropriate to consider the following:

1. The current youth culture may meet the immediate needs of youth, but it often represents values and standards *other* than those of the Christian faith. Youth culture offers much

positive help to Christian youth, but it isn't a Christian youth culture. At times, it can be accurately viewed as anti-Christian. It certainly will not Christianize youth any more than American culture Christianizes adults. Tensions between Christian youth and the larger youth subculture must be faced and dealt with by Christian parents and youth leaders.

2. While peer pressure is not new to the current generation of youth, it remains particularly powerful. Given the need youth have for acceptance and belonging, Christian ideals and mandates such as "in the world but not of the world," and "be not conformed but transformed" are not easily followed in the face of the demands of youth subculture. This powerful pull is supplemented by the equally powerful media, which seek further conformity from youth.

3. Christian youth can live as part of loving sympathetic Christian families and still experience generational conflict, identity crisis, and role confusion. This occurs because Christian youth are not immune to environmental and peer influence. Christian leaders must learn that delayed adulthood, generational conflict, identity formation problems, and role confusion do not invalidate faith. Such problems are typical developmental problems common to all youth.

4. Don't expect more from youth than our culture allows. This is especially significant in regard to occupational choice. Recalling the difference between occupation (earning a living) and vocation (a call to minister for Christ) will help. All youth can and must be challenged during adolescence to the Biblically mandated vocation (call) of ministry. Youth experience difficulties in occupational choice because of the specialized socioeconomic structure characteristic of our post-industrial society. In the meantime, youth must be challenged to minister through an occupation. But impatient adult demands that youth decide "what they are going to do" would be better replaced with challenge to Christian mission and vocation *now*, which can be implemented through later occupational choice.

5. Rather than piously denying the existence of generational differences and conflicts, allow the gospel to work there also. Denying such conflicts merely postpones the day of reckoning, and in the meantime tends to aggravate the real issue. On the other hand, it is equally disabling to presume the existence of conflicts and differences where none exist. Jesus helps us live with the realities of history and our own lives.

6. Youth need a knowledge of the relationship to God through Jesus Christ. That will best and most appropriately be experienced through a nurturing and accepting congregation. In such a community of Christians, identity can emerge through knowledge of God and through active roles in the congregation.

7. Parents should not be left out of the picture. They not only need understanding, but at times, sympathy. The implications of rapid change also affect parents. Even the most competent and well-meaning parents experience surprise, frustration, and anguish as they try to lead, relate to, and communicate with youth in a world quite different from the one in which they experienced adolescence.

8. All who work with and raise youth must be hopeful and positive. We can complain as did Hesiod and Aristotle, but Christian leaders should couple their concern for youth to a positive view of modern life and culture. Wringing hands over days gone by, the lost innocence of youth, and a world gone berserk, offers very little to youth who instead want guidance for a troubled present and help in living in an unforeseen tomorrow. Christian love and truth will serve youth better than crying for a lost yesterday.

All Christian leaders must claim the Biblical truth that God is Lord of all history: every personal history, every culture, every subculture, every society, every change in life, and even tomorrow. While that reality doesn't deliver anyone, youth included, from problems and conflicts, it keeps modern youth culture in perspective. That perspective centers in Christian faith, which helps every youth live out a personal history with dignity and triumph.

---

[1]*The Rhetoric*, II, 12

[2]John R. Gillis, *Youth and History: Tradition and Change in European Age Relations: 1770-Present.* New York: Academic Press, 1974, pp. 3-9.

[3]Daniel Bell, *The Coming of Post-Industrial Society.* New York: Basic Books, 1973.

[4]Hans Sebald, *Adolescence: A Social Psychological Analysis* (second edition). Englewood Cliffs, New Jersey: Prentice-Hall, 1977, p. 31. This is a particularly helpful book.

[5]Rolf Muuss (ed.), *Adolescent Behavior and Society: A Book of Readings.* New York: Random House, 1971, p. 39.

[6]Theodore Roszak, *The Making of a Counter Culture.* Garden City, New York: Doubleday, 1971, p. 39.

[7]Kenneth Keniston, *Youth and Dissent: The Rise of a New Opposition.* New York: Harcourt, Brace, and Jovanovich, 1971, pp. 3-21.

[8]See also Keniston, *Youth and Dissent,* "The Speedup of Change."

[9]Randolf Bourne, *Youth and Life.* Boston: Houghton-Mifflin, 1913, pp. 3-7.

[10]John Janeway Conger, "A World They Never Knew: The Family and Social Change," *Daedalus,* Fall 1971.

[11]*Ibid.,* p. 1132.

[12]Richard L. Rapson, *The Cult of Youth in Middle Class America.* Lexington, Massachusetts: D. C. Heath and Co., 1971, pp. 16-25.

[13]Edward A. Krug, *The Shaping of the American High School: 1880-1920.* Madison, Wisconsin: University of Wisconsin Press, 1969, p. 169.

[14]David Baken, "Adolescence in America: From Idea to Social Fact," *Daedalus,* Fall 1971.

[15]Krug, *op. cit.,* pp. 169, 447. The number of high schools in America had risen from 2,526 in 1890 to over 14,000 by 1920.

Ellwood P. Cubberley, *Public Foundation in the United States* (revised edition). Boston: Houghton-Mifflin, 1962, pp. 627,628. Student population had risen from 202,963 in 1890 (or three per 1,000 population) to 1.8 million in 1920 (twenty-one per 1,000 population).

[16]Oscar and Mary Handlin, *Facing Life: Youth and the Family in American History.* New York: Little and Brown, 1971, pp. 220ff.

[17]Roszak, *op. cit.,* Chapter One.

[18]See also Keniston, *op. cit.;* and Keniston, *The Uncommitted: Alienated Youth in American Society.* New York: Dell, 1965.

[19]Charles Reich, *The Greening of America.* New York: Random House, 1970, was the most optimistic, sympathetic, and widely read view of youth cultures in the late 1960's. See also Francois Revel, *Without Marx or Jesus: The New American Revolution Has Begun.* New York: Doubleday, 1971.

[20]John W. Aldridge, *In the Country of the Young.* New York: Harper and Row, 1964.

[21]Willard Dalrymple, "The Youth Revolution: It Is Over and It Has Won," *Intellectual Digest,* July 1972, pp. 80ff.

[22]Gerald C. Tiffin, "A Cultural Interpretation of the Jesus People," *Rides et Historia,* Spring, 1973, pp. 79-86.

[23]Keniston, *Youth and Dissent.*

[24]"Freshmen Show a Conservative Shift," *Chronicle of Higher Education,* February 12, 1973, p. 1.

[25]Daniel Yankelovich, *The New Morality: A Profile of American Youth in the 70's.* New York: McGraw-Hill, 1974.

[26]Louis Seagull, *Youth and Change in American Politics.* New York: Franklin Watts, 1977, p. 96.

[27]Roger Karsk, *Teenagers in the Next America.* Columbia, Maryland: New Community Press, 1977, Chapter 12.

[28]*Los Angeles Times,* September 19, 1975, Sec. IV, p. 1.

[29]Sebald, *op. cit.,* pp. 231, 232.

[30]Francis Schaeffer, *How Should We Then Live?* Old Tappan, New Jersey: Revell, 1976, Chapter 11.

[31]Clifford Kirkpatrick, *The Family as a Process and Institution.* New York: Ronald Press, 1955, pp. 266, 267.

CHAPTER

2

The Person of
the Youth Minister

by Don Hinkle

As you read, think about these questions:
—How does your personality directly affect your ministry's success?
—In what ways can you best obtain God's help and direction for your
    ministry?
—What ways will your relationship to your own family spill over into
    your youth ministry?

You see the youth culture—the trends, both positive and
negative, the tragedies of broken homes and lives, and the potential of transformed lives. You get excited about it. You want
to be involved. You figure it will not be easy, and you're
right—there is much to do. In most church situations, you need
to keep a lot of things going simultaneously: recruit and train
counselors; spend time with them; counsel with the youth;
plan the youth group lesson; contact the visitors; encourage the
regulars; call parents on the phone; plan the projects and activities; go to the games on Friday; get a bus driver for the
retreat; figure out when to schedule the counselor's meeting
so all can be there, and then remember to go yourself; make
eight calls to reach one guy who then says he doesn't want to
go this time; preview the film so you don't get surprised; compile or write the appropriate material for camp; set up your

growth groups; write the inevitable weekly youth column; learn to work as a member of a ministry team; deal with the expectations (both real and imagined) of the church leaders. The list goes on, and your time grows shorter and shorter. At times you'll feel like the circus performer who starts one plate spinning on a long pole, then starts another on a second pole while keeping the first plate spinning—until finally, running from one to another, he has all ten plates spinning. At the end of the act, he's exhausted and the plates, perhaps, are all intact.

Ministry to young people is a demanding challenge, but it's exciting—it's something you need to willingly, lovingly involve yourself in.

The most important factor in youth work, however, is who you are as a person. That takes precedence over any method or program. You soon discover you cannot build a program without committed people. Luke records one of the scariest things Jesus ever said: "A pupil is not above his teacher; but everyone, after he has been fully trained, will be like his teacher."[1] Paul echoes the same concept in his advice to Timothy: "Pay close attention to yourself and to your teaching."[2] Who you are carries more weight than what you say.

This lesson runs throughout Scripture. One of the most compelling passages is in Jeremiah 23. In that chapter Jeremiah shows that the scattering and destruction of God's people can be directly traced to the spiritual leaders. "For both prophet and priest are polluted, ... from the prophets of Jerusalem, pollution has gone forth into all the land."[3] Pollution in all its forms has become a way of life in our society and in the youth culture. Before we can ever begin to be effective in bringing cleansing to others, we must be pure ourselves. Values, attitudes, relationships, conduct—all are transmitted by a modeling process, and need spiritual cleanliness.

The Word of God, our effectiveness in ministering to young people, and our own spiritual health all demand that we be models of a balanced Christian life, especially in our relationships with God and with our family. Chuck Miller, in discipleship seminars held across the country, stresses that before we can do the work of God, we must be the people of God. This process takes time and constant evaluation and the wisdom to recognize that periodically we'll suffer setbacks. We'll never perfectly be the people of God, or have everything in perfect balance, but that must be the goal.

His Relationship With God

What does it take to be in a right relationship with God? There are no surprising answers: quiet times alone with God; a study of Scripture for personal growth; the commitment to communicate through prayer. Most youth ministers can give their groups powerful challenges and lessons on the subject. But again, change does not come simply from true information. Change requires truth lived out in practice.

David learned the truth that his life was to focus squarely upon God. He says, "I shall behold Thy face in righteousness; I will be satisfied with Thy likeness when I awake."[4] We are to love God, not just the things of God or the work of God, with all our being. It is easy at times to love the involvement, the interaction of being with young people, and the emotional lift they can provide, so much that God is overlooked. Satisfaction must be centered in Him.

Study and meditation on God's Word is another factor in a strong relationship with Him. Jeremiah explains in greater detail the misleading lifestyle of Israel's spiritual leaders:

Thus says the Lord of hosts,
Do not listen to the words of the prophets who are prophesying to you.
They are leading you into futility;
They speak a vision of their own imagination,
Not from the mouth of the Lord.[5]

Time must be given to a personal study of God's Word— giving heed and listening. If not, ministry is not done in God's power or direction, but only in man's. The challenge is to do the Lord's work in the Lord's way:

I did not send these prophets,
But they ran.
I did not speak to them,
But they prophesied.
But if they had stood in My council,
Then they would have announced My words to My people,
And would have turned them back from their evil way
And from the evil of their deeds.[6]

Take the time to stand in God's council. See and hear His Word. Set aside a place in your schedule where you will read and meditate on God's Word for the sake of *your own* life. Study at another time for lesson preparation.

The commitment to pray and time spent in prayer is also an integral part of our relationship with God. Scriptures teach much about its power and necessity. E. M. Bounds has a book entitled *The Power of Prayer* that should be in both the library and life of every youth worker. In addition to having a spirit of prayer throughout the day, you need to set aside specific, consistent times for prayer. Whether you use an old formula like A.C.T.S. (adoration, confession, thanksgiving, supplication) or the Model Prayer, or another method—take the time. In Psalm 5, David says, "In the morning, O Lord, Thou wilt hear my voice; in the morning I will order my prayer to Thee and eagerly watch."[7] Prayer requires an ordering, a self-discipline.

It is deceptively easy to lead others without adequate preparation. And for a time it appears to be successful. We can, as Jeremiah says, borrow or steal words from others. At times you can go to a meeting with no preparation and everything goes well. Several reasons contribute to that. For one thing, you may have done preparation much earlier and the material is still in your mind; for another, you may be taking one thought and sharing your life concerning it, as well as the Scriptural truth. This has a positive effect if your life is in the right relationship with God. The third reason is of real concern. If a lesson that has neither recent preparation nor a committed life behind it goes well, it might be that Satan is doing all he can to give it the appearance of success. He knows, even if we forget, that if leaders are lulled into letting their own lives slide, momentarily deceived by the surface success of lessons and programs, in time, youth will be affected by what the leaders have really become, not what they teach. Satan well understands the principles of changing lives. So must we. The overriding concern in youth work is the person of the youth worker.

His Relationship With His Family

Attaining balance in your life involves the right quality and quantity of time with God. That must be true with your family as well. Many of you may not yet be married. Perhaps you will be, perhaps not—but you will be involved in teaching both parents and young people the importance of a right relationship with family. And realistically, you will be in a family relationship—either with your own husband or wife and children, or if unmarried, special friends who become your family circle.

God's plan still stresses the sharing of values and ideals with your family and through your family to others. Who we are in relationship to our family has a major bearing on our effectiveness with others. Satan's trap is to lead us to believe that so much needs to be done that we dare not take time off for anything—including family.

Guard your family time closely. Your wife should know that she is more important to you than any of the high school or college girls you work with. Your own children should understand that their needs and activities are more important to you than those of the youth you work with. Remember, the first youth you should work with are your own children. Your family will understand that at times you need to postpone or shuffle family events. Just make certain that they also see you cancel being at a youth outing to be with them occasionally. Let your family *win* some of the schedule conflicts. Better still, avoid the conflicts by scheduling in advance special times with your family. For example, write 'family' or your wife or husband's name on some day—once a week or two or three times a month. Then if you're asked to do something on that day, you can just say 'I'm already booked for then.' If you explain it's a family commitment, many people will try to get you to change it. But if you are willing to explain your position, it's an excellent teaching opportunity. Tell others about your commitment to your family not as an apology, but as an example.

Recently many books have been written on the subject of the family. Much good information and recommendations are available. For now, just keep two things in mind.

First, take time for them. Take your day off—a lot of people can cover those twenty-four hours you miss, but no one else can be a husband to your wife or a father to your children. Don't miss out on any age they go through; take your children, one at a time, to special places—or just set aside times for them. Do the same for your wife—set up a date night. Robert Schuller, one of the most active ministers in the country, takes time each week to have a date with his wife, and nothing is allowed to interfere with that. He also takes his children with him on calls occasionally. You could take walks or rides, go to games, play games at home, watch your children play ball, get involved with their activities, just go home and be there. Set aside family nights. The family time didn't start with one particular religious group. It's been God's design for a long time that families be united. The quantity of time is important, but more important is the quality of that time. Secondly, home isn't where your ministry ends, it's where it ought to begin. *Listen* to your family talk to you. Pay attention to what's going on. Ask specific questions that show you're aware of what takes place around the house and at school. Marvel at the way your children grow— they are a gift from God.

A right understanding and relationship with your own family will provide essential insight into the families of the youth you work with. It will also keep your view of yourself in proper perspective. You're not a grown-up teenager; you have responsibilities at home.

Time for Himself

A third area of growth in the development of your own life as a youth worker is the time you spend with yourself. This includes a continuing emphasis on physical, emotional, intellectual, and social growth. In practice, it means you need time to provide for your own needs and nurture your own capabilities. Again, the emphasis is on sufficient time. "Sufficient" is the key—you can't be constantly in introspection, discovering who you are. That's not the point. You do need time in your schedule just to relax and allow God to create again and again within you His Spirit and direction and life. God does not expect you to be in constant motion in order to be pleasing to Him. A Sunday afternoon nap instead of calling does not cancel your salvation—even if Jesus returns while you're napping. It is O.K. to relax—more than that, it is essential. A compulsively busy person cannot be creative, and certainly in youth work creativity is a prized possession.

Furthermore, do all you can to maintain good health. See a doctor on a regular basis. The attitude of "I'm O.K. as long as I don't go to the doctor" is not wise.

Get away by yourself once in a while.

Don't give up "play time" either. Just face the truth: it's fun! Adults tend to find excuses or reasons for having fun. God's plan is that we enjoy life. One poster I have carries this message—"The great man is he who does not lose his child's heart." The message probably meant two things: First, greatness means we keep the love and trust of our own children; second, greatness comes to those who maintain a childlike confidence.

Allowing some rest and growth time for yourself is not selfish. Your goal in youth work is not just to take care of number one—but to most effectively minister to young people. To do that most effectively requires the full development of the person you are.

As you continue to build your ministry with young people, keep as your motto this statement of Paul's: "Follow me as I follow Christ." Live it out before your group in relationships with God, your family, and yourself.

---

[1]Luke 6:40
[2]1 Timothy 4:16
[3]Jeremiah 23:11, 15
[4]Psalm 17:15
[5]Jeremiah 23:16
[6]Jeremiah 23:21, 22
[7]Psalm 5:3

CHAPTER

3

The Goal of
Youth Ministry

by Dick Alexander

As you read, think about these questions:
—In what way can you define the "Christlike" growth that should be
the goal of a youth ministry?
—What changes must occur in the lives of you and your students to
exemplify progress toward a Christ-centered life?

Seeing the Goal

Even though we can't get where we're going unless we have
pinpointed our destination, church leaders do not agree on the
goal of youth work in the local church.

The goal of youth ministry is the goal of the entire church:
maturity—"the stature which belongs to the fullness of
Christ."[1] Youth ministry does not operate in a vacuum. It is
concerned with, and is part of, the total body of Christ, and has
as its focus the single goal of producing Christlikeness. Its goal
is not recreation, socialization, patriotism, or even evangelism.

To say the goal of the church is evangelism is roughly akin to
saying the mark of good parenting is having babies. The task is
not merely to proliferate newborns who will be left un-
nourished, but to develop growing, dynamic, maturing youth
who share Christ from the fullness of their lives. If evangelism
is the natural, inevitable overflow of a Christ-filled life, could it

be that part of the reason for the current lack of evangelism in many circles is that we're asking the starving to give bread? Conversion is a step on the road to Christlikeness, but only one of many.

Some contrast evangelism and nurture, seeing them in conflict. It is more Biblical, though, to see them as a continuum. Granted that any lineal diagram of spiritual reality leaves something to be desired, the accompanying models may be of some help. The vertical scale represents "spirituality," the horizontal base line represents time in a person's life, and the cross is the point of conversion.

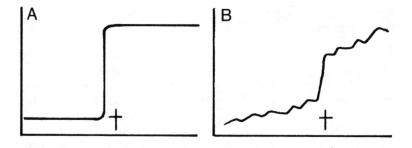

Figure 3-1. Two representations of spiritual growth.

Those whose only concern is evangelism might see spiritual growth as represented in Figure A. At conversion everything that really counts takes place. Concern about Christian growth is seen as self-serving and dangerous, in that it distracts from evangelism.

Figure B presents a long process of growth in relation to God. As in physical life, there is life before spiritual birth. A person becomes open to Christ. He questions. He searches. He prays. There are the beginnings of relationship. At conversion there is a dramatic change as he is forgiven, reconciled to God and regeneration takes place in his spirit. Life begins, real life. But it just begins.

The task of the church in regard to the newborn is neither to drop him and look for more births, nor to expect the newborn to run with the ball. The spiritual baby can and should tell what he knows, and that will bring some conversions. But why have many of those who've been Christians several years ceased sharing the bread of life? Has starvation set in? One reason for lack of effective evangelism is lack of effective nurture. Those concerned with evangelism should not fear nurture, but welcome it. In the long term, *all genuine spiritual growth reproduces itself.* Christ has no interest in comfortable, self-serving bodies of believers who learn facts and do no work. He has every interest in the continual transformation of a person into a loving individual, who, because of his relationship with the Lord, is capable of handling his own problems in such a way that he is able to give himself to others in the name of Christ. This kind of life is attractive to the world. People excited about a continually growing relationship with Christ will not be difficult to motivate for evangelism. Paul saw the total purpose of his life as bringing people to maturity in Christ.[2] That means taking each person wherever he is on the continuum, before or after conversion, and moving him to the next step.

"Christlikeness" means right beliefs and right behavior, although many have a very narrow view of both. We know the tests of orthodoxy—does a person believe the right things about baptism, the Lord's supper, etc. Yet many who could pass the true/false Sunday-school final wind up in the pit of sin. The Christian way is more than knowing certain information and giving mental assent.

Behavior is most commonly defined in negatives. Christian behavior to many is what a person doesn't do. We think we know what a Christian doesn't do, but what *does* he do? Christ was not noted for His abstinence (in fact, He was criticized for alleged indulgence) but was set apart by His positive concern for suffering individuals. Although He didn't smoke or swear (as far as we know), that was not central. His behavior was different. He cared.

Too many define Christianity in terms of externals. But "good Christians," while sometimes respected, don't attract many nonbelievers to Jesus. "Good Christians" don't change the world.

The goal is transformation to Christlikeness.

Characteristics of Implementation

What is our model for encouraging growth in people? A business? A school? The home? Most people would say the home is far and away the best setting for transmitting the Christian life. If that's true, *why are our churches patterned after schools?*

Picture a dynamic Christian teenager whose home life was exemplary. Hypothesize what it was in the family life that sparked his commitment and enthusiasm. Could it be the following scenario?

> One Sunday Dad comes home from worship with a deep conviction about his role as family leader. He announces that Tuesday after dinner he'll be teaching minor prophets for the whole family. Thursday after dinner he'll teach restoration history, followed by Mom's class in Bible geography. Saturdays, everyone will be up at 6:00 a.m. for personal prayer. From 8:00 to 10:00, Dad will lead an evangelism seminar, after which the family will fan out in the neighborhood to pass out tracts.

If it seems ridiculous that the formal education pattern used in a home would produce a dynamic Christian youth, why do we think that using it in a church building will produce much better results? We begin with the assumption that the home, not the school, is the basic pattern for the church.

Six factors significantly affect a person's transformation to Christlikeness. Each of the six must be operative to bring noticeable change. A breakdown at any one reduces effectiveness to a small fraction of the whole.

Scripture

The first component of change is Scripture. To be effective, Scripture must be seen for its unique nature—truth to be lived, not information to be learned.

Christian teaching is not like public school teaching (it is a mistake to assume that public school teachers automatically make good Bible teachers). If a student knows the War of 1812 was fought in 1812, he has learned. Yet he may score a perfect mark on a Bible proficiency test and not have learned in a Biblical sense of knowledge.

There is absolutely no credit with the Lord for learning Bible facts apart from application and obedience. Some have the erroneous idea that if young people store up Bible truth, someday when they need it, they'll have it.

The Word of God is not neutral, but active. When obeyed it is the seed that germinates into character change. When it is disobeyed or ignored, hardness of heart will result. The Pharisees were the most knowledgeable people of their day in Scripture, and were the hardest group for Jesus to reach. The toughest kids to get through to are often the ones who grew up in the church.

One of the worst things a church can do for its youth is to teach Bible facts without adequate application and encouragement for response. Ordinarily it takes at least as long to apply a fact as it does to discover one. In an average Bible lesson, we might figure two to five times as much time for application as discovery. This schedule allows no room for fifty minutes of Bible information, a quick encouragement to apply it, and a closing prayer.

Many Christian teachers do not take the Bible seriously. They adopt systems that reward learning Bible facts alone. The Word of God is not learned until it is *lived*. Teaching children and youth that they have done well because they have memorized verses or recalled information is to encourage them to stop short of truly learning Scripture. The Word will bring change in life when it is applied and obeyed.

We must also place teaching people *how to study* the Bible on a higher priority than teaching the Bible itself. If you come to my house and find me shoveling applesauce into my six-year-old's mouth, you might conclude he's handicapped. We have populated churches with generations of spiritually handicapped people who depend on their preacher or Sunday-school teacher for their regular spoon feedings.

It is possible (and desirable) for a person to regularly read and study the Bible on his own by the time he's in ninth grade. It is much more important for the church to provide him the tools for Bible study than to nurse him along without them. Group Bible study provides a supplement and balance to personal study—it is never a substitute.

The Holy Spirit

The second component of transformation is the Holy Spirit. Apart from Him, we are nothing; with Him, we have life.[3]

The church is desperately in need of positive teaching on the Holy Spirit. Some give so much attention to a few spectacular gifts they miss His power to change lives. Others are so concerned with refuting Pentecostal error and establishing correct doctrine that *they* miss His power to change lives.

It is in the Spirit that Christ is with us and dwells in us. The character change we seek is His fruit.[4] It is by His power that we rise above mundane human existence to be the people of God.[5] It is in His strength, not our own, that we live moment by moment.

Example

The third component of change is a living example. Paul wrote to the Thessalonians to follow the example of Silvanus, Timothy, and himself.[6] It is one thing to picture the beauty of a principle, but another to see one lived out.

This modeling is easily the scariest of the factors of growth. Being a model of the Christian life makes demands that many do not want to face. It is not hard to talk about Jesus. It is difficult, though, to *live* like Him. When we make a person a youth leader in a church, we are really saying to the kids, "Be like him."

We're concerned because we're not reaching more youth. Could one reason be that they don't find the lives of adults in the churches very attractive? *The major test of the effectiveness of a professional youth worker is his ability to develop quality adult youth leaders in the congregation.* This represents a major change in orientation for most youth ministers who see their jobs as working with kids. While a love for young people is the prime motivation for entering youth ministry, it is also the prime motivator for making adult leaders the main priority of youth ministry.

Relationship

Transformation takes place when Scripture is brought to life by the Spirit in the life of a person who has a living example (model) of Christian growth and comes into a close relationship with that leader. This fourth factor (relationship) determines the amount of effect the leader will have on the learner. Larry Richards in *A Theology of Christian Education* lists the qualities of a relationship likely to promote the learning of a lifestyle:

First, there must be frequent, long-term contact with the leader. The key words are *frequent* and *long-term*. What does this say about the life-changing effect of the hour-a-week Sunday-school teacher? What does this say about the one-year "contract" for a youth sponsor? And what does this say for the growth of adult youth leaders when the youth minister changes every year and a half?

Second, there must be a warm, loving relationship with the leader. How do kids know their parents love them? Because they provide food, clothing, shelter, and an allowance? Certainly not. Kids don't see that as love—that's merely what parents are supposed to do. How do kids know leaders love them? Because they show up, are on time, and have well-prepared lessons? Certainly not. That's what leaders are expected to do. Our question is what they *perceive* as love.

Third, the youth needs to see the leader in a variety of life situations. The key word is *variety*. If we wanted to show them how to teach Sunday school, we established a good structure for doing so, but some leaders show them little else.

Next, there must be exposure to the inner life of the leader. Instruction must accompany shared experience. The learner must not only see the behavior of the leader, but hear the feelings, values, and motives behind it. My father was an excellent husband model, but I didn't learn much from his example. During eighteen years in the same house with him, his example didn't rub off on me. I wish so much now we'd taken time to discuss what makes a good husband before I had to learn the hard way. Actions must be explained, motives revealed.

It is also essential to share failure as well as success. We have an illusion that leaders need to show perfection. My reaction to seeing leaders confess weakness has been great relief in knowing I wasn't the only sinner. Seeing our leaders fail, but grow through their failure, gives us hope. The kids know the leaders blow it, anyway, so the leaders might as well be honest.

Life Situation

The fifth major factor in growth is the life situation. The emphasis of Jesus in training the twelve was on what we have come to call the "teachable moment"—an informal conversation that arises out of sharing a life experience.

Suppose we could interview Peter, a coward who became a model of courage. We like Peter because we relate to him. His mistakes were so evident. Yet from this fallen warrior Jesus built a powerful preacher and servant, so we ask Peter, "What did it? What made the change?"

I think Peter could quickly take us to some turning points in his life. One would be when he told the Lord He shouldn't be crucified, and Jesus called him "Satan." No doubt this was a memorable experience, one filled with hurt, but one prompting deep thought and reflection.

I believe Peter would also take us to Galilee following the resurrection. Following his denial of Jesus, he now stands face-to-face with the risen Lord. Christ asks if Peter loves Him. He repeats the question. He asks if Peter even really likes Him. Racked by guilt, Peter struggles to answer. But at what may have been the low point of his life, Jesus commissions Peter to care for His sheep. Peter's worth is reaffirmed.

The great life-changing events for most people are not sermons and lessons. A young man who had been blessed by four years of my best teaching and preaching had the gall to tell me several years later that he didn't remember one Sunday-school lesson I'd taught. He couldn't remember a single sermon I'd preached. Just before my heart shattered, however, he told me he remembered many conversations we'd had over a Coke and on the golf course.

Consider Jesus' ministry. Suppose He'd have been able to do only one facet of His work—either the public (large group preaching and teaching), or the private (working with the twelve). Which would He have chosen? Had He taken the public, the church would probably not ever have gotten off the ground. Had He chosen the private, the church would have begun much more slowly than it did, but would still have had a solid foundation.

A balanced ministry uses both the formal teaching and preaching setting and the small group or one-to-one informal discussion that arises from shared experience. It *focuses* on the informal, realizing that therein lies the greater potential for change. A person is most likely to change when he is in a state of disequilibrium—some level of mental or emotional imbalance caused by a recent experience. His interest level is higher because he is already involved in the experience.

A young man gets into a loud argument at a church softball game. Two girls are jealous of each other over a shared boyfriend. A youth sponsor wants to quit because the group's not going anywhere. Our personal discussions of temper, jealousy, and commitment in these settings with the people involved will have far more effect than good sermons on the same subject next month. The solution is not to quit public preaching and teaching, but to see the full range of Jesus' ministry.

If we see Sunday school, youth meetings, and midweek Bible study as the backbone of our youth program, either we know something Jesus didn't or we're on the wrong track. The work of Jesus with the twelve and real-life setting of the Christian home are our examples. Our job is to foster those kinds of situations with youth.

Time

The final factor in transformation is time. True spiritual growth always takes time, usually lots of it. Look how long it has taken you to become such a fine person! Adult leaders sometimes expect high school kids to act like they're thirty. A high school person can be serious, sophisticated, and mature one day, and the next day (or minute) act like a sixth grader.

Programs can grow quickly. Given an adequate budget, any youth worker worth his salary can produce a group of two hundred to three hundred kids in six months. But that's merely a body count. Jesus was never interested in those kinds of numbers. The reason we resort to contests, promotions, gimmicks, and the "big event" is simply that we don't trust God. We plant and water and expect an immediate harvest.

If the Scripture is taught for response, the Holy Spirit is given free reign in people's lives, and adult models are building loving relationships with youth and sharing many life experiences with them, over a period of time young people will come to live the kind of lives we've dreamed of. If these conditions are not met, no program, however attractive and well-attended, will have any worth.

---

[1]Ephesians 4:13
[2]Colossians 1:28, 29
[3]2 Corinthians 3:4-6
[4]Galatians 5:22, 23
[5]Ephesians 3:20, 21
[6]2 Thessalonians 3:7, 9

4

Practical Structures for Reaching the Goal

A. Discipling for Depth

by Dick Alexander

As you read, think about these questions:
—How can a leader define and create a "discipling" youth ministry?
—In what ways will the training of the discipled leaders differ from the training of youth and adult leaders in general?

The Bible is a *method* book, not just a *message* book. If a young man had just turned sixteen, but had received no driver's training whatever, would parents of sound mind give him the keys to a new 280ZX and wish him luck? The history of man is one of bungling the plans of God. Is it conceivable that God would give us the most precious treasure in the history of the universe and expect us to *figure out* a plan for getting out the gospel?

Jesus' life provides us not only with an example of how to live as individuals; it is also a model for ministry. He showed us precisely how to work.

Discipling has become a catchword in recent years. In some circles it is quite faddish to speak of discipling. To some, discipling means only evangelism. To others it means anything we do with people to encourage maturing. But discipling in the context of Jesus' life means what He did to train the disciples, especially the twelve. This chapter will give a foundation for a discipling ministry, basic principles of discipling from Jesus' life, and some suggestions for implementing those principles in youth work.

Our Lord's ministry focused on the small group. He ministered to the masses, but chose twelve for intensive training.

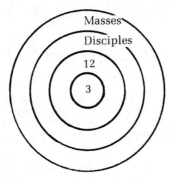

Figure 4-1. Jesus' relationships

He taught thousands. But from those thousands there were some people like Mary, Martha, Lazarus, with whom He spent more time. From the disciples He chose twelve men as traveling companions. Even in the group of twelve, Peter, James, and John were accorded special experiences (the transfiguration, the inner garden). It might be appropriate to add one more circle at the center of the target with a "1" in it for John, who was the disciple Jesus loved. *The closer we get to the center of the circles, the more time Christ spent with the people involved.* Those who see the preacher's main job as visiting non-Christians and disinterested church members are not following Jesus' example. He spent some time with each kind of people, but His priority was leadership training. The apostles were troubled by petty jealousies, but Christ would not permit His training plan to be curtailed by their immaturity.

A discipling ministry focuses on the few in order to reach the masses. Pouring one's life into a small group is not a dodge for the lazy who don't want a big job or for those who lack faith that God can reach many. Giving one's life in depth to a small group can never be permitted to turn into an "our gang" clique living in their self-contained Christian ghetto. Jesus' school of ministry was not a bomb shelter where the fainthearted could escape the reality of life in a pagan world, but a caring community of people oriented toward inward growth that would produce outward ministry. Working with a few is not a retreat to smallness but a preparation in the most significant way for bigness. The final product of discipling is *multiplication* of Christlike people. The task of the discipler is not to win converts, but to *reproduce reproducers.*[1]

Occasionally the quantity/quality debate emerges—do we want to be big or spiritual? The answer to the question is, of course, *both*. Contrary to popular opinion, they are not mutually exclusive—when we follow Biblical principles. The question is not which one, but which one *first?* The answer is again clear: quality. The first priority of our ministry should always be depth of spiritual life, since genuine spiritual growth always reproduces itself.

Let's create a situation for the purpose of discussion. Your goal is to grow the greatest number of quality people in the shortest time. You have a choice between two churches to which you have been called as youth minister. One has a group of one hundred kids, all spiritual zeroes. The other has a youth group of one kid, but he's committed. Which do you take? With the one committed kid, you're ahead to start with. If we count *disciples*, not bodies, you've got one. In the "big" group you've got none. Many youth leaders in small churches are discouraged because they don't have a large group. But if a group is not deep, it's easier to change a small group than a big one. The large group has more inertia—as someone breaks out of the mold, the group pulls him back down to their level. To reach the world, start where Jesus did, discipling a few who will then disciple others.

Some churches, in a hurry to have a recognized youth program, immediately whip up a program to bring in more kids. By adding more babies to a crowded spiritual nursery (alias "youth group"), they multiply the existing problem. Programs don't produce commitment. Godly people do. If we have the godly people, they'll reproduce. If we don't, we can't program around it.

Growing quantities of quality people means we must be the people of God before we can do the work of God. If we have assumed that our large group meetings were adequately growing our leaders, we have taken too much for granted. Our shortsightedness is seen by our frequent lament over lack of quality leaders. In Matthew 10 we find the account of Jesus commissioning the twelve. His "leadership training seminar" covered five general subjects: the "how to's," facing opposition, security in God, the cost of discipleship, and His care for them. Four-fifths of the content was personal growth related, one-fifth task related. *Christian leadership training focuses on the life of the worker first, skills second.*

Principles of Discipling

Jesus laid out a pattern of ministry designed for every church. In His work with the twelve, He demonstrated in detail how we are to minister. While thick volumes have been written on this subject, the following is a brief summary of four broad principles of discipling people to maturity.

Association
Christ began by making broad contacts as He traveled. From all those He met, He chose twelve after a night of prayer.

We wonder, why these twelve? Considering the diversity of abilities and personality types, it seems the single common denominator was teachability—they were willing to learn. There weren't many quarterbacks and homecoming queens, just mostly smelly fishermen. A fairly unlikely crew of world changers.

He chose these twelve to be *with* Him. Probably the most important verse in the second chapter of John in terms of its long-range impact on Christianity is the only verse from that chapter on which you've never heard a sermon. We know well the wedding at Cana of Galilee and the cleansing of the temple. But John 2:12 tells us that after the wedding feast Jesus went with His mother, His brothers, *and His disciples* to Capernaum and *stayed there a few days.* The disciples there observed Christ with His own family, most of whom did not accept His lordship at that time!

In Mark 7:31, we might pass quickly over the mention of a journey from Tyre through Sidon to the Sea of Galilee. Many Bible teachers believe that journey of Jesus with the twelve took four to eight months. What took place during that time? Probably some teaching and healing. But certainly there would have been hours and days of informal conversation.

The most significant transforming experiences in the lives of the twelve grew out of shared life. This could only happen because of much time spent *together*.

Our discipling relationships are fundamentally different from those of Christ with the apostles, in two ways. The first is that with everyone but Christ, discipling is mutual. There is one Lord, the rest are brothers. Jesus did not need to be discipled, although Peter tried occasionally. A person leading others by discipling them learns much from those he leads. The freedom to reprove, rebuke, and correct is mutual. The second difference in our ministry is that *together* we are the body of Christ. In the one person, Jesus, lived the embodiment of all the fruit and gifts of the Spirit. Since no individual demonstrates the fullness of Christ by himself, a person must be exposed over a period of time to a variety of leaders in the church.

Commitment

The first major concern of Jesus' ministry was association, the building of quality relationships by spending much time together. The second concern was commitment. We will see the commitment we desire so much (and find so rarely) in the contemporary church when we build commitment as Jesus did.

We know that Christ called the twelve to leave all and follow Him. What we don't often realize is that He'd spent a year with them first. In the first year of their relationship, Jesus asked little but time together.

We find a fascinating account in Luke 5:1-11. Before He called the fishermen, He gave them a great catch of fish. He first helped them to their goal, then invited them to His. Jesus invested great time and energy with them before asking anything from them. Most contemporary churches give little before demanding commitment. We love Him, however, because He *first* loved us.

Jesus saw commitment as progressive. The twelve grew in their level of dedication (witness Peter's denial and subsequent return and growth). Talk of total commitment sounds inspiring, but nobody suddenly jumps from zero to one hundred on the spirituality scale.

Jesus committed people to a cause, not an organization. He made them "fishers of men," not "bus captains." The question is not, "Will you teach junior highs because we have a vacancy?" but "Do you have an interest in junior-high-age youth and their growth?" The difference in the questions reflects vastly different views of ministry.

Training

The priorities in growing people are always their personal lives first, ministry skills second. The priorities in training methods are informal teaching first, formal teaching second.

The essence of discipling is the "teachable moment"—using a present experience for a lab in which truth is experienced. Formal teaching (a pre-planned lesson) goes from Scripture to life. Informal teaching goes from actual life to Scripture and immediately back to life. The interest level is much higher because the learner brings to the discussion a level of emotional involvement and anticipates immediate, accurate application. An open relationship is essential. "Speaking the truth in love"[2] is a regular feature of a significant relationship.

As the twelve began to grow, Jesus transferred responsibility to them for ministry. At first it was very simple. Arrange the people in groups. Pass out bread. He had them use existing, common skills while He showed them new ones. In the third year of their relationship Jesus began sending them out to teach and heal.

Jesus first demonstrated what He wanted done, then gradually involved the twelve in doing it. A common, useful description of the flow of responsibility from leader to learner is shown this way:

leader's role	learner's role
do	watch
do	help
help	do
watch	do

Christ followed demonstration with delegation and maintained supervision. People in specialized ministry (the paid professionals) are notorious for doing it all themselves. The results are seen in their fatigue, the immaturity of the troops and the impotence of the churches. Youth sponsors in many churches are punch and cookie people. In a valid youth ministry the adult youth leaders, not the paid youth minister, are doing the bulk of the teaching and counseling, with many of the young people involved in significant peer counseling with one another, and doing most of the shepherding and evangelistic work for their age group as well as having other ministry to the church at large. Three attitudes are necessary on the part of the leader in a specialized ministry if the "regular folks" are to do more than chaperone: he must get over his "messiah complex;" he must give them freedom to fail; he must be as excited about their success as his own.

Reproduction

The twelve were chosen to bear fruit.[3] The final test of discipling is that the learner becomes the leader and passes on his own growth. The Lord invested three years in the apostles and then turned them loose. Their lives were no longer directed by Him personally, but by their commitment to well-learned principles, the Holy Spirit, and accountability to one another.

The method of Jesus' ministry is the right method for ours. If you're a youth worker just beginning a ministry in a church, you will want to begin building relationships with adult leaders, prospective adult youth leaders, and youth. Since discipling focuses on the informal, share your meals, recreation, home life. Your key consideration should be "What am I doing that could be shared with others?" Some of these people are chosen for further training. It is not a question of picking people from a lineup, but of lives gravitating together.

The ages of the people involved is a factor. The leader generally must be older than the learner in this type of relationship. It is difficult for a young youth worker to "disciple" a middle-aged adult leader. He can, however, contribute to the growth of the adult if he is wise enough to ask questions instead of making statements.

Getting Started

Candidates for Discipleship

With whom do we start? There are two answers: the official leaders, and the hungry.

Begin with those already in leadership positions. Too often, they're not the ones eager to grow, but we must make every effort to reach those already designated as leaders. We give first priority to adults, then to youth, beginning with the oldest age group and working down. The leaders first, then other hungry people.

It's difficult to know how many to attempt to work with at a time. The Lord thought He could handle twelve effectively, so our number will be something less. These are people we work with very closely. Remember, Christ also gave himself to many other disciples and the masses. Some youth workers will work simultaneously with a small group of adults and a small group of youth. The most common mistake is to try to work with too many at once and not really affect anybody.

When adult leaders begin to disciple, they choose youth from the age group they work with; for example, a junior high male Bible-school teacher will choose a few boys from his class. Experience indicates that boys be with male leaders and girls with females, in groups of two to five, three or four being optimum. Not only are the masculine and feminine role models important, but people tend to be somewhat less concerned with impressing others and are therefore more honest with people of their own sex. Some churches prefer to focus on one-to-one discipling, rather than working with groups. The adult leader builds an aunt or uncle type of relationship with the youth, being a "significant other" adult, never a substitute parent.

Commitment

The commitment level asked from the people depends on their maturity. Initially a person is asked simply to spend some time with the leader and group. As their interest develops, the group is asked to put in time outside the regular group meeting in reading and study. Opportunities for serving are presented, and each individual is encouraged into a consistent ministry.

When people new to discipling are first approached, considerable time is spent in relationship building. When young people have been involved in being discipled previously, the leader may ask them in the fall to make a year's commitment to him for spending time together, studying, and ministry.

During teen years, a youth may need a series of discipling leaders (junior high, high school, college, or career) but an unhealthy dependency could also develop, fostered in part by the adult's need to be needed. The mature adult leader can give two to four years of his life to a youth and then pass on the young person to another leader, recognizing that together we're the body of Christ.

Activities

The leader begins building the group, as a group and as individuals, into his existing schedule (meals, recreation, etc.). Also, a regular meeting time of one to two hours, depending on age and interest level, is set for the group each week at a time the group agrees on. This is the formal part of discipling and forms a structure for group sharing and discussion. The leader encourages openness and honesty and sets the pace with his own example. Although the group meets regularly, the focus is on informal times outside the regular meeting.

Training the troops begins with their needs. The more quality time spent living, working, sharing, and discussing, the better the learners' lives come into focus and the clearer the understanding of their needs by the leader. As these needs are revealed, the discipler turns first to his own experience for resources that have helped him. The first answer to the question, "What do I study with them?" is a question: "What are their needs?" The second answer is also a question: "What has helped me?" He may then also seek other resources.

The regular, structured time each week is built on the detailed application of material the group is studying together. It may be Scripture study, Bible related books, other Christian books, tapes, or workbooks. Initially a part of the group time may be spent in doing the study. As soon as possible, the group should begin to study in advance for meetings, so that the time together can be spent on implications and application.

Objections and Answers

Some youth ministers just contemplating discipling the youth in their church will see the task as hopeless because they have trouble getting one good adult leader for every fifteen kids, much less one for every three or four. But we don't cancel visitation just because we don't have enough callers to visit every house in the city in one night. Start where you are, discipling the best available adults and then turn them loose on the peer youth leaders first and then on other hungry kids, until you reach the fringes of your church and beyond.

Some object to discipling because it sounds like it would make cliques worse. Cliques are the product of immaturity. Most find that the maturity brought through a discipling relationship reduces the insecurity that produces cliques. Existing barriers in their youth groups begin to dissolve as discipling progresses.

Some who are most drawn to lead in discipling are least qualified. Because of their own psychological needs, some are drawn to this role from a desire to dominate another person. Discipling is not like a mother duck followed around by her babies. They are not our disciples, but His. These are people with whom we spend a few years and share all we know about Christ, and then turn loose. A leader has no authority in the life of the person he works with. Contrary to some popular trends, he is not a spiritual father to be obeyed. The leader's role is to stimulate, not smother.

You As Discipler

As you work with the troops, open your home. Spend much time together. Play golf, tennis, racquet ball. Go shopping or to a game. Jog together. Diet together.

Let them observe your ministry and help. Give them major responsibilities. Ask for reports. Discuss. Evaluate. Encourage them into ministries of their own. Give them plenty of rope. Push them gently into challenging situations.

Confront openly. Use teachable moments. Welcome adversity as opportunities for advancement. Encourage much.

Disciples regularly fail (witness the twelve). Deal with failure graciously, and keep pressing on.

Finally, turn them loose. Maintain contact.

Conclusion

Discipling is not *a* way of ministry. It is not just an *option* for us, if Jesus' example means anything.

Discipling is not a "program." It is not one more thing to be built into the church schedule or another series of meetings. It is a *lifestyle,* affecting our whole way of approaching the body of Christ. It is not merely a group meeting, unless we permit it to deteriorate to that, but focuses on shared life and informal teaching.

Discipling is not working with Christians. Discipling is

building a relationship that results in moving a person toward Christlikeness, whether he is a growing Christian or a disinterested nonbeliever in need of rebirth.

Discipling is not smallness. It is not a safe retreat for the fainthearted. It is concerned with reaching *all nations.*

Discipling is not new. It may have been recently rediscovered, but it permeates both the gospel and history of the early church in the epistles and Acts.

Many honest Christian youth leaders lament the lack of depth in both adults and youth in their churches, yet remain tied to conventional programming. The answer may not be in trying harder, or finding better bands, more balloons, and wilder activities. A Biblical lifestyle will be developed by a Biblical approach to ministry.

To begin discipling in a church that has, in the past, run a YMCA-style program requires a firm belief that discipling is Biblical. Results are slow at first. Changes in churches come slowly because people change slowly. Beginning with a few to reach the masses means that for a while the numbers may not be impressive, but it also means that few changes in existing church programs will be necessary at first. Jesus did not announce to the world He was working with a few men. He just did it.

---

[1] 2 Timothy 2:2
[2] Ephesians 4:15
[3] John 15:16

B. A Creative Approach
to Effective Bible Study

by Ed Fine

As you read, think about these questions:
—What specific methods can be utilized in practical Bible study classes?
—What specific strengths and benefits stem from each method?

Bible Study and Exposure to Bible Content

The idea of determining what the Bible means is not limited to the minister and the scholar. More Christians today seem to be interested in finding out for themselves both what the Bible says and the applicable meaning of its words.

The Bible is not the only document that must be studied to be understood. One of the classic examples of such a document is the Constitution of our United States. Throughout our history, the justices of the Supreme Court have given full time to interpreting what the Constitution said and meant when it was written and what it actually means today. We must use the greatest care in interpreting the Bible, for we are dealing with material of infinite worth—the very message and revelation of God.

Through the 60's, Christian and public educators focused primarily on the teacher, teacher education, and instructional techniques. But in the 70's, the focus turned toward an emphasis on the learner. The wise teacher's primary concern is how a person learns and how he, as the teacher, can best help the learner.

The Bible teaches us that "a wise teacher makes learning a joy."[4] For this reason, it behooves a teacher to plan for his learners' changed behaviors.

Young people are inquisitive by nature. Their eyes must see,

their ears hear, and their hands move. An old adage wisely says: What I Hear, I Forget;
What I See, I Remember;
What I Do, I Understand.

The basic task of the Sunday school and the youth hour is to teach the Bible. This task can be accomplished in many different ways. Any one method used over and over soon loses its effectiveness and causes boredom. However, if one uses a variety of ways to teach and involve his learners, covering what the Bible says, the Bible becomes, as it is in reality, exciting to study and relevant to the learner's life.

Involvement and relevancy can be accomplished through the use of "Bible learning activities." A Bible learning activity is a method or orderly way of teaching. The activity must be purposeful. It is a learning activity, one that causes learning to take place. It is a learning activity that involves the Bible. The Scripture and its relevance to our lives is the center of every Bible learning activity.

Types of Bible Learning Activities

The following Bible study methods will help children, youth, and adults discover the wonders of God's love and the value of His truth for their lives.

Discussion is a deliberate conversation between two or more people on an assigned topic.

Most discussion techniques can be used best in small groups. Starting a discussion and keeping it going is easy if a teacher follows one basic rule: Ask an open-ended question that cannot be answered with "yes" or "no."

Research activities involve learners in reading, studying various resources, and collecting and analyzing data to arrive at an answer.

Research assignments give the opportunity to assign Bible exploration and conclusion/decision questions. Such work develops thinking and reasoning habits in the learners and helps guide the learners in applying the Scripture to their own lives.

Research assignments are limited only by the imagination of the teacher and learner. Research can be an individual or small group assignment and can be done in or out of class.

Lecture techniques are those in which the communication is one way, that is, from teacher to learners.

Lecture is best used to relay a quantity or "block" of information in a short period of time.

Whenever possible, lectures should be accompanied by illustrative audiovisuals to maintain the learners' interest and make the learning more lasting. However, research shows that over-use of any lecture method eventually creates negative feelings in the learners because they have no opportunity to contribute to the discussion.

Written activities are primarily those in which learners use pencil and paper to express their ideas through creative writing. It also provides the kinesthetic approach to learning.

Pencil and paper activities can be used to clarify feelings, thoughts, and ideas, to stimulate thinking, and to allow for individual expression.

A written idea can be shared, analyzed, and evaluated much more easily than a verbal thought can.

A large class can be divided into subgroups, each of which determines some common ideas about an assigned topic. Each subgroup can work as a team in preparing its contribution, which is shared with the other subgroups.

Dramatic activities involve learners in acting out assigned or chosen roles as a learning experience.

Dramatic activities build strong group spirit and help learners gain insight and understanding on their own.

Dramatic presentations strongly reinforce the learning that has taken place during the preparation period prior to the actual presentation.

One popular dramatic activity is role-playing. A problem/concept situation is briefly acted out, with emphasis placed on individuals identifying with the characters. This is followed by a discussion of the problem/concept presented.

Another dramatic activity that is especially effective today is the use of puppets, which enables the learner to express ideas he might not otherwise reveal.

Art is any pictorial, graphic, or symbolic expression of a theme, a story, a feeling, or an idea—including paintings, doodlings, drawings, and designs.

Art activities can be used to capture the interest and stimulate the imagination of the learners by allowing creative, non-verbal expression of ideas.

An important principle to remember in using art is that the process is more important than the product.

Music-related activities involve learners in studying or composing songs. We are taught to "make a joyful noise unto the Lord," so we should encourage all learners to contribute.

Music should be recognized as a learning medium. These activities can be used to teach Bible facts, explore the meaning and place of music in learning, translate a form of entertainment into learning experiences, and express ideas, thoughts, and emotions.

Utilization of as many methods of Bible teaching as possible further insures success. The subject never changes, but the teaching procedures evolve with the needs of the learners.

Teachers must always select the activity according to the aim of the lesson and plan a variety of activities within the curriculum.

In conclusion, several results are achieved when the teacher uses appropriate methods in the Sunday school and youth hour:

1. The teacher's role is that of guiding and helping the learner in learning from the Bible. The learner takes the responsibility of learning and therefore, he learns more.

2. Retention is greater when the learner becomes involved. Research shows that we retain twelve percent of what we hear and ninety percent of what we do.

3. The learner relates the Bible to his own experiences, and applies its truth to his own daily life.

Today is the day we must help our youth to find the joy of discovering what the Bible says by using activities in our Sunday school/youth hour that are helping to change attitudes and lives.

---

[4]Proverbs 15:2, The Living Bible

C. Koinonia (Fellowship) in Process

by Paul Schlieker

As you read, think about these questions:
—What is the Biblical mandate for Christian fellowship?
—What groupings and methods will most likely cause the desired
  koinonia to develop in your youth groups?

Biblical Precedent

God has always valued fellowship at the human level. In fact, our relationship to one another is so important that Jesus said "loving our neighbor" is second only to "loving God."

As told in the book of Genesis, the first sin destroyed the fellowship between man and God. Adam and Eve were banished from the Garden of Eden, and they forfeited the relationship they enjoyed with their creator.[5] Sin destroyed the fellowship between man and his fellow man when Cain, with bitter envy, killed his brother Abel.[6] With these two sins, fellowship between God, man, and his brother was destroyed.

The Israelites thought they pleased God with all their burnt offerings, Sabbath assemblies, feasts, and prayers, but God said these had become a burden to Him. He hated their solemn assembly mixed with iniquity. The Israelites' problem was in their relationships with one another. They had oppressed the poor and the widows and orphans of their day; their hands were full of blood.[7]

The Good Samaritan was commended over the priest and the Levite because he took time to help his neighbor.

The early church was committed to fellowship.[8] Their fellowship included the whole of life. They purposed to meet each other's spiritual, emotional, and physical needs. This "common life" was not merely an experiment in Jerusalem, but it became a distinguishing mark of the first century church.

John said, "If any man says 'I love God,' and hates his brother, he is a liar."[9] Jesus said, "By this will all men know that you are my disciples, if you have love for one another."[10]

So from the Garden of Eden to the book of Revelation, our fellowship with one another is of major importance to our standing with God. Not only that, our positive relationship with one another in the body of Christ is essential for spiritual growth. No man can do a "solo" in the kingdom of God. No "private" treks can be made to Heaven. God has given us the gift of community.

Thanks be to God for providing a plan for total reconciliation! He wants us to be reconciled to one another in the family of God, the church. These two basic relationships are essential for any Christian: failure to mature in either love toward God or love for a brother spells disaster for a person's spiritual life.

Unfortunately, many Christians today equate fellowship with a potluck dinner. Biblical fellowship (koinonia) is not an option for the church, it is a command. Listed below are just some of the activities of Biblical fellowship.

John 13:32—Love one another
Romans 12:10—Be devoted to one another
Romans 12:10—Honor one another
Romans 15:7—Accept one another
Romans 15:10—Be of the same mind with one another
1 Corinthians 12:26—Weep and rejoice with one another
Galatians 5:13—Serve one another
Galatians 6:1—Restore one another
Galatians 6:2—Bear one another's burdens
Ephesians 5:21—Submit to one another
Ephesians 6:18—Pray for one another
1 Thessalonians 5:11—Encourage one another
Hebrews 10:24, 25—Stir one another up to love
James 5:16—Confess sins to one another

These actions of fellowship create the necessary environment for spiritual growth. Without the habitual practice of the above mentioned concepts, our churches will deteriorate into mere social clubs.

The muffled cry of millions is expressed in a song by Ken Medema: "Don't tell me I have a friend in Jesus until I have a friend in you." We long to find a group in which we can find identity, acceptance, and strength. That group should and must be the church.

In youth ministry, the mark of a mature youth group is the ability to love one another. The members of a youth group can know more Scripture than the apostle Paul, have a teen choir that surpasses the Mormon Tabernacle Choir, and include every student in the local high school. But without *love*, that youth group is nothing, a "noisy gong," a zero in the kingdom. Our goal with young people is more than filling them with Bible knowledge. We must equip them with Biblical *attitudes* of love and sensitivity toward one another. When we begin balancing their love for God with their love for one another, we will be closer to the kingdom than we were before.

Practical Application

In a youth program, fellowship must be expressed in a diversity of forms and structures. Young people need both small group (three to six people) and large group (fifteen to fifty-plus) experiences. The youth program that only has "big" youth meetings, with no opportunity for small group sharing, greatly limits the development of intimate fellowship. On the other hand, the youth program that allows for only small group expression tends to become ingrown and stagnant.

A youth group should meet together in a large group for the following reasons:

1. The large group develops that total group identity.
2. A large group is often more exciting than a small one, and can often motivate through sheer numbers.
3. The large group provides the opportunity to teach that we need every member of the body of Christ. If we see only our closest friends, we're never stretched to learn to accept those who are different from us.

However, don't forget to aim for balance. Small group structures are important too:

1. In a small group, the adult can focus his attention on the needs of a few, and thus be a more effective leader.
2. Small groups provide the best environment for the most intimate kind of Christian fellowship. We often don't

want to open up in front of a large group. We feel threatened. A smaller group makes us feel more comfortable; more willing to share and to express needs.

Large Groups

At First Christian Church our high school youth group meets every Sunday evening after the service as a large group. We call it "Senior High Koinonia." We usually meet in a person's home. The purpose of our gathering is relational. Though we discuss the Scriptures, our main purpose is not to have another Sunday school. Our main focus is people. We try to learn more about one another. It's a time of large group interaction. We stress the importance of being the body of Christ and loving and accepting one another. We openly discuss our differences and emphasize how those differences are positive. We emphasize the strength that comes from unity. This weekly meeting complements our Sunday-school hour and small groups. We strive to provide variety without losing our relational goal.

Some of the activities at "Koinonia" include singing, games, sharing, confessing, and praying. Sometimes one person talks to the whole group, and then we divide into smaller groups to discuss what was said. At other times, we share what God has been teaching us in our personal devotions. Some nights are filled with laughter, others with tears. The time is one of love, openness, and growth in the body of Christ.

Small Groups

We also encourage our young people to participate in a midweek program called "Discipling Groups." We feel these face-to-face groups are essential if we are to deepen our trust and commitment to one another.

The groups of three to six members organize every September. The young people help select the adult leader for their group. The role of the adult leader is to model a consistent Christian life with his group. It isn't necessary for him to be perfect, but to be in a process of spiritual maturity and growth.

The role of the student is that of a participant who ministers to the other members of the group. They encourage through listening, sharing, and confessing their own weaknesses.

Resources

Some groups study a Bible book. However, most groups have

some kind of study guide that they use along with their Bible. Resources include:

1. *Discussion Manual for Student Relationships* (three volumes) by Dawson McAllister
2. *Discussion Manual for Student Discipleship* by Dawson McAllister
3. *Profile for Christian Maturity* by Gene Getz
4. *Profile for the Christian Lifestyle* by Gene Getz
5. *The Measure of a Man* by Gene Getz
6. *Now That I'm a Christian* (two volumes) by Chuck Miller
7. *Bound For Joy* by Stuart Briscoe
8. *At the Testing Tree* by Ward Patterson
9. *Christian Use of Emotional Power* by H. Norman Wright
10. *Celebration of Discipline* by Richard Foster
11. *Be Joyful* by Warren Wiersbe (Warren Wiersbe has a complete "Be . . ." series published by Victor Books)
12. *Spiritual Warfare* by Ray Stedman

These discipling groups are patterned after Jesus' example of discipleship in the New Testament. We attempt to provide a structure in which Biblical content and loving relationships can be intricately combined as He did with the twelve.

Supplemental Activities
The discipling group leaders are encouraged to look for informal opportunities for contact along with their weekly meeting. Attending plays, concerts, sports events, going out for breakfast or lunch, and working together are just some of the opportunities available for fellowship and ministry.

Many other activities can help reach the relational goals of youth ministry. Summer camps, retreats, youth trips, wilderness backpacking, youth banquets, picnics, bike hikes, work projects, and many other special activities all have a relational dimension. When used properly, they can bring people closer to one another.

Conclusion

The church is not the home, nor is it a replacement for the home. But with proper planning and willing adults, the church can supplement family ties by providing meaningful relationships within the body of Christ.

In his book *Dare to Discipline*, James Dobson says that the person who isn't loved dies! Evidence of this fact, he writes, was observed in the 13th century when Frederick II conducted an experiment with fifty babies. He wanted to see what language they would speak if they never heard a spoken word. The babies were fed and kept warm, but never talked to. All fifty babies died. Love and fellowship are as essential to our life as the air we breathe and the food we eat.

May we ever be committed to providing fellowship opportunities in which the love of God can be seen, felt, and experienced.

---

[5]Genesis 3:23, 24
[6]Genesis 4:8
[7]Isaiah 1:10-17
[8]Acts 2:42-47
[9]1 John 4:20
[10]John 13:35

D. Authentic Service
by the Youth Group

by Gene Shepherd

As you read, think about these questions:
—How do the examples of Paul and Christ illustrate what "service" really means?
—What plausible projects can put the theory of Christian service into action?

"Service" is not merely something that is to be done, but a way of life. In fact, Paul pointed out this attitude of Christ as being vital to our own Christian experience. The role of the youth worker is to develop (in others) eyes that see authentic service opportunities and willing hands that move to minister in the name of Christ.

In the second chapter of Philippians, Paul discusses the essence of Christian living: do nothing out of selfishness, regard others as being more important than yourself, keep a close check on your own personal interests. Then he points to Christ as the perfect embodiment of what he has suggested. Christ was God, yet He used His position to better man's lot, even though it meant great personal injury. While others might have used their rank to escape responsibility, Christ did what was best for mankind and took the form of a slave. Man's need was His primary concern, and He gave up all to fulfill that need. Servanthood, as defined by the life of Christ, is doing what is best for an individual regardless of the consequences. It is love in action.

Few would disagree with this definition of service, but daily implementation of the concept is sadly lacking in the average high school youth group. What are we doing? Carefully evaluate a few typical service projects: a money-making activity for a youth trip, Bible Bowl, painting and buying curtains for the youth room, the midweek Bible study, and the Fall retreat. These can be valuable projects. The problem comes when they monopolize the vast majority of our young people's time. Why? Because these projects are "self" directed. A token trip to the nursing home does not change the condemnation leveled by Paul in Philippians 2.

"That's just fine, but kids don't want to do anything unless it's fun," goes the usual response. But careful selection and planning of service projects, over a long period of time, can teach youth that service *is* fun. "Joy in Serving Jesus" is not just a hymn title, but a reality. The true servant of Christ has a purpose for life because of his ministry. There is a great satisfaction in that ministry as well as fellowship. Indeed, it is fun.

The best place to begin is where something needs to be done. Evaluate your congregation. Where is help needed? Are you overlooking areas of service? Are certain age-group or class needs going unmet? Find an area and begin serving that need.

One congregation did it this way. They had eighty-five shut-ins, 200-plus members over sixty-five, and no programs geared to this age level besides the regular Sunday-school classes. The leaders agreed that the youth could fill in some of the gaps.

The junior youth group's major thrust now is to the shut-ins. Their young people make holiday greeting cards each evening in youth group as a presession activity. Everything from Christmas to Halloween is utilized as an excuse for saying, "The Juniors are concerned about you." Every shut-in receives a handmade card every three or four weeks. Besides this outreach, the juniors call on shut-ins three times a year. The children sing, read Scripture, and pray for the shut-in before they leave. It is not unusual to find a shut-in's curtain or wall pinned full of the kids' homemade cards.

The junior-high group also ministers to shut-ins, but in a more specific way. They spend time, during the fall and spring, doing odd jobs for the elderly. Leaves are raked, windows are washed, and hedges are trimmed in the name of Christ. In each situation, the youth try to communicate a real concern for the individual. Junior highers also write and visit those in the hospital for extended periods of time. This is especially needed in the winter when so many elderly folks are sick or feeling forgotten.

The high-school group elects a senior citizen officer. Working with a family group, he plans and carries out a whole program of ministry to the aged. Under this group's guidance, the high schoolers plan and conduct a monthly chapel service for an area nursing home. They visit all eighty-five of the congregation's shut-ins at least twice a year. The teens individually visit and write personal letters to both shut-ins and nursing home residents three times a year. The group also plans and runs a Senior Citizen Carnival in the fall and a Senior Citizen Banquet in the spring, open to anyone who feels like a senior citizen.

The college-age fellowship ministers to two apartment buildings for the elderly. They visit, conduct special services, plan fellowship meals, and do odd jobs for the residents.

A few results of this program make a fitting conclusion. After the senior citizens found out the youth really weren't trying to finance a trip with their Senior Citizens Banquet, interesting things began to happen. The most enthusiastic supporters of the youth program were over sixty-five. Cakes and brownies came pouring in any time they were needed. When the youth did take a trip, senior citizens planned a special prayer chain to remember each young person daily for a two-week period. Encouraging notes and letters were frequently sent to the youth by their older brothers and sisters in Christ. Retired women often volunteered to go on retreats as cooks.

This ministry was not initiated to get something back in return. Lives were touched, and an exciting two-way ministry evolved into a blessing for the whole congregation. All the while, the young peoples' interest and participation in authentic service has remained high. They like being the hands of Christ.

Some Possible Service Projects

Juniors
—Shut-in visitation
—Make greeting cards for shut-ins, college students, and servicemen
—Set up chairs for fellowship events
—Straighten and clean hymnal racks
—Sharpen pencils for pew racks
—Decorate auditorium for holiday services

—Make centerpieces for church banquets
—Plant and maintain a flower bed at the church
—Fold the church paper and bulletins
—Stock church pantry by earning canned goods
—Write notes to absentees
—Play preludes on the piano for junior worship
—Make tray favors for nursing home or hospital
—Pass out bulletins

Junior High
—House and yard work for shut-ins
—Writing letters to college students, servicemen and missionaries
—Stuffing envelopes for bulk mailings
—Address the church paper
—Make posters to promote church functions
—Be greeters for a service
—Yard work at the church building
—Snow removal for church and shut-ins
—Nursing home visitation
—Repair toddler-room toys
—Polish church handbells
—Change bulletin board each month
—Distribute promotional material for VBS and revivals
—Set up tables and chairs for banquets
—Keep church buses clean
—Call on junior high youth
—Wash communionware
—Distribute Sunday-school papers
—Read to the blind
—Clean out the baptistery
—Adopt a grandparent
—Prepare drinks for church potluck dinner
—Change message on outdoor sign

High School
—General cleaning tasks for church building
—Typing jobs
—Baby-sit for adult group meetings
—Conduct nursing-home services
—Phone survey work
—Hospital visitation

—Run errands for shut-ins
—Play piano for youth church and graded choirs
—Service camp cleanup/fixup
—Pick up riders for church events
—Take publicity shots of church events
—Assist in food preparation and cleanup
—Youth calling
—Live nativity Christmas presentation
—Weekly participation in worship choir
—Run a "Fifth Quarter" outreach
—Music secretary
—Church librarian
—VBS workers
—Ushers
—Run chair lift for handicapped
—Coach junior basketball team
—"Sign" services for the deaf
—Work at First Chance camps
—Conduct revivals for area churches
—Man puppets for junior worship

Part Two

THE YOUTH PROGRAM IN THE LOCAL CHURCH

Section Outline

CHAPTER

5

Recruiting, Training, and Developing an Adult Volunteer Staff

by David Roadcup

As you read, think about these questions:
—What factors compel the youth minister to develop a pool of adult volunteers?
—What character traits in potential youth leaders show the greatest promise for success with youth?
—How can counselor recruitment be organized into an efficient, self-sustaining program?
—How can youth counselors, once selected, be trained in initial and ongoing programs for spiritual growth?

The superstructure of any solid youth ministry is the development of a qualified adult volunteer staff. These significant adults are the most effective teaching tools you will have at your disposal, and will require much of your time and effort. They will be helping to transform the young people of your church into the image of Christ.

The teaching, learning, and living of the Word of God is the foundation of any credible youth program. The framework for that foundation is found in the adult volunteer staff. These people are called sponsors, leaders, coaches, or counselors. They will be referred to in this chapter as "counselors" or "adult leaders."

Why Adult Leaders Should Be Cultivated

Every member of the church is a minister. The New Testament clearly teaches that every member of the body of Christ is a minister to that body. Each has a significant ministry to perform. Each is an integral part of the functioning of the church.

In Old Testament times, only men from the tribe of Levi who met certain qualifications were allowed to serve as priests. In the New Testament dispensation, all of God's people became ministers. Hebrews 4:14 says that now, Jesus is the ultimate High Priest and that we are all "a royal priesthood." Every person in the body of Christ is a minister. Each has duties and obligations to perform. Our gifts were given us "for the equipping of the saints for the work of service, to the building up of the body of Christ."[1] Each saint is to be prepared to minister, so the body can be built up.

Several significant adults in a congregation could assume a leadership role in the development of that congregation's young people. This form of ministry is one of the most important functions in the church.

It is impossible to do the job by yourself. Many youth workers are called to congregations "to work with our young people." They frequently do the bulk of the work themselves because that's what they think they were called to do and what the church expects of them. Other youth workers do most of the work themselves because they are the best qualified to do it. Both of these concepts are incorrect. It is illogical and impossible to do the entire job by yourself.

An excellent example of this principle is seen in the life of Moses. In Exodus 18 we find Moses judging disputes among the people of Israel. Moses is facing a severe problem: there are many more cases than he has time to handle, and he is inundated by the work load!

His father-in-law, Jethro, a wise man and "the original management consultant"[2] gave him some advice: "Moses' father-in-law said to him, 'the thing that you are doing is not good.' " What was Moses doing that was "not good"? He was trying to do all the work himself!

Sound familiar? How many youth ministers (and other ministers as well) are trying to carry their entire work load by themselves? Their number is legion! Alas, modern-day Moseses!

We so easily fall into the pattern of running, day after day, attending staff meetings, luncheon engagements, counseling appointments, planning meetings, hospital calls, church services, weddings, and social events, trying to maintain and build our relationship to the Lord, plus being good parents at the same time! We are like the man in the circus who has started numerous plates spinning atop sticks and must frantically run from one to another to keep all of them spinning.

Secondly, Jethro says to Moses, "You will surely wear out." Wearing out results from the type of work load described above. Moses was handling the disputes from morning till evening with no time off. Little leisure or relaxation.

Many ministers suffer from ulcers, nervous breakdowns, exhaustion, and extreme tension because they do not heed the admonition of Jethro, "You will wear out."

Thirdly, Jethro tells Moses, "The task is too heavy for you. You cannot do it alone." The work load was simply too great for Moses to handle by himself. He had not learned the important principle of involving and training others for the execution of a large task.

At this point, Jethro gave Moses a workable plan. First, Moses was to tell the people how to observe the statutes and laws and what work they were to do. Second, Moses was to divide the tribes up into thousands, hundreds, fifties, and tens, and assign honorable men to judge minor matters and disputes. This would leave Moses with the major cases to judge.

Jesus used this delegation principle extensively. He spent the majority of His time training His disciples and others to do the work that He was doing.

Paul also surrounded himself with men he was constantly training. He admonished Timothy to train others when he wrote to him and said, "And the things which you have heard from me in the presence of many witnesses, these entrust to faithful men, who will be able to teach others also."[3]

The major thought behind this story plus the examples of Jesus and Paul is this: the youth worker who tries to do the entire job by himself, who does not make a major attempt at teaching and training adult volunteer workers, is not following a logical or Biblical guideline for effective ministry. "The work of Christian leadership is [that of] preparing the people of God to minister."[4]

What are you going to leave behind? One of the acid tests of a good ministry is what you have left behind.

Many churches have become accustomed to the following style of youth ministry performed by a professional youth worker from a local Bible college: The new youth man comes into the congregation, establishes some quickie programs, runs on his personality, uses a lot of balloons, Kool Aid, and cookies, exhausts his "bag of tricks," and then is "called" to another ministry in which he does the same thing. This immature form of ministry and these quick moves cause a number of negative things to happen. First, it is almost impossible for any solid program to be established when a man moves every one or two years. Second, it severely damages the confidence the church develops in the youth ministry position and program. Adults may feel there is little reason to work in a program when its direction and emphasis changes with each new man.

I heartily recommend that a man take a congregation and remain there until he has done the following things: 1) established a staff of trained adult workers (counselors) who could function independently of his leadership; 2) developed and taught the congregation an approach to ministry based on Scriptural principles; and 3) established an extensive resource center that contains books, tapes, records, movie order catalogs, resource information, periodicals, curriculum materials, and filmstrips to be used in the work of youth ministry.

Many adults will grow because of their involvement in the youth program. Involvement in and exposure to ministry with young people will, in many cases, stimulate growth in the lives of the adults who are working in the youth program.

Continuous exposure to Bible studies, retreats, fellowship, counseling, and other forms of ministry to young people will cause adults to begin growing in areas that had been dormant for years. The time involvement, stress, and challenge of ministering to youth will lead adults into Christian growth and maturity. Paul told Timothy, "Pay close attention to yourself and to your teaching; persevere in these things; for as you do this you will insure salvation both for yourself and for those who hear you."[5]

The Effective Youth Counselor

Growing Relationship With Christ

It is absolutely impossible to

—Give something away you do not possess

—Feed someone if you yourself are starving

—Lead someone in places where you have never been

If an adult leader does not know the Lord, it will not take very long for the young people to discover that fact. It is impossible to create discipleship in the lives of our young people if we are not disciples ourselves.

Leaders of young people need to be deeply rooted in the Lord. They should know the Lord in a personal way. They should be striving daily to understand what the lordship of Jesus Christ means in their lives. Adult leaders must be dedicated Christians.

In his book *Knowing God* J. I. Packer says,

> What were we made for? To know God. What aim should we set ourselves in life? To know God. What is the "eternal life" that Jesus gives? Knowledge of God. "This is life eternal, that they might know thee, the only true God, and Jesus Christ, whom thou hast sent" (John 17:3).[6]

Sterling Example

The power of an exemplary life is awesome!

There is no way to measure the importance of example (or modeling) in teaching and maturing young people in Christ.

Whenever adults are placed in a leadership position of any sort, they are scrutinized by their learners. Young people watch what the adults say, what they wear, how they drive, how they treat others, what their lifestyle is like. Their way of life (example) is their greatest teaching tool.

Jesus taught mainly by His example. Over and over again, He demonstrated for the disciples how they were to act and react in different situations. He taught them with words, but He mainly taught them as they watched what He did.

The apostle Paul also taught in this fashion and understood this very important principle. In several different Scripture passages he tells his readers, "Follow me as I follow Christ."[7] What did he mean by that? Had he become perfect? No. He meant that when a person begins to mature in Christ, his life comes to the place where he can begin to model the life of Christ to others. Paul was at that place. The Lord also expects us to grow until, although not perfect, we can say to others, "follow my example as I follow Christ."

Nothing is more devastating in the church than leaders

(especially those working with young people) who teach great and meaningful things but avoid living the life themselves.

Love for Young People

Learning how to show a sincere love for the young people with whom you are working is one of the most significant methods of ministry you can employ. In an age of shattering divorce and the two-paycheck marriage, thousands of young people are crying out for love and attention.

One of the most important ways to show love and concern for young people is to spend quality time with them. Another is to show a genuine interest in them. Still another important display of love is to discipline your group with understanding. Making a phone call, sending a card, or just listening are also ways of letting young people know you care.

I have worked with adults in the past who declined to be volunteer workers in youth ministry because they felt they were not gifted at teaching or singing, athletics, or the production of visual aids. Therefore, they thought they were not able to serve effectively. But the ability to show mature concern and loving compassion stands out head and shoulders above other attributes in developing relationships with young people.

Emotional Maturity

Emotionally unstable youth need the stability that mature adults can and must provide. The youth counselor who has an acceptable level of emotional maturity, who loves from his mind as well as his heart, who exercises patience and control in stressful situations, who knows where and when to call a halt to fun that is getting out of hand, and who has developed a sense of humor, is a valuable asset to any youth program.

Sensitivity and Understanding

One of the most outstanding character traits of our Lord was His incredible sensitivity in dealing with others. The woman at the well, the woman taken in adultery, Zaccheus, the Gadarene demoniac, and Mary and Martha at the tomb of Lazarus are all beneficiaries of Jesus' great capacity for feeling with others.

Taking time to read faces and listening closely for hidden meanings are all part of developing a sensitive spirit. Having the courage to walk into one of their lives and offer help when they are crying out silently is part of showing gentle concern.

Creativity

What oil is to a set of gears, creativity is to the youth counselor. Our teaching, serving, loving, and ministering will all take on new dimensions when we work from a creative frame of reference.

God, our Father, is our example in creativity. In the opening pages of Genesis, we see Him creating. All through the Old Testament, God is creating a people prepared to receive the Messiah. In the New Testament, we see Him creating a physical Savior to provide our recovery. In Acts and the epistles, we see Him creating the church. At the end of Revelation, He is creating a new Heaven and a new earth.

Let us sand the rust from our imaginations and rekindle the flame of creation that lies within each of us.

Knowledge of Developmental Characteristics

The youth counselor must know the mental, physical, spiritual, and emotional traits of the age group with which he works. Understanding the needs, desires, drives, interests, and struggles of those with whom we are working is imperative for good teaching, communication, and understanding of where our youth are.

Dependability

Dependability is a critical factor in the lives of those involved in a volunteer capacity. If dependablity is not a growing characteristic in his life, a counselor will not only limit his ministry but will also lose credibility with the people with whom he is working.

Ability to Fail Successfully

Howard Hendricks writes, "Failure is one of the uglies of life. We deny it, run away from it, or upon being overtaken, fall into permanent paralyzing fear. Probably because of our reluctance to face it, not much is written about the anatomy of failure. As Christians, we wave our visionary banners proclaiming 'Victory in Christ,' refusing often even to admit that the path to ultimate victory may include intermediate bloody noses."[8]

Failure is occasionally a part of life. I know of no better opportunity for growth than failure. Our failures can destroy our direction for ministry and maim our creativity for life, or they can be looked upon as excellent learning opportunities.

Remember not to let negative experiences get you down. When one comes along, endure it, learn from it, and press on.

Counselor Recruitment

Planning for good recruitment will insure more effective training for the staff and clarify the job description for their ministry. Both of these items are vital for beginning the training process.

In the past, volunteer workers have been recruited in one of two ways.

The first (and wrong) method called for the youth worker to go to the home of the prospective counselor, lay the youth material on the coffee table and ask them to become counselors, usually "because no one else will do the job." This method sometimes works, but the usual result is that, because of a lack of proper training and motivation, the counseling couple quits after the third or fourth month.

The preferred method of recruitment is described below.

Step 1—*pray hard!* Begin your sponsor recruitment effort by bathing it in prayer! The Lord can move in the hearts of people in your congregation and lead them to your program. Pray for the following things:

—Pray for the Lord to lead you to people who have compassion for young people.

—Pray for adults who are willing to learn.

—Pray for good judgment in approaching people about working on the youth ministry staff.

Fervent prayer does work. Several years ago, I needed another married couple to work with the junior girls in our program. I had spotted a couple who were dedicated Christians who I felt would work out well in that slot. I prayed for several days and prayed again as I was driving to their home. When I arrived, I told them of our need. The husband told me that they knew why I was coming and had already discussed the matter. They decided that it would not be feasible for them at that particular time to take the job. Trusting their judgment, I told them that I would contact them at a later date. The woman of the house then offered me a piece of cake and a cup of coffee. While we were sharing together at their table, the man of the family asked me to give him some specifics about sponsoring the junior girls, and I told him what would be required. I put no pressure on the couple, but by the time I left, they had agreed to work with the junior girls! I sincerely believe that the Lord was working in that situation.

In congregations where there has been no youth program or where the youth program has been very weak, there may be problems getting qualified adults to help. Strong, specific prayer could be the agent in helping many of these potential workers to say yes.

Step 2—*determine your need.* As your plans begin to solidify, start to determine what your adult leader needs will be. To discover that, consider the following questions:

1. For how many groups will you be responsible? Are you in charge of only preteen groups (preschool through sixth grade), only junior high through college, or all age groups?

How you divide your groups will depend on the size of your congregation and the number of workers available. Usually, the more distinct the breakdown, the more effective your approach will be..

2. How many young people do you foresee in each group? If there has been a youth program in the past, you should have some idea of the number of young people you will have in each group—hopefully, allowing for significant growth. If there has been no previous program, examine the Sunday-school roll and arrive at a workable figure.

3. How many adult workers do you need in each group? I recommend that you recruit married couples when possible, for two reasons: First, if the couple has a strong marriage, this presents an excellent model for the young people to consider. Second, a married couple can encourage and strengthen each other as they work.

At the same time, singles can do an effective job because of their relative freedom.

In preteen groups (sixth grade and below), the accepted ratio is one adult worker to every five young people. This figure should be followed, but if you have never had an active program before, do not be disappointed if it takes you several years to reach it. In ministering to junior high age and above, the number of adults would depend on the approach that you are planning to use. I recommend a minimum of two adult couples to each group. If you are using a discipling approach (see Chapter 4A), the number of adults would have to be significantly increased.

Step 3—*begin looking for prospects*. Next, start searching for potential counselors. Begin looking in the Sunday school or church fellowship. The young married couples class is an excellent place to start. The usual age spread is 20-30. These couples are usually active and in many cases show a sincere interest in youth work. Next, go to a college-career group. Mature college-career young people make excellent counselors. They can identify readily with junior-high and senior-high youth.

Adults in the 30-40 age bracket also make excellent counselors. In many cases, they have children involved in the program and have a genuine interest in what is being done with and for their children.

The 40-50 and 50-60-year-old age groups also have excellent potential to work as counselors.

At this point, the question invariably comes, "Should parents work in the same groups as their children?" That question has several variables.

With four- and five-year-olds, it is definitely better to separate the children from their parents. With school-aged children, it depends on the relationship the children have with their parents. I usually ask the child in a very low-key way, how he or she would feel about a parent working as a counselor in the group in which he is a member. Most preteen children do not seem to mind, and the parents work out well in those groups. More junior high and senior high youth are opposed to the idea, and this is normal. The situation depends on the relationship the parent has with the child.

Be careful not to rule out the 60-70 age group; many people in that age group are interested in young people. This is an excellent age because of the grandparent image and the wisdom that can come from older saints who are intimately acquainted with the Lord.

If your congregation takes a yearly talent survey and tabulates the results, place the entry "Working with young people in a counselor capacity" on the survey sheet, and see if anyone you have overlooked might be interested.

I would also ask the other members of the church staff for prospects. If you are in a large congregation, the distribution of talent should be worked out with the other staff members so that a relative few members are not being bombarded with church service requests. Sharing the talent between departments and staff members is an important point to keep in mind.

You also may want to ask the young people themselves, or the youth committee, for suggestions as to adult counselors. Many times they will come up with names you have overlooked.

Make the search for adult workers one of the major priorities of your ministry all year long. Even after the staff is completed, I would still be on the lookout for prospects for possible future openings.

Step 4—*inform the congregation.* The need for adult workers should be brought before the congregation. You can do this by announcing your need at a board meeting and asking for the prayers and support of the church leadership in your recruitment effort. Have the minister preach a sermon on the need for qualified adults to serve. Announcements in church publications may also be helpful.

Step 5—*compile a list of prospects.*

Step 6—*visit prospective sponsors.* A personal visit not only shows the importance of the job, but it provides an opportunity for better communication—both verbal and nonverbal communication are possible.

Call and make an appointment with the potential counselor or couple. This insures that the potential counselors will be at home, and you will not offend anyone by just dropping in.

When you visit them, share the following information with the potential counselors:

1. You are trying to formulate the very best program you can.
2. It is impossible to do the job by yourself.
3. You would like them to consider becoming youth counselors.

Invite them to a training seminar that will be conducted at the church, to give them a clear picture of what a counselor is and does. At this first encounter, do not actually ask them to become counselors.

Step 7—*conduct the counselor training seminar.* At the seminar, explain what a counselor does, what the job expectations are for being a counselor, and how the counselor can do the best job possible.

For information on the details of the seminar see below.

Step 8—*second call.* After the counselor training seminar is concluded, make a second call on the prospective counselors and discuss the material covered and expectations shared. Was there anything that was not clear? Make sure the counselors have a clear understanding of your expectations.

Then ask them for a commitment of service for a definite period of time (a minimum time period would be one year). In many Bible-school class settings, when you "sign on," it winds up being for life. It is impossible to quit or change roles. Give your potential counselors the option of stepping down after a specific time period; a "light at the end of the tunnel." If someone on your volunteer staff has to be replaced, this can also take place at this time.

Counselor Training

The youth worker who wants to have a quality program knows the value of thorough and consistent training for the counselors ministering with him.

Three basic ideas should form the foundation of your training program.

Quality staff training should go on all year long. Adequate training does not take place once a year just before the "program" begins. It takes place consistently in various forms and different approaches throughout the year.

Impart to the counselors the quality information they need for working with young people. Counselors need to know about characteristic development of the age groups with which they are working, Bible study techniques, methods of discipline, and other topics needed for effective ministry to youth. Work hard to give your staff good information and direction in these areas.

Build the lives of the counselors as well as imparting knowledge to them about their jobs. Building the devotional life, marriage, parenting ability, character, and witnessing talent of the counselor is more important than teaching him how to conduct a successful social or how to use a 16-millimeter projector.

Since the life of the counselor is his most critical teaching tool, put much effort into building his life as well as what he knows about young people.

The Initial Training Seminar: A Workable Model

Assuming your youth year runs from September to August, and assuming your personnel have been recruited, begin your counselor training in late summer or early fall with a weekend seminar. After recruiting your workers, conduct a formal teaching seminar where you acquaint the counselors with the major objectives of the approach to ministry you plan to use, how you plan to meet those objectives, and how they as functioning workers will help meet those objectives.

Objectives. Three general objectives should be accomplished in the initial seminar (you will want to teach many other things as time allows in the future).

—The major goals you have planned for the program
—How you plan to reach those goals
—The counselors' role in reaching those goals

Time. The month before your program is to begin, select a weekend in which you can secure the greatest amount of participation by your anticipated workers.

If a weekend is not workable, try conducting the seminar two evenings a week for two weeks, working two hours each session. If this cannot be arranged, try one night a week for four weeks—two hours each session. For those who cannot make the training sessions, you might tape the sessions and allow them to listen later.

Place. Your church building will probably be the most advantageous place to meet, because of the availability of audiovisual equipment and meeting rooms. Or you might choose a large home. You may want to hold a weekend seminar in a retreat setting at a Christian service camp or a retreat house.

Preparation. Have lectures, discussions, and visuals thoroughly planned in advance. Be sure the room size will facilitate the size of the crowd. Check room temperature, lighting, and room arrangement. If you plan to use resource persons, be sure to secure them early. Inform them of the specific times and dates of the seminar. Make sure they know precisely what topics you want them to handle.

Content. In this initial seminar, try to cover the following topics:

—The importance of youth ministry
—A description of the job of youth counselor
—Characteristics of an effective youth worker
—Major and minor goals in youth work
—Structuring to reach our goals
    1. Discipleship—the foundation
    2. Effective Bible teaching

3. Fellowship for growth

4. Service and ministry

Listed below are additional topics you will want to share with your people throughout the year to come.

—Resources for ministry available to you

—Youth evangelism

—Socials

—Developmental characteristics of age groups

—Creativity and youth work

—Counseling youth

—Discipline in structured and nonstructured situations

—Involving parents in the program

You may want to use this volume as curriculum. I also recommend the following volumes:

Youth Ministry by Larry Richards (Zondervan)

A Theology of Christian Education by Larry Richards (Zondervan)

Youth Education in the Church Today by Zuck and Benson (Moody)

Creative Youth Leadership by Jan Corbitt (Judson Press)

Youth Ministry Sunday, Monday and Everyday by Carroll and Ignatius (Judson Press)

Quarterly Sponsor's Conference:
Training Beyond the Seminar

The purpose of the conference is to offer extended training opportunities throughout the year. This meeting should also provide fellowship and a time of encouragement. The conference should include three main parts: an "input session," a time for refreshments, and a fellowship and sharing time.

The "input session" could include a lecture or discussion. During this session, take a topic your counselors need to know about, and work through it with them. You may also want to bring in a resource person to share during this period.

The refreshment time following should offer a time for informal discussion.

The fellowship and sharing period can be organized in several ways. You may want to have a worship time together, a small group experience, or group sharing, ending with a time of prayer for the young people, their parents, and the program.

Some may be tempted to omit the fellowship segment of the format. Remember that one of the main objectives you have for your sponsors is to build their lives as well as giving them information. This time of sharing will strengthen and encourage your workers for their task.

Counselors' Retreat:
An Intensive Sharing and Growth Time

The counselors' retreat should accomplish the same objectives as the Quarterly Sponsor's Conference. The main difference is the time allotment for these activities. The retreat should provide for additional training opportunities, and allow time for worship, fellowship, and recreation.

Always take people other than your retreat attenders to do the cooking. If your participants prepare the meals, those involved in preparation will miss much of what is offered in the sessions.

I recommend that the counselors' retreat be held sometime in the spring.

Sponsor Resource Center

Select an area of your office, the church library, or some other area of the church facility and establish a *Sponsor Resource Center*. Stock this area with the following materials:

Books—secure as many books dealing with youth ministry as possible and have them available for checkout.

Magazines—order several magazines that deal with ministering to youth or youth-related issues.

Resource information—teaching aids, "canned materials," ideas books, and other helpful tools should be kept on file.

Cassette tapes—cassette tapes can be one of the best continuing education tools you can secure. Order tapes of seminars and sessions from schools, colleges, and conventions that deal with youth work.

Three important items will help your resource center to function properly and be used extensively: First, you must motivate people to *use* the center. Second, keep your workers informed about the materials available there and new materials coming in. Third, be sure the materials are checked out and returned. Poor management of the filed materials will soon result in the depletion of what you have amassed.

Clinics, Workshops, and Conventions

An additional way to continue the training of your people all year round is by taking them to seminars, clinics, workshops, and conventions whenever possible during the year.

Informal times (traveling, eating together, etc.) are also excellent times for building relationships and strengthening one another.

It would be good for the church to help with the expenses of sending your staff to any of these gatherings.

Counselor Development

In many ministries, the recruiting and training of the volunteer staff is handled well. Many ministers, however, forget about the all important area of staff development. It is critical that we also develop our people after they say "yes" to our request.

Staff development is the idea of working with the members of your staff in helping them continue to grow. They need additional training, encouragement, and help.

Below are some helpful suggestions that may facilitate positive development in your volunteer workers:

Spend personal and social time with your sponsor staff. Doing informal things together with individuals from your staff will give you excellent opportunities for discipling them. I always try to make the youth counselors good friends as well as "fellow workers."

On one occasion, many of our junior-high young people were participating in a band and choir program at the junior high school. I called our junior-high counselors, and we all attended the event together. What a response we received from our junior-high young people! After the event the sponsors came to our home for some light refreshments. It was a great evening together!

Bowling, a cookout, or other informal opportunities will provide good chances for building bridges. You can do hundreds of things on a social basis to build good relationships with your volunteer staff. This is a crucial part of building a good corps of workers.

Build and maintain the self-esteem level of your staff. Youth ministers make a major mistake if they take advantage of their volunteer workers. Working volunteers until they drop, without a word of thanks, is not healthy for the workers or your program. A sincere display of gratitude for service and hard

work is a strong Biblical mandate. Paul tells us to "Give preference to one another in honor."[9] A kind, thoughtful word of
thanks will go a long way towards making someone feel ap-
preciated for hard work.

In addition to verbal thank-yous, I also recommend hand-
written, personal letters and notes of appreciation. These are
appropriate ways to show gratitude to your counselors for their
labors of love.

In addition to showing appreciation, be open to the suggestions and ideas of your staff members. Work hard at developing
the creative input of your people. Remember that the minds
and ideas of your staff members are one of your most valuable
resources.

You may also want to devote one Sunday to showing appreciation to your volunteer staff. Introduce them to the congregation in the morning service. Have a dinner for them after
church, prepared and served by the parents of the youth whom
the sponsors have been serving all year. If you want to use that
day to its fullest, have a Sponsor Appreciation Service. In this
service, the young people, parents, and others can express appreciation and share specific instances of ministry that the
sponsors have performed. This not only provides a way of saying "thank you" to the staff members who have worked all
year, but it also allows the congregation members (parents,
grandparents, and others) to get to know the sponsors who are
working with their young people.

Another way to help maintain the self-esteem level of your
sponsors is to have them fill out a questionnaire that asks for
personal data, such as family and hobbies. At the end, ask them
to write a paragraph stating the reasons they feel working with
young people is important. Put this information into a brief
article for your weekly church publication.

The above two ideas are additionally valuable because both
let the parents in the church get acquainted with the adults
who are working with their children.

Conclusion

The foundation of any good youth ministry is the Word of
God. The superstructure of that ministry is a qualified and
trained staff of volunteer adult workers.

The youth minister who recruits, disciples, trains, encour-

ages, and loves his counselor staff is well on his way to building an effective youth ministry in the local church.

---

[1]Ephesians 4:12
[2]Edwin C. Bliss, *Getting Things Done.* New York: Charles Scribner's Sons,
1976, p. 28.
[3]2 Timothy 2:2
[4]Paul Benjamin, *The Growing Congregation.* Lincoln, Illinois: Lincoln Christian
College Press, 1972, p. 28.
[5]1 Timothy 4:16
[6]J. I. Packer, *Knowing God.* Downers Grove, Illinois: InterVarsity Press, 1973,
p. 29.
[7]1 Corinthians 4:16; 11:1; Philippians 3:17; 4:19; others
[8]Erwin Lutzer, *Failure: the Back Door to Success.* Chicago: Moody Press, 1975,
p. 9.
[9]Romans 12:10

6

Getting Started in Youth Ministry

by Les Christie

As you read, think about these questions:
—What important considerations should I weigh when I am deciding how to respond to a call for a youth ministry?
—What relevant questions should I ask in an interview for a youth minister's position?
—How can I get a practical, responsive youth program going?
—How can I measure the "success" achieved in my ministry?

June is "National Hire a Youth Minister" month, when a seminarian leaves the cloistered confines to enter the "real world," and is hired (called) to his first church. Too often July is "National Disenchantment With the Church" month, and December or (at the latest) May becomes "Leave the Church for Greener Pastures" month, and the cycle repeats itself.

Your First Youth Ministry

Much of the problem could be avoided if the youth minister had a clear understanding of the job, the church, and the senior pastor. I would ask myself three key questions before applying for a job as a youth minister: 1) Do I really want to be a youth minister? 2) Do I feel this is the church God wants me to work in? 3) Do I get along with and respect the senior minister?

Do I Really Want to Be a Youth Minister?

Many fresh, young, energetic, enthusiastic seminary graduates want to be youth ministers. They just get started in their first ministry, and their bubble bursts. They discover that being a youth minister is not all fun and games. All kinds of things go on in the local church youth group that floor them! Things school could never teach them.

One of the saddest statistics I know is the length of time the average youth minister stays with a local congregation. In California it is one year; across the country it is two years. That's sad! This occurs for many reasons. Many people, it seems, treat the youth ministry as a stepping-stone to the "real ministry." The youth ministry *is* the real ministry. This is where the action is. Certainly, it is a specialized ministry, but that doesn't make it any less of a ministry.

I hope you have a vision of just how important you are in God's kingdom. We need more older, mature, stable youth ministers. I plan to be a youth minister for life. If God wants to move me, that's fine, but my goal is working with kids. I love it. We youth ministers also need to stay long enough to see our failures, so we can learn by them.

When youth work is looked at merely as a stepping-stone to something else, then the youth leader cheats the kids he is working with. He can't possibly be giving all his time and energy to those kids, if in the back of his mind he is looking for some other ministry. Also, if this turnover goes on long enough in a youth group, with a new guy coming every couple of years, then those kids will question the next person who comes along, wondering how long he will last.

Another reason a person leaves the youth ministry is that he often times starts off as a part-time employee in a small church and gets discouraged. I hope this chapter will help you overcome that discouragement. Remember, these small churches may not have the vision you have, but never get so discouraged that you throw in the towel completely.

Another reason a youth minister leaves the youth ministry is that he doesn't like being low man on the totem pole—last one in the pecking order of a church staff. He can take only so many little ladies asking, "When are you going to be a real minister?" or saying, "You'll make a fine minister some day." After a while this can really wear on a man until he feels as if his position really isn't a ministry. So he leaves the ministry and ends up assistant manager of a McDonald's franchise. Or pride gets to him and he leaves for a senior pastorate.

Another reason the youth worker leaves is the sudden realization that youth ministry is not the area of service God is calling him to. Before he accepts a position in a church, he should diligently ask God to show him His will as to his area of service.

Scripture mentions many instances in which adults worked with kids, such as Barnabas with John Mark and Paul with Timothy. The closest thing to a youth minister might be Timothy's grandmother, Lois. She lived with her daughter and grandson and conveyed the gospel message with her life as well as her words. The worst youth minister is mentioned in 2 Kings 2:23, where Elisha came in contact with a number of kids who kept calling him "old baldy." Yikes! That kind of youth minister we can do without.

Is This Church Where God Wants Me to Work?

Many books on the market today can adequately cover the topic to finding God's will for one's life. However, some youth workers think of God as a celestial party pooper looking down out of Heaven. If He sees someone enjoying their ministry, He hits them on the head and yells, "Quit having a good time— this is a ministry!" Some youth ministers with this belief select a church that they have no desire to serve so that they can be living sacrifices acceptable to God.

It is inconceivable to me that a loving God would ask you to step into an obviously mismatched situation just to prove to God, yourself, and others, that you are really sacrificing. You would be of little service to the Lord or others in that area. God wants your needs and desires met as well as those with whom you will be working.

Could you bring your family to this church for strength, comfort, and good teaching, so that they will become mature, whole and complete in Christ? Are the people behind you? Will they support you in your ministry (not just financially)? What has been the experience of the previous youth minister, and why isn't he still there?

Do I Get Along With the Senior Pastor?

This is crucial. You must support him if your ministry is to be effective. Is this a man you respect and admire? Is he someone you can point the kids to as an example of a man trying to live the Christian life? Is his preaching motivating, Biblical, enthusiastic, challenging, and loving to you? If it isn't, how will you ever convince kids to come and hear him?

Will this man stand behind you when you fall on your face? Will he back you in front of the church board? Is he willing to open his life to you and are you willing to open your life to him so that you can minister to each other?

You may not agree on every issue with him, but are you together on the basic doctrines of the church? Is he a team man, or does he work best alone? Can he share a portion of the flock God has given him with someone else? Can you? Do your personalities clash, or complement each other?

Interview

If the above checks out, then meet with the commitee that does the hiring for the church. You will be a little nervous at that meeting, but remember, the folks who will be interviewing you will probably be a little nervous also. You should try to find answers to two types of questions at this meeting: those dealing with personal considerations, and those dealing with the ministry itself. Be yourself, the best you can, at this meeting. Be positive and honest with them about your own experience in youth work. Share with them your goals, expectations, desires, and dreams of working with their kids.

Personal Considerations

Job description. Is one clarified and written down? (Important!) To whom am I responsible? Am I working *for* a committee or *with* a committee? In this work relationship the youth minister should answer directly to the senior pastor. Some youth men have too many bosses.

Staff meetings. When and where are they held?

Salary. Does it include: conference allowance, Social Security, auto allowance, housing, hospitalization, retirement, and cost of living increase? (Full time salaries in this field are now running from $9,000 to $30,000 a year. The guidelines being used by some churches are that of the public education sector in the area of the church. It should be taken into consideration that the Minister of Youth Education is a teacher and a planning administrator.)

Vacation. Is it clearly understood what constitutes a vacation? A week or two at camp or some conference is not a vacation. You must take time with your family that *they* can call their own. After a person is established in youth work, *three weeks a year* seems a reasonable amount of time. Some are getting four weeks, and some even more.

Day or days off. What is the policy? Sometimes the pastor or the staff members will not take their time off. This leaves the youth minister with a cloud of guilt if he does take his day or days off. If he is working early morning to late evening five days a week, two days is not too much to have off. Many of us are involved in early morning studies and planning and our day is not finished until the last kid has gone home at 10:00 p.m., or later, on other nights.

Study time is not time off. I don't squander my days off on study. This would cheat my family and I would not be able to carry out my responsibilities at home with them.

Conferences and camps. What is the policy? Many guys find themselves in camps and conferences sixty-plus days a year. This is working time and the church should understand this before you go. This is two months' time away from the local ministry. Some churches are jealous of this.

Services. What part in the public services will I need to take? Is preaching expected? If so, then more study time must be allowed for this during the week.

The Ministry Itself

Camp. Where do we have to go to camp? Can I have the freedom to develop my own camping program?

Curriculum. What curriculum is being used? Who must approve it? Is the curriculum compatible with my ministry?

Freedom to make changes. Are there any sacred cows here? Do we always have to have our meetings at a certain time? What rooms can be used? Are certain rooms off limits to kids?

I will never forget an experience at a church I had just begun serving. We had decided to paint the room we used for our youth Bible school class. We met at the church at 3:00 a.m. (more kids will come out at this time than at 11:00 a.m. on Saturday). We could not make up our minds what color to paint the room, so we painted it the four colors we had with us— white, black, red, and blue. What I didn't realize then, but found out Sunday, was that that room was also used for one of the adult Bible school classes—and that they had used that same room for the last ten years. The minister warned me of the situation and I went directly to their class just before it ended. I don't need to tell you what that day's topic was! I tried to think fast, and my message sounded something like this: "You have probably noticed your room has been painted. Well, I just want you to know how spiritual your kids are. They painted the back wall black to represent leaving sin behind, the front wall white, for facing Christ, the side wall red, for the blood of Christ, and the other side wall blue, to remind them of Heaven. I'm just so glad to work with such spiritual kids." What could they say! They loved it. (That room is still those colors today.)

Budget. A sufficient budget will be needed for the following:

1. To train a staff, help them with expenses for camps, etc.
2. For conferences for the minister himself.
3. For curriculum and other materials for Sunday morning and evening.
4. For programs—that is, speakers, music groups, etc.
5. For camps—underwriting and helping kids go who can't afford to go, helping underwrite staff costs, etc.
6. Books for the youth minister to work from.

If the congregation doesn't have a youth budget, suggest starting one, but make it a small amount and increase it slowly each year.

Starting Your Ministry

Now that you have the job as youth minister, what do you do? The following ten-week timetable can help you get the youth program rolling. During the ten weeks, keep the existing program going as it is.

First week: Get four individuals who are highly respected in the church for their Christian character to serve on a committee to help you. At least one should be an elder. These people should excel in areas where you do not. This group at our church consists of an executive who works with computers (he's my organizer), a doctor (he's got wisdom), a junior high school teacher (he's got the guts to leap out in faith), and a college teacher (he's got a big heart and loves kids). These people, together, form a bionic man. I bounce my ideas off them for their insights. They also help get many of my ideas passed at the general board meeting.

Weeks two through four: Get names of potential youth workers from your four-man committee, church secretary, senior pastor, custodian—anyone. Then send each potential worker a recruitment letter like this one:

Mr. John Doe
777 Youth Lane
U.S.A.

Dear John,

Hallelujah! Praise the Lord! Hosanna! (and any other theologically oriented exclamatory phrases) Your name has been handed to me as one who just might be interested in working with God's kids through our great Junior High—College age youth program. That's exciting—well, it's exciting to me, because we need some Christian folks to help us in some of our youth activities.

Who gave me your name? I'll never tell, for fear you might attempt some drastic retaliatory measures against them!

Seriously, your name was mentioned to me as one who has the ability and possibly the interest in working with our youth. That's good for two reasons: first, because we need you; second, because you need us. You need an avenue of service for your Master; that is, you need one if you don't already have one.

Do you? Are you actively serving Christ in some way? I'm praying that you will consider the investment of some of your life in the lives of some of God's kids, so that our church and God's kingdom might have a bright and promising future.

If you are not interested and my information source was erroneous, will you kindly give me a call at the church and tell me? If you're not sure, or if you are sure that you are interested, you may do one of two things: Call me and talk with me about it, or wait for further information in the near future.

We will be offering a training course for four Sunday afternoons from 4:30 p.m.—6:00 p.m. on November 30—December 20, which you are invited to attend. It does not obligate you in any way; it only informs you about actual involvement in youth sponsoring. Youth sponsoring is a unique ministry that involves youth and adults working together in such a way that blesses the lives of both.

Thanks for your time. I hope you're interested.

All glory to Him who specializes
in the impossible,

Les J. Christie
Youth Minister

Since many adults in the church would love to work with kids, but are not known to the above people, make announcements from the pulpit each Sunday telling about the upcoming sponsor training. Put reinforcing articles in all church publications. In order to have a successful youth ministry, you not only need to flow into the lives of the youth, but also into adult men and women who have the same burning desire to reach kids that you have.

On the next Sunday morning, have the entire congregation fill out a youth sponsor training card during the worship service. The senior minister should preach on the need to reach youth. Collect the cards and send a letter to those who signed up, reminding them that the training begins next week.

YOUTH SPONSOR TRAINING

(This does not commit you to be a sponsor)

- ☐ I want to take the Youth Sponsor Training on the three Sunday afternoons (list dates).
- ☐ I would like to take the training, but cannot come on the above dates.
- ☐ I'm not sure. I would like to talk to the youth minister about taking the training.
- ☐ I will not be able to take the training at this time.

_____   _____
NAME   TELEPHONE

Fourth through seventh weeks: Take them through the sponsor training found elsewhere in this book. At the end of the training they are given an opportunity to sign up to be youth sponsors.

Eighth week: Visit each home of those who have signed up to be sponsors after taking the training. I take a photograph of each sponsor and draw a map showing how to get to his house.

Ninth week: All those interested in working with each particular age group get together and plan their first kickoff meeting.

On the next Sunday, the youth program begins.

Success in Youth Ministry

Many people judge success by the following four areas:
1. Attendance.
2. Spiritual growth in kids and coaches.
3. How close you kept to Scripture.
4. How involved the kids are in the total church program.

All of these are important, but I think three other areas are far more important to test your success in youth work and in the youth program.

1. What will these kids be doing twenty, thirty, and forty years from now? Will they still have that commitment to Christ?
2. "Wealth, notoriety, place and power are no measure of success whatever. The only true measure of success is the ratio between what we might have done and what we might have been on the one hand, and the things we have done and the things we have made of ourselves on the other" (H. G. Wells).
3. When we get to Heaven and Christ says, "Well done, thou good and faithful [doesn't say *successful*] servant."

7

How to Plan
a Year's Approach
in Advance

by Roy Reiswig

As you read, think about these questions:
—What tested, workable methods can I employ to organize my personal time and talents in this ministry?
—What elements of planning and production go into structuring and coordinating a vibrant, full-year youth program?
—Starting with a simple good idea, what steps should I take to bring it into fruition as a youth project?

"Advance planning spells the difference between mediocre uneventfulness and a solid meaningful program."

How many times have we heard statements like this one, and yet continued just as before? We tend to do whatever project is the most urgent—just getting done what must be done today, and never really feeling like we've got the situation under control.

While it may be unrealistic to expect to have our work *completely* under control, it is possible to feel better about it than many do.

As youth ministers, we all want to be accepted and respected as adults. We want credibility; we want parents to trust us. I believe that effective planning and organizing will help develop that respect, trust, and credibility.

Don't try to do everything exactly as stated in this chapter.

Adapt, don't adopt, what's being said. Read the material, think about it, and then adapt the principles to your situation. It's also important that we not let organizational techniques use us, but that we use them.

Personal Planning and Organizing

Before we can talk about how to organize a youth program, we must first discuss our personal work schedules.

Do you approach Monday morning with any kind of plan, or do you just start with the top thing on the desk and go from there? What you do on Monday morning will set the pace for the rest of the week.

Let me share some ideas that have helped me feel like I know what I'm doing and where I'm going.

Back Dating

Many of the activities that youth ministers develop should be worked on over a six- to twelve-month period of time. A week of camp, a summer youth trip, a choir tour, and an area-wide retreat are all activities that require long-term planning. The problem is that we don't always remember to do the right thing at the right time, and we end up in a mess.

Back dating is a simple way to help prevent that from happening. Deaning a week of camp can be used as an example.

As soon as you are given the responsibility to dean a week of camp, you should write down everything that will need to be done to make camp effective.

—Prepare tentative schedule
—Finalize theme and class topics
—Order movie
—Send letter to campers
—Prepare for first faculty meeting
—Write to prospective faculty
—Make teaching assignments
—Send final letter to faculty
—Finalize and print schedule
—Write for Bible college group

After you have written down everything you can possibly think of that will need to be done, select a date to work on each one. Next rearrange the list in chronological order—now you have a backdated calendar.

Dec. 1—Write to prospective faculty
Dec. 1—Write for Bible college group
Jan. 15—Finalize theme and class topics
Feb. 3—Make teaching assignments
Feb. 12—Order movie
April 1—Prepare tentative schedule
May 4—Send final letter to faculty
May 15—Finalize and print schedule
June 3—Send letter to campers
June 3—Prepare for first faculty meeting

This should be done for every activity that requires several months of preparation. My preference is to use the date of each Monday; therefore it becomes a project for that week.

Weekly Plan Sheet

The weekly plan sheet is a good way to keep from getting behind on the planning of a particular activity. Divide a piece of typing paper into ten rectangles (two across and five down) and print consecutive Monday dates in each square. Several sheets like this will give you a whole year in advance.

Then transfer each item on the back dated calendar to the corresponding week on the weekly plan sheet. After this is done, you can put your camp file away and rest assured that when it's time to do something for camp, your weekly plan sheet will remind you. This method is also helpful for ideas you'd like to work on later, or anything else that pops into your mind that needs to be done, but not right now.

If you use a desk calendar with a double page for each week, you might use a section of each page for the weekly plan sheet. This has proven to be a valuable tool in helping me keep on top of things.

Daily "To-Do" Lists

Each Monday morning you should spend some time with God and your calendar before organizing a plan of action for the week.

First, make a list of everything that needs to be done. Check your weekly plan sheet and include those items also. Be sure you get everything written down.

Then assign projects to various days. Don't schedule all the fun, easy projects on Monday and Tuesday and then all the heavy difficult things on Wednesday and Thursday. Mix them up. Give yourself some variety. Also, be careful not to get too long a list for each day; it's a terrible feeling to fail to get that list done.

As you look at each day's schedule, do the more difficult mental work when you're most alert. For me, the best time is in the morning; you'll know when it is best for you. Save physical tasks like going to the bookstore or putting things in the classrooms for a time when you're beginning to get drowsy and need to wake up. Also, force yourself to get the unpleasant tasks done first; then when they're completed you can enjoy the day.

One caution: Remember that your real ministry is with people, not programs. It's impossible to put "people time" on daily to-do lists. Telephone calls, kids or adults dropping in to talk, and other such things should never be viewed as interruptions—things that keep you from completing your "list" for the day. They are the *whole point* of your ministry.

Youth Lists

One of the first things that should be done when you begin a new ministry is to secure name, address, phone number, and grade level for every young person who is currently active or has recently attended your program. Then a separate list should be prepared for each grade level with two sections: one for members and another for nonmembers. Make eight or ten copies of each list and distribute them to Sunday-school teachers, youth sponsors, VBS directors, etc. These lists are valuable when anyone needs a list of those in a specific age group (for graduation gifts, Bible college mailing lists, and so on).

We have found many uses for the lists and have found that updating them once a year saves a lot of time and effort. The lists also encourage teachers and sponsors to contact the kids.

Card File

From the youth lists, we prepare a corresponding card file with name, address, and phone number, and indicate whether the youth is a member or prospect. These cards are then used when calling on kids. A short report is recorded on the card after each call.

Filing System

A personal filing system, adapted to the needs of your ministry, can be a valuable tool, but many have a "piling system," which is useless. When ideas and articles are put in a pile or a box, they're seldom seen again.

The structure of your system should meet the needs of your current ministry. My file system is in a constant state of change (as is my ministry). That's how it ought to be.

Begin by making a list of all the file topics you need. Then try to group them under major headings, similar to an outline with main points and sub-points. Give yourself several weeks to write, rewrite, arrange, rearrange, put in, and take out, till you become comfortable with the list.

If you have a huge pile of material to file you may need to go through it piece by piece and add those categories to the list.

Next prepare dividers, like taller file folders, for each major category; then prepare file folder for each topic and arrange them alphabetically (or however is best for you).

After your personal files are well organized, check on the church files. A permanent file of all activities for future reference should be kept in the church office. This file helps the church maintain information about various ministries even when ministers move.

A few miscellaneous comments on filing:

—If it can't be filed, throw it away.

—Do filing when you need a change of pace activity.

—Keep a place for "things to be filed," but do not let it get too full.

—Keep individual files small. If you get a lot in a file, divide it.

—Always have new folders available. Try to file things immediately.

Be sure to develop your own system. It's fine to look at someone else's, but your filing system needs to match your ministry.

Total Youth Program Planning and Organizing

Begin Early

This is one of the most basic principles we must learn, and yet one of the most difficult to put into practice.

When we're used to planning a week ahead of time, it's difficult to change and think about next year. You may need to let things just happen as they will for two or three months while you begin working on future plans. As the youth minister, you should be thinking six or twelve months ahead, always watching for new needs, new opportunities, and new ideas. Your work with the sponsors should be a couple of months in advance of when their activities are to take place.

Seasonal Planning

Some youth ministers plan one month at a time. Then they're always planning. Other youth ministers plan a full year at a time. I think it's difficult to determine what each group needs that far in advance.

My preference is seasonal planning.

Fall Season: September, October, November, December (two or three week break for Christmas and New Year's)

Spring Season: January, February, March, April, May (two week break for graduations and Memorial Day)

Summer Season: June, July, August (two or three week break for school opening and Labor Day)

Let me remind you of the importance for you to adapt, not adopt. This schedule may or may not work for you.

The basic concept is to provide units of three to five months with natural breaks for holidays. (It's my belief that it is not necessary to have youth groups fifty-two weeks each year.)

Involving Sponsors and Youth

The natural inclination for most young youth ministers is to try to do everything: plan and teach every lesson; plan and execute every social; take the kids to every youth rally. It seems easier if we don't have to have three or four meetings explaining what to do and how to do it. But most youth ministers begin to realize, sooner or later, that they're not "bionic" and they do need some help.

If we ask adults to serve as youth sponsors, it's important that we encourage them to take a major role in planning and leading activities. The development of high-school youth as leaders in their own group is discussed in another chapter. They also should be included in planning and leading activities.

On the other hand, don't dump the entire responsibility on the volunteer leadership and just leave them. Your role as youth minister should be to provide general oversight, resources, creative thought, and motivation. You may have to begin by doing most of the work, but always move toward giving them more and more to do.

Determine Needs

Our first inclination in planning youth activities for the year is to think of "neat" party ideas and different lesson topics to get the kids to come, but there is a better place to start. We should determine some basic areas of need and then program accordingly.

You may want to prepare a questionnaire for the young people to fill out, or talk with teenagers and parents about needs. Ask the youth sponsors and/or officers about the areas of need.

Establish Objectives

After determining your needs, decide which ones to work on during that particular season. Young people have many different needs, and you can't hope to minister to every need in three or four months. So you should work on various needs at various times.

Select Lessons and Activities

After needs are determined and priorities set for the specific season, lessons and activities can be selected to meet the needs. If needs and priorities are wrestled with first, then the selection of lessons and activities will be much more simple.

Most churches have stacks of youth group lesson books collecting dust. Get some volunteer help and take the books apart, filing each lesson under the appropriate topic. Then you can go to the lesson resource file to find materials that deal with the specific needs. If your church has no materials there, it's the youth minister's responsiblity to find resources.

Service projects, socials, and other activities should also be planned to help meet the needs of the group.

Calendar

We must be careful to coordinate youth activities with other church activities, so that conflicts don't arise.

This is especially true when the group wants to use the fellowship hall or a church bus or van. Activities should be coordinated with other ministerial staff and the all-church calendar.

Printed Information

A printed brochure should be available to help parents, young people, other church members, and visitors to know what's going on in the youth program.

You may want to print one brochure that explains your entire youth program. Or you may want to prepare a brochure for each group each season. This would include lesson topics, as well as dates, times, and costs for socials, trips, retreats, and other activities. It should also include a list of sponsors and times of church services.

Proper Channels for New Ideas

One of the greatest temptations youth ministers face is trying to start a new program too quickly. We get a good idea from a book, or we hear a good speaker at a convention, or we talk to another youth minister, and we are ready to "can" the old program and start something new—immediately.

The exact steps to take in securing approval for a new idea will be different in every congregation, but let me relate how it's done in our congregation:

Start early. Be sure to give yourself several months to think about a new idea. You must have a firm idea about what you want to do before you can tell anyone else.

Secure complete information. If you're considering a new program, become thoroughly acquainted with it. Write to churches who are involved in it. Talk to youth ministers. Get your facts together.

Discuss with the ministerial staff. Present the idea to the other ministers. Let them "shoot it full of holes." Better to find the weak spots there than in a board meeting.

Prepare a written proposal. It should explain what, when, why, how, how much, for whom, and anything else you can think of. This will help you determine your approach of presentation.

Youth committee. Share your written plan with them. Ask for their questions and reactions. Revise accordingly.

Elders. By this time you know exactly what you intend, and you can take a well-thought-out plan to the elders. You'll have the answers to most of their questions, and chances are your plan will be approved.

Teenagers. The last group to know about a new program or activity ought to be the kids. If you tell them ahead of time and it isn't approved, then they're not only disappointed, but they're upset with the elders. Wait until all details are worked out and approved, then tell the young people.

One of the things that troubles youth ministers the most is their desire to be treated like adults. If this is true, then let's *act* like adults. The techniques for planning and organizing that we've looked at will help us to "stay on top of things." When people begin to notice this, they'll begin to treat us like adults. We'll feel better about our ministries and do a more quality job of "presenting every teenager complete in Christ."

Youth Evangelism

by Les Christie

As you read, think about these questions:
—How can youth be trained as effective evangelists to their peers?
—What spiritual benefits can you and your youth accrue in an evange-
listic program?
—What really is a testimony to Christ, and how can a youth best
present this witness to others?
—Once a youngster is won for Christ, how can his conversion be
followed up to strengthen his growth in the church?

If a youth program is to be effective, there must be an ongoing evangelism program. The Bible tells us that "Christ Jesus
came into the world to save sinners,"[1] and "the Son of man is
come to seek and to save that which was lost."[2] As a shepherd
looks for a lost sheep, a woman looks for a lost coin, and a
father for a wayward son, so we are to be looking for young
people who are spiritually lost. The word "evangelize" means
"to bear a good message." Nothing is more thrilling than bearing that message, and seeing someone respond to Jesus Christ.

Motivation for Evangelism

The population of the United States is growing at a rate of
60,000 people a week. One-third of its citizens claim no reli-

gious affiliation. Yet ninety-five percent of our church members have never led someone to Christ.

Love

Our goal as youth ministers is to "equip the saints for the work of service."[3] Those who share their faith with neighbors, friends, and youth, should not look at evangelism as going on an Indian raid into enemy territory, bringing back spiritual scalps. We are to minister to the whole person. We must be concerned with people's needs and desires. In order to be effective in evangelism, we must have a genuine love for people.

Dawson Trotman, founder of the Navigators, had this kind of love. Dawson died in a boating accident trying to lift two struggling girls up out of the water into a ski boat. *Life* magazine said the best way to sum up Dawson's life would be to say "he was always lifting others up!"

I hope you genuinely care for people. How sad to read the psalmist's words, "No one cares for my soul."[4] I hope you have a burning desire to reach the lost. Not with an attitude of superiority, but of one beggar telling another where to find bread or one friend telling another where to find *the* Friend. I don't want to give you guilt feelings if you are not evangelizing or to pressure you into verbally sharing your faith. Evangelism cannot be effective from an "I ought to" attitude but must come from an inner "I must."

Jesus gave us a tremendous example of this when He agonized, "O Jerusalem, Jerusalem, who kills the prophets and stones those who are sent to her! How often I wanted to gather your children together, the way a hen gathers her chicks under her wings, and you were unwilling."[5] Jesus had a genuine love for people and a desire to minister to them.

Paul wrote, "I have great sorrow and unceasing grief in my heart. For I could wish that I myself were accursed, separated from Christ for the sake of my brethren."[6] Wow! Think of it! Paul would have gone to Hell if it would have helped his brethren come to Christ. Paul further showed his compassion for the lost when he wrote, "Therefore, we are ambassadors for Christ, as though God were entreating through us; we beg you on behalf of Christ, be reconciled to God."[7]

Paul was a man of God with a burning passion for evangelism. But who motivated Paul? I think it was Barnabas, the one who brought Paul in when the rest of the disciples questioned

Paul's conversion. Barnabas was person-oriented. He loved people. Barnabas also had the gift of discernment: He could look beyond what a person was and could see what he could become. Barnabas knew that a youngster who was sharp enough to get into trouble was probably creative enough to become someone significant.

I hope as you get ready to share your faith with youth that you are doing it out of a deep love. You need to let people know you love them for their own sake and for Christ's sake, and that your relationship with them does not hinge on how they respond to Christ. You cannot be like the insurance salesman who gets their signatures and then forgets them. Your motivation must come from an inward love for God and people. The acid test to see if you really love someone is the way you respond to that youth who does not respond favorably to your invitation to receive Christ. Do you still care about him, or do you just write him off? Jesus knew what was in man, yet He loved man. The apostle John, in summing up all the reasons why he loved Jesus, said it was because Jesus loved him first.[8]

Simply putting out a sign saying "Welcome Young Sinners" and then sitting back and waiting for them to flood into the church will not get the job done. We must go where they are. For that reason, I go to every sports activity, play, or music presentation at our kids' schools that I can. I can't find a verse of Scripture that commands a lost person to go to church, but I can find a dozen verses that tell us ministers to go out into the world. The reason we go where the kids are, at school and in homes, is simply because we feel comfortable in the church setting, but a high-school kid who is visiting us may feel threatened. I feel a little uncomfortable at the local high school, but the kids feel comfortable because it's their home turf. Kids will be more open where they feel most comfortable.

You, as the youth minister, are not the only one who is to flow into the lives of kids and share the gospel with them, but your sponsors (adults) and the kids in your group can also share Christ verbally and with their lives. We as youth ministers have tended to become keepers of the aquarium instead of fishers of men, and our kids are bloated from always taking in Christ's love but never giving it out. There is no such thing as a "gift" of witnessing. We are all expected to do it. Everyone who is a Christian is some kind of witness for Christ, so the question is not *will* we witness, but *how* we will witness. Total witnessing involves how we live and what we do, as well as what we say. Jesus said, "This people honor Me with their lips, but their heart is far away from Me."[9] If we are to be effective, our lives must back up what our lips proclaim.

Convictions

In sharing with others effectively we not only need love but some firm convictions about what we believe.

There is a big difference between beliefs and convictions. Beliefs say "I think . . ." or "I feel. . . ." Convictions say "I know. . . ." Beliefs are something you hold, convictions are something that hold you. The crucial question we must answer is the one posed by Jesus, "Who do you say that I am?" I hope you can say with conviction, "I *know* that Jesus is the *only* way." You must be able to agree with Christ's words, "Apart from Me you can do nothing."[10] God is not looking for glib people, but people with a burning conviction that they have the truth and the truth has them.

How to Get Started

We began an evangelism program with our youth about eight years ago. We saw many kids coming to church, but then slipping right out the back door. Our group was large enough that someone could easily get lost in the crowd and eventually drop out, and no one would realize it until weeks later. So an adult sponsors and I began taking kids with us when we called on visitors. There was no arm twisting. The kids who went had the desire to go (in fact, they asked us to let them go with us).

At first we had some lessons designed to help the kids call on visitors more effectively. The kids were quickly bored with the classes, and we thus learned two important lessons. First, we had to let them see the need for the classes before offering them. So we had them call on visitors by themselves, cold turkey, with no help from us. They were frustrated (to say the least) because they didn't know the answers to some of the questions the visitors were asking, so they soon saw the need for the classes. Second, we learned that evangelism is more caught than taught. You don't really learn it in the classroom, but in the field. In the classroom we don't give them the whole ball of wax, but just a little teaching—then we send them out; then a little more teaching and send them out again.

The Organizational Structure of the Evangelism Program

When a visitor comes to one of our youth activities, several things occur. First, he fills out a visitor card and a map to the visitor's home is made. Second, I write him a letter welcoming him into our group. Third, our high-school secretary (youth), calls him on Monday and welcomes him, and asks him if he wants to be on our youth mailing list. Fourth, on Thursday all of our kids who are interested meet together in the evening for our calling program.

The calling night begins at 6:30 at the church with all the youth callers together in one room. I usually get an elder to come in. He begins the session with a five-minute devotion. Then we divide the kids into cars. We do let some youth drive if they are reliable drivers, or we have willing adults drive the cars. We send them out in twos or threes with one person doing the talking. It is far more effective, we found, if you phone the young person you are calling one hour before you will be there. This makes sure he will be home and anticipating your presentation. When telephoning before we go, I ask the person if we could come by to explain our activities at the church, and if they would mind helping us by letting our kids practice sharing their faith. This prepares them for the gospel presentation. After the calls are made we try to get back to the church by 8:30 p.m. The calls are shared and we have a time of prayer.

Go With Someone

Our kids go in small groups with one youth as the presenter. This way, the other two can learn by observing and they don't feel threatened to have to say anything. After going out a couple of times, the one doing the talking may ask one of the others to share his own testimony. Basically, though, the "silent partners" are to take care of any distractions. For example, if there are tiny kids in the home, the silent partner will play with them so the speaker will not be disturbed by distractions.

We have girls and guys call together. Never have three girls called on a guy or vice versa, because this may be threatening to the one being called on, or the one being visited may make a decision for the wrong motive. Nor should you have more than three people go to the door of a visitor. A whole troop might scare him.

Once the youth have gotten into the home, they should be genuinely complimentary about the home or that person.

After finding out how he came to the youth activity they attended, the visitor is asked if the callers can share what it means to be a Christian.

Using the Bible in the Gospel Presentation

The designated talker then makes a gospel presentation. There are several ways of presenting the gospel. I use the "Roman Road" plan. I like it because it stays in one book of the Bible.

Romans 3:10
        3:23   to show we are sinners
        5:12
        6:23   to show the price of sin
         5:8   to show that Jesus paid the price
  10:9, 10   to show the need to confess Him before men
     6:2, 3   to show the need for baptism

These verses should be learned within their context and not simply used as proof texts. We need to know what's in our Bibles.

Select the presentation that suits you best, but decide on some plan and use it. It is helpful to mark your Bible with the order the verses come in. Whatever plan you use, practice the KISS method (not the rock group): Keep It Simple, Stupid! Don't try to teach a visitor everything in one night. The kids are to be sensitive to the visitors' needs and moods. They are to welcome interruptions and questions.

It's important that your kids use the Word of God in sharing their faith. The Bible says in Romans 10:17, "Faith comes from hearing and hearing by the word of Christ." God's Word is a powerful tool.

Go Believing

Many of your kids will be afraid to share their faith verbally. Don't force them! Have them go as silent partners if they wish. Timidity is the norm for the beginning soul winner. Most of us are shy and scared. Assure them that Christ is with them as they go.

I want my kids to get a lofty view of their ministry. What they are doing is important! Share with them Ecclesiastes 9:10, "Whatever your hand finds to do, verily, do it with all your might." Teach them that this isn't a hundred-yard dash but a twenty-six mile marathon, so they should not let minor discouragements throw them. They also need to be enthusiastic about their task. Enthusiasm means "God in us." As Christians, God is in us, so we should be the most enthusiastic people around!

Look Your Best

Our Christian kids are ambassadors for Christ, so they should look the part. Make sure they have combed their hair, brushed their teeth, and checked their deodorant. You may even want to slip a Certs into each mouth before they leave to go calling. They should dress nicely—they need not wear a tuxedo, but they should look presentable so the prospect is not turned off by the callers' appearances.

Be Your Best

If we want to communicate with our world effectively we need to keep intelligently informed about what's happening in our world. It is blasphemous thing to saddle the Holy Spirit with the blame for rambling, wearisome, unprepared mumblings. Our visiting youth need to be well read and well prepared for their calls.

As Christians we have many things for which to be happy. Psalm 126:3 says, "The Lord has done great things for us; we are glad." When we share our faith, this joy should be reflected in our faces. The person the youth are calling on does not want to hear all about their problems. Jesus told the demoniac, "Return to your house and describe what great things God has done for you."[11] He was told to emphasize the positive. Some of us need to quit looking like Pepsi that's lost its fizz.

One further thought: The Bible says that the servant of the Lord must avoid foolish arguments.[12] We cannot argue someone into the kingdom of God. Don't be drawn into a religious argument. The best way to win an argument is to avoid one. Avoid them like the plague.

Training Callers

I share with our callers some obvious things that seem obvious to me only because I've learned them the hard way:

—Don't be afraid to say "I don't know."
—Don't act superior. Be humble.
—Answer questions, but try to stay on subject—the main issue.
—Look the person in the eye when talking to him.
—Learn to listen. Don't do all the talking. Ask questions they will enjoy answering about themselves. Make them feel comfortable by showing them you are genuinely concerned about their thoughts.
—Don't be in a hurry for a decision.
—Find out at least where they are spiritually before leaving their home.
—Don't get a big head because people you have shared with are coming to Christ. First Corinthians 3:6 tells us, "I have planted, Apollos watered; but God gave the increase."
—Don't carry a large Bible. To a non-Christian, it looks like you're carrying a gun.
—Don't be critical of other congregations, and be sure to be modest about the church you attend.
—Pray before going.

Some good Biblical examples on how to share your faith include Jesus' approach with the Samaritan woman at the well (John 4), and Philip's approach with the Ethiopian eunuch (Acts 8). Andrew is only mentioned four times in Scripture, but each time he is bringing someone to see Jesus.

Other topics you may want to cover during the training times are witnessing to relatives and Jewish friends, cults, why you believe as you do, and knowing the Bible as the Word of God. After the training, I have the kids practice sharing their faith verbally with one another.

Try to make sure that your kids are learning to proclaim the gospel and not sell the gospel. There is a difference. As your kids go out calling, remember that their job and ours is to make *real needs* into *felt needs*. We know eating is a real need, but when it becomes a felt need, we eat. We know Jesus is a *real need* in kids' lives, but Jesus must also become a *felt need*.

Some of your kids may not be able to handle a calling situation by going into someone's house to share, but they can make maps to the homes or write letters to visitors. They can pray for individuals to come to Christ, and for those going calling on visitors.

Benefits

Our motivation for sharing our faith is our love for Jesus Christ and for people. We have a burning desire for others to meet the One who has made a difference in our lives. We share out of love. There are, however, five extra benefits from sharing your faith:

1. You'll have beautiful feet in God's eyes (really): "How beautiful are the feet of those who bring glad tidings of good things!"[13]

2. You'll have joy. "Those who sow in tears shall reap with joyful shouting. He who goes to and fro weeping, carrying his bag of seed, shall indeed come again with a shout of joy, bringing his sheaves with him."[14]

3. You'll shine like the stars: "Those who have insight will shine brightly like the brightness of the expanse of heaven, and those who lead the many to righteousness, like the stars forever and ever."[15]

4. Christ promises to be with you: ". . . I am with you always, even to the end of the age."[16]

5. Christ will recognize your faithfulness in Heaven: "Well done, good and faithful servant."[17]

What's My Testimony?

Definition

Webster gives four definitions for a testimony. These include:

An open acknowledgment before people. "Everyone therefore who shall confess Me before men, I will also confess him before My Father who is in heaven."[18] We are to do this anywhere we can: at school, home, church, laundromats, anywhere! We are to do this any time we have an opportunity.

To give evidence. "Quietly trust yourself to Christ your Lord and if anybody asks why you believe as you do, be ready to tell them, and do it in a gentle and respectful way."[19] This verse is the reason my church taught a ten week series on "Why Believe the Bible?" We want our kids to be ready if someone questions what they believe. I give my kids a hard time by firing tough, hard questions at them during this series. I would rather have them fail in the classroom than in the world.

A solemn declaration. I want my kids to know that when they give their testimony, it is not a joke, but serious business.

A testimony has three parts: 1) your old life before you came to Christ; 2) how you became a Christian; 3) how your life is now with Christ (be honest). The center of a youngster's testimony is to be Christ, not himself. When people walk away after hearing your testimony, they are to be drawn closer to Christ, not necessarily to you. When Christ is lifted up, He will draw all men to Him. As it was stated in 1 Corinthians 1:6, "The testimony concerning Christ was confirmed in you."

Our kids' testimonies should be their own and not someone else's, even if theirs do not seem very dramatic. We have to put the blame for this dramatic expectation on ourselves. Who gave the last testimony you heard? It was probably an ex-drug user, ex-Hell's Angel, basketball star, movie star, or someone who had a dramatic conversion in a traffic accident, in which he fell out of the car with his finger landing on John 3:16. No wonder our kids are reluctant to share their blah testimony or have a tendency to exaggerate it. Wouldn't it be tremendous if some kid reared in a Christian family, who saw his need to make Christ Lord of his life and did so, gave his testimony? More youth could identify with that witness than with the ex-Hell's Angel, or with the testimony that contains a description of unbridled passion and depravity.

I'm not putting down the ex-Hell's Angel's testimony, but less dramatic examples are important as well. Compare Paul's with Timothy's conversion in the New Testament. Does a person always have to sink into chronic depression before coming to Christ? I, for example, had a great time before I came to Christ. Christ has made a difference in my life, but I wasn't miserable before I became a Christian. I just knew I was a sinner who needed Christ to make my life whole.

It's also important that we stop trying to imitate others when we give our Christian testimony. I used to want to be like those guys who could get on a plane and share their testimony with the person next to them. In my own flights around the country, I felt guilty when I wouldn't share with a fellow passenger. Then I realized that I couldn't always, but if someone else *can* witness on a plane, then praise the Lord!

Firsthand authentication of a fact. A witness speaks about what he knows, not hopes or feels. We cannot communicate out of a vacuum. The only way people will believe our testimony is if we have the facts straight, we say them clearly, and our lives back up what we say.

People are watching our lives. Our lives are part of our testimony to the world. We may have all the facts together, but if our lives are in shambles, it is a waste. We shouldn't need to ask, "Will you give your testimony?" because a Christian should be giving a living testimony all the time. Asking that question has isolated one's witness from the rest of his life and distorted the idea of what a New Testament witness is.

Follow-Up Evangelism

Too much evangelism stops when the person becomes a Christian, but that is the very time when a new Christian needs extra attention. Failing to support and teach a new Christian is like leaving a baby alone to fend for himself. The apostle Paul followed up with new believers by:
   —Praying for them regularly.[20]
   —Visiting them personally when possible.[21]
   —Sending others in his place where he could not go.[22]
   —Writing letters: nine recorded letters to young churches and four letters to individuals.
We offer a four-week series of lessons every three months for new believers; we also use an eight-week series in the home with a one-on-one situation for one hour a week.
In these sessions we teach Christian doctrine and an overview of the Bible, and also cover the "one another's" in the Bible (honor, greet, accept, serve, and encourage one another). Knowing the rules isn't playing the game, however, so those who have been through the eight-week series are asked if they would like to take someone else who has just become a Christian through the same eight-week series.

Miscellaneous Ideas

Have household evangelism meetings. Meet in someone's home with friends and neighbors. Limit the group to eight and have a time to share about Christ and do appropriate activities.
Last year, I taught eight high-school kids a Bible-study lesson from the Gospel of John on Wednesday nights. They in turn taught the same lesson on each following Monday night, teaching small groups in four different homes. It was a tremendous time of growth for these eight kids as well as those who came to their Bible studies.

I don't agree with those who compromise their Biblical principles in order to win someone to Christ. Going into a bar and
drinking to win a drunk or okaying premarital sex to a couple
so they will listen to the gospel message is wrong! We are to go
where the non-Christians are, but we are not to condone or
participate in those activities to win them. When Paul said, "I
have become all things to all men, that I may by all means save
some,"[23] he was not talking about compromising Biblical principles.

Have a non-Christian social every few months, where the
only way you can come is to bring a non-Christian.

Take a picture of visitors and whoever brought them, put
their names on the picture, and put it on a bulletin board.

Print youth directories every few months, with names, tele-
phones, addresses, grades, schools, and birthdays.

The following article by Mike Yaconelli hits home to those of
us who are youth ministers:

The Little Boy Who Wanted to Fight Fires[24]

Once there was a little boy who ever since he could remember
wanted to be a fireman. The shrill of the siren and the deep rumble
of the racing fire truck had filled his dreams almost every night.
Deep in his heart there was a longing to some day be able to help
people; to save people from the ravaging grasp of a fire. It was not
the whim of childhood fantasy. His was the unmistakable call of
destiny.

Growing up never changed his mind. To be sure, he had gone
through all the indecision and doubts of adolescence, the well-
meaning questions of friends and family who "wondered whether
he could be happy as a fireman." But he never wavered. He was to
be a fireman. He was to put out fires.

Oh, how he longed for the day when he would no longer be a
spectator, but could participate actively as a firefighter. Now all he
could do was watch.

Then the big day arrived. He was accepted at one of the best
fireman schools in the country. For three years he immersed himself
in his schooling. He spent hours honing his skills on practice fires.
He studied fire-fighting theory long into the nights. His teachers
were world-renowned.

But still, after all these years, he had never fought a real fire. As
graduation approached, he realized that the long-awaited moment
was within reach.

But suddenly, he began to have doubts. For the first time in his life, he was unsure, afraid, and worse yet, questioning whether he ought to be a fireman at all.

It was then that one of his professors suggested he travel to Europe and study under one of the greatest fireman theorists of all time. He would be recommended by his professors and would receive the finest training available. It would last for two years.

The not-so-little boy decided to travel to Europe, and for two years he exhausted himself in dedicated study and became one of the most brilliantly educated firemen in the world. But all he had ever done was put out practice fires. Once again, graduation loomed before him. And once again he was haunted by indecision. He knew all about fires and could tell anyone how to fight one; in fact, he knew so much he began to feel that his superior knowledge did, in fact, place him a notch above "ordinary" firemen. He became increasingly concerned that he might have to fight fires with "uneducated" firemen, which could result in him being exposed to unnecessary danger.

It was then that he was offered a position to teach at one of the most respected fireman's schools in the country. He accepted. And for twenty-five years, he taught with honors and received recognition worldwide. He died last year and when they read his memories they came across a strange passage written while on his deathbed:

I lie here today reviewing my life. I still remember my dream, my passion to be a fireman. More than anything else I wanted to put out fires . . . but I realized something today. I have never put out a real fire. . . . Never.

I pray God richly blesses your ministry as you reach young men and women for Jesus Christ.

---

[1] Timothy 1:15
[2] Luke 19:10
[3] Ephesians 4:12
[4] Psalm 142:4
[5] Matthew 23:37
[6] Romans 9:2, 3
[7] 2 Corinthians 5:20
[8] 1 John 4:19
[9] Matthew 15:8
[10] John 15:5
[11] Luke 8:39
[12] 2 Timothy 2:23
[13] Romans 10:15

[14]Psalm 126:5, 6
[15]Daniel 12:3
[16]Matthew 28:19, 20
[17]Matthew 25:21
[18]Matthew 10:32
[19]1 Peter 3:15
[20]Colossians 1:9
[21]Acts 15:36
[22]Philippians 2:19, 20
[23]1 Corinthians 9:22
[24]Reprinted.with permission from *The Wittenburg Door,* published by Youth Specialties in San Diego, California.

CHAPTER

9

Developing Leadership in Youth

by Les Christie

As you read, think about these questions:
—How can you select youth leaders who have the greatest potential to help the group thrive?
—How can you break down and assign leadership roles for best group effectiveness?
—What are some ways to motivate youth leaders and followers to actively participate in activities?

My ultimate goal as a youth minister is to bring youth to maturity in Christ; to prepare, disciple, and train them to serve God. The best way to motivate youth to serve in the local congregation is to give them real responsibility when they are young. This is not a new idea. The Bible says, "It is good for a man that he should bear the yoke in his youth."[1] Young people must learn how to handle burdens and responsibilities.

A yoke is usually made for *two* animals. The word *yoke* implies more than one person together in a similar task, striving for similar goals.

The Bible says, "Train up a child in the way he should go, even when he is old he will not depart from it."[2] Most of us have been quick to claim the promise without heeding the command. The words "train up," in Hebrew, mean *to create a desire.* It is our task as youth ministers and youth sponsors to create a desire within young people to live for Christ.

Selecting a Core of Youth Leaders

How do we select the special kids, the inner circle into whose lives we as youth ministers will flow? Many youth groups carry out their leadership elections in unscriptural ways. A youth group may have three guys running for president; when one wins, the other two are out. What a waste of two sharp guys! Perhaps we make one of the guys a "vice-president," a do-nothing job similar to being a blackboard monitor. I am convinced, after thirteen years in youth ministry, that kids want tasks that will stretch them (the tougher the better) and place real responsibility on them to fail or succeed. In most youth groups, though, election time is often a time of political speeches and posters, which result in jealousy, contention, and hurt feelings.

We sometimes select a problem youth to be a leader, feeling that a leadership position might help straighten him out. That's one of the dumbest ideas I've heard! What does such action do to the kid who's been coming to your group for the past two years and wants desperately to serve, but gets ignored because he's quiet and well-behaved?

Scripture doesn't set down a definite pattern for the selection of leaders. God's leaders are chosen primarily on the strength of their spiritual lives, not their natural abilities. God uses and develops the talents of those people who are living in obedience to Him. God wants available people who are willing to be used by Him. Sure, He can use the beauty queens and the great athletes, but God uses guys and gals as suits of clothes, always available in His ready-to-wear department for the Holy Spirit to slip into and use at any time. If He could use you or me, He could use anyone. Then how should we select this special group that will lead the other youth?

Several weeks before the election, encourage prayers for the selection of the right people. On election night, request that only those who are members of the youth group should vote. This graciously eliminates non-Christians from voting. Give each voter an alphabetical-order list of the members of the group. Each voter is to circle the nominees he thinks God wants to lead the youth group. Before the actual vote, you may also wish to go over some Scriptural characteristics of a man or woman of God.[3]

The ballots should be tabulated by the youth minister and sponsors, who scan the list to see if someone has been elected whom they feel should not be in a given position. If this occurs (it rarely does), then the person with the next highest number of votes is put into that office. This makes it a combination democracy and dictatorship!

The youth minister then phones all of the parents of the newly-elected leaders before telling the kids. He needs to check with the youth's folks to see if they will let their youth hold office (parents really appreciate this). Their kids must be able to come to all activities, spend as much time as needed, and they are required to keep a quiet-time diary. If the folks approve, then notify the elected youth and visit each home individually, going over the job description with the parents and the youth. Then, at a leaders' meeting, everyone describes his task to the others, to clarify their roles and relationships.

Establishing the Leadership Roles

These elected officers are to be servant-leaders. The servant-leaders do not have elevated positions, but lowly ones. Their main task is to flow into the lives of the fringe kids as well as the other leaders. They are to get to know and love the kids in the total group. Through living a Christlike life, their greatest impact on the total group (and their school campuses) will be felt. These positions will cost them much time, hard work, and demands that stretch these leaders to their capacity.

Each leader selects a group of kids he is to work with, disciple, and train the rest of the year. One adult sponsor is put with each youth leader and group. Each group is responsible for a specific task. These positions are thus both person- and task-oriented.

The ultimate goal that each leader is striving for in his life and the lives of the kids he is flowing into is Christian growth. When he thinks of an activity, he must consider, "Will this bring someone closer to maturity in Christ?" If it won't, then the idea is scrapped.

The following list covers seven offices that correspond to seven areas of work in a youth group. You develop whatever tasks best meet the needs of your particular youth group.

Calling Chairperson

This position is responsible for seeing that every visitor feels welcome. This officer introduces visitors to regular members and tries to make the visitor feel important and comfortable. He insures that the visitor is called upon at home within one week of his attendance at a youth group function. The chairperson also draws maps for the callers to locate prospects' homes. He keeps a filing system on results of calls for future reference. He also holds clinics on how to make home calls. The calling chairperson's goal is to *introduce* people to Christ.

Project Chairperson

Project ministries are designed to help your kids put into practice all they have learned in other youth group activities. Project ministries are organized group activities, aimed at specific and attainable goals. Young people are directly involved in meeting the spiritual or social needs of others, while also developing their own spiritual skills.

Some projects that last only a few days include:

Work around church. Do some painting inside and outside the church, or some yard work, or wash the church buses.

Distribute flowers. Take little handmade gifts or flowers to church shut-ins.

Secret missions. Find people in your church who need things done (such as mowing the lawn). Then do them when the people aren't there, and put a little card on their door saying, "Some Christians from your church did this because they love you."

Work for city. If you call up the local Chamber of Commerce, they will give you worthwhile work to do around the city.

Can night. Collect cans of food for needy. Challenge your kids to go canvass the area and get a certain number in just one hour.

Pumpkin caroling. At Halloween, sing pumpkin carols to the elderly (Hallmark Cards has a Peanuts card with these in them). Also, take the listeners seasonal treats.

Drive-through nativity. Have kids dress up like Mary, Joseph, and others with live sheep in a lean-to stable. Have this display on the church parking lot where cars can drive by. Play music out of a loudspeaker and hand each car a tract made by the kids.

Christmas in July. Give gifts to poor kids in the community in July, because they are usually swamped during December and then forgotten the rest of the year.

Some projects that last a longer period of time:

Adopt a grandparent. Many grandparents in our church have their grandchildren clear across the country, and many of our high schoolers have distant grandparents. This project brings these two generations together. Match up a grandparent (they don't have to be grandparents, just around that age) with a kid. Withhold the grandparent's identity from the youth for a while. They do little deeds for each other, write encouraging letters, then later they enjoy a Revealing Party.

Adopt an orphan. Many organizations will allow your group to adopt an orphan for about twenty dollars a month. They can write to the child and sometimes even bring him out for a visit.

Work in mission field. You could put on a VBS program there, or paint buildings. Plan well in advance, and make sure the people want you to come. Don't go with a superior attitude. Have a definite goal in mind.

Sewing. Have little old ladies in church and your teenagers meet once a week to sew and knit. The older ladies can teach the youngsters. The finished products make nice gifts.

Filmmaking. Plan and create short movies, or take slides and match them with some Scripture.

Puppets. Learn how to make puppets and use them in short skits to be presented to the young kids.

Chalk drawings. Learn how to do chalk drawings (Bill Gothard) and present them to a different group.

Hospital Headliners. Visit a convalescent hospital, mentally retarded hospital, physically handicapped hospital or a children's hospital once a month. Develop a relationship with those in these hospitals.

Saturday morning movies. Five of our kids, after seeing *The Bad News Bears* (a "G" rated picture that was gross), said we needed to provide something better for little kids. They ordered some Walt Disney pictures to show on Saturday morning during the summer. They learned how to operate a 16mm projector and make popcorn. They printed up tracts to hand out around the neighborhood, and, at the end of the movie, described the activities our church had for the age group. Many kids became Christians through this ministry.

Secretary
The secretary keeps an up-to-date list of where everyone lives and of who is attending what activities. He mails out all publicity—an important function. Secretaries also send out notes to those who have not attended in a while and welcoming letters from the youth minister to visitors.

Historian
The historian keeps records (in words and photos) of the youth group activities each week in a large scrapbook that is taken to every function.

Social Chairperson
The social chairman plans all socials, including dates, times, activities, guests, food, locations, and cost. The goal of these socials is always to bring non-Christians to Jesus Christ.

Members are not motivated to come on the basis of whether or not they like the particular activity. They come because they want to help people to come to Christ.

Publicity Chairperson
This person takes care of all advertising of youth activities. This includes monthly calendars, advertising in church and local papers, radio spots, posters in Bible-school classes, and special mailouts.

Bible-Study Chairperson
This person, and others on his committee, meet with a sponsor or youth minister to study a portion of Scripture. The following week, these kids lead studies on those Scriptures to groups of ten to fifteen of their peers.

Motivating Youth to Participate

Show Them Why, Then How
A few of our kids once expressed a desire to go calling on people to share Christ with them. I was thrilled! I set up four lessons on *how* to call, but they sat bored through the first session. They didn't see *why* they needed lessons. So, I sent them out to witness to strangers. They came back saying, "Ohhh, we couldn't remember one verse, and this atheist chewed us up." Then they knew *why* they needed the lessons,

and they were on the edge of their seats the next time I showed them *how* to call. You may have tremendous programs, but unless the kids see *why* they need to be there they will not come.

I go through a regimented process of exchange to convey ideas to my leaders:

—I do it, they watch
—I do it, they help
—They do it, I help
—They do it, I watch
—They do it

This process can be seen with the training of our publicity people. For the first piece of publicity, I do it and they watch. The second piece, I do it and they help. The third piece, they select the kind of picture to use, the type, the layout, and the paper, and I help. The fourth piece of publicity they do, then show to me when they are finished. From then on they do it all with little advice (unless they ask for it).

I also allow my kids to fail. They are responsible for what they do. We learn a great deal through failure. I don't do anything for a kid that he is capable of doing himself, because if I do I will be creating an emotional cripple. I want him to learn to trust in God, not in my coming to his rescue. This is the most difficult part of our job for the youth minister or sponsor because we feel we could do it better. We would love to do it for them, but we can't, if this is to be a youth-centered youth group.

Give Them Encouragement

Always look for something positive you can point out to kids. Kids never forget a good word you have said about them. One of the reasons I'm a youth minister is because my fourth grade Sunday-school teacher said, "I bet you'd make a good youth minister." That's all she said, but I never forgot it. This praise motivates kids beyond belief. The only time Jesus rebuked his disciples was for lack of faith. He was an encourager. I hope my kids feel about my sponsors and myself the way these early disciples felt about Jesus—"We love him because he first loved us."[4]

If you want to motivate kids, look at them with God's eyes, seeing what they can become. I had one sponsor who motivated kids like this. She asked a little second grader what he wanted to be. He said, "President of the United States." The youth sponsor didn't lift an eyebrow but got on her knees next to that kid and said, "Let's think of the godly qualities that a president should have," and they listed them together. Then they prayed that those qualities would be in that boy's life. Wow! He may never become President, but then again. . . .

I am convinced that our kids are not only the leaders of tomorrow but are capable of being the leaders of today. Let's train and motivate them in the way they should go, and when they are old, they will not depart from it.

---

[1]Lamentations 3:27
[2]Proverbs 22:6
[3]For example, Galatians 5:22, 23; Titus 1:7-9; 1 Timothy 3:8-13
[4]1 John 4:19, *King James Version*

Part Three

AGE CHARACTERISTICS AND SPECIAL ACTIVITIES

Section Outline

10. Ministry to Age Groups
    A. Preschool
       1. How Preschoolers Develop
       2. Preschoolers' Needs
       3. Our Attitude About Teaching
       4. Youth Ministry With Preschoolers
    B. Primary
       1. Primary Learning Development
       2. Age Characteristics of Primaries
       3. Strategy for Ministry
    C. Juniors
       1. Teaching Is Ministry
       2. Conclusion
    D. Junior High
       1. Physical Development in Early Adolescents
       2. Social Development in Early Adolescents
       3. Mental Development in Early Adolescents
       4. Emotional Development in Early Adolescents
    E. Senior Highs
       1. Pressures
       2. Keys to Ministering With High-School Youth

CHAPTER

10

Ministry to Age Groups

A. Preschool

by Richard H. Hicks

As you read, think about these questions:
—How is the physical development of preschoolers related to the curriculum we can provide them?
—What basic needs must we meet in order to effectively teach this age group?

Butterscotch pudding, an eggbeater, Noah's ark, and excited "coaches" (youth sponsors) await the arrival of that first bundle of energy. The hall door opens and footsteps can be heard. In walks little Chris, diaper bag in one hand and Bible in the other. His eyes survey the room as the coach welcomes him. This child represents the preschool ministry. Chris is a unique individual with physical, spiritual, emotional, mental, and social needs.

One summer evening, Amy and her family were returning home from church. Amy began singing a line from a Sun-

day-school tune: "Who made the moon?" She immediately answered her own question with a resounding, "God did!" As
Amy repeated the song, everyone in the car joined in singing
these praises to the Lord. This little girl shared her personal
excitement about God with those she loved!

Preschool ministry in the local congregation can be described with one phrase: "Never a dull moment!" It's true! We
are dealing with precious children just beginning their personal adventures of life. Nothing is more fulfilling than being
used by God to build these lives in His image.

How Preschoolers Develop

Jean Piaget, noted psychologist, identifies four stages of
child development that have great implications. Preschool
ministry is concerned with Piaget's first two stages: the *sen-
sorimotor* period and the *preoperational period.*

The Sensorimotor Period

The first stage extends from birth to approximately two
years. This age child depends on direct contact between his
senses and the learning activity. Learning must be accomplished in the present rather than depending on past experiences.

Implications for Preschool Ministry: 1. Effective teaching experiences for this age child must include objects to discover
with his senses. One such tool to accomplish this is a
homemade "Teaching Box" that includes a variety of creative
resources: different colors and textures of cloth to touch, a flip
chart illustrating simple finger plays and songs, a mirror, large
animal pictures, cotton balls that have been dipped in different
flavorings to smell, and a cassette recording of common sounds
to identify.

2. A preschooler, lacking a good memory, must experience
firsthand the concepts being communicated. Guided play,
music, and large muscle building toys can be used as teaching
tools. Effective teaching must maximize present sensory experiences.

The Preoperational Period

This second stage of development includes ages two through
approximately seven. This child's thinking process can only

focus on one aspect of a situation at a time. He can only view things from his own perspective. His words illustrate his thought process.

Implications for Preschool Ministry: 1. Learning aims must be chosen with one focus in mind. Many lessons can be learned from the Biblical account of the boy Samuel, for example, but we must choose only one lesson aim. A good learning aim relevant to the preschooler would be, "I can obey." The child will know Samuel obeyed, feel he should obey, and respond by identifying actual obedience in his own life.

2. Viewing experiences only from his own perspective can affect how a preschooler relates to others. For example, Tim hits Lynn, but he doesn't understand he has hurt her. We need to broaden his perspective by pointing out the correct behavior.

3. Talking with the child gives the coach information identifying his level of understanding, and enables the coach to help the child develop his thinking process. For example, Jimmy is looking at a book. He sees a picture of Noah's Ark and says, "I went to the zoo!" The coach capitalizes on his response and replies, "What animals did you see? Noah had two of each of these on the ark." The coach acknowledged the child's thinking process and broadened it.

Piaget proved that each child passes through these developmental stages. The role of the coach is to plan discovery learning experiences in light of the child's development.

Preschoolers' Needs

Four major needs of the preschooler are love, security, self worth, and meeting physical needs. How are these needs met?

Love

A familiar bumper sticker reads: "Have you hugged your kid today?" These large red letters communicate the basic need of every preschooler. The coach who loves the children is concerned about their total being. Love is demonstrated by physical contact, such as a hug, holding the child in your lap, or placing your hand on his shoulder. Body language communicates attitudes. Patience must also be a characteristic of every preschool worker.

Preschoolers learn the meaning of love through our personal example. Through special activities such as making cards for shut-ins and even delivering them, young children can grasp an understanding of love.

Self Worth

Bill Gaither's song, "I Am A Promise," is the theme song of every child! The preschool coach must plan learning activities developing the potential God has given every child.

One way to develop self worth is to encourage the preschooler to accept responsibility. For example, youth group refreshments can be prepared at home by the child and his parents. Then, the child is the official "host" at snack time during youth group, distributing cups, napkins, and the goodies. Children should also be taught that with privileges comes responsibility. Cleanup can be a learning tool as the coach demonstrates and gives simple directions for the child to follow.

The effective coach will acknowledge the individual's self worth. When the child arrives, he welcomes him by using his first name and facing him at his eye level. He acknowledges the child's feelings. For example, if a child drops a block on his foot, the coach might respond, "Jimmy, I know that block hurt your foot."

Additional ways to build a child's self worth include recognition of birthdays (preschoolers enjoy receiving their own mail), regular home visits (which give insight into a child's behavior), and public recognition. Personalize preschool ministry in every way possible.

Security

Preschoolers relate their church experiences to the home. Husband-wife coaching teams communicate a home atmosphere. Male coaches communicate that church is not just for women and children. Preschoolers also need to see familiar faces at Sunday school to feel secure.

A home living center in the classroom provides not only excellent learning experiences, but a familiar environment. A home living center can consist of a child-size "play" sink and stove, table and chairs, and other homey touches.

The preschool coach can communicate security by being ready to greet the first early arriver. This insures a good youth meeting from the beginning. Children need a familiar routine each week—but some surprises are exciting!

Concern must also be given for the child's safety. Each coach should know where the first aid kit is, and where parents can be found. Fire exit plans should be posted and explained to everyone.

Materials for the child should be located at his eye level—easily accessible. Coach supplies should be placed well above the child's sight and reach.

Physical Needs

Children learn through planned activity. However, if a "quiet-active" sequence does not exist, attention can become minimal and behavioral challenges maximal. God equipped every preschooler with custom-made wiggles! Plan learning activities with preschool muscle development in mind. (For example, scissors are not appropriate for younger children.)

When their needs are met, a preschooler can begin to understand spiritual insights. He can best learn about God through the personal ministry of his coach. He associates what he sees in his coach as attributes of God. The preschool coach is God's representative!

Our Attitude About Teaching

Two key words best describe the preschool worker's attitude about his personal ministry—opportunity and investment!

Preschool ministry is more than paper dolls and Pampers. Jesus made time for children. Jesus considered his involvement with children as a definite ministry.

Can preschool workers become frustrated with their ministry? Certainly! Behavior challenges and lack of adequate staff can be major frustrations. If this personal frustration is communicated to the children, though, your teaching opportunity is lost.

Frustration can be avoided in at least two ways. First, preschool workers must realize their motivation for ministry is a commitment to Jesus Christ. Second, the preschool coach must be committed as a fellow Christian to others who share in coaching leadership.

Monthly "Equip Nights" provide personal Bible study and prayer for the coaching/sponsoring staff. Specific prayer requests should be considered. Victories and needs are shared as a functioning team. By ministering to the needs of one another, coaches ensure a powerful, positive experience for the children. Equip Night also provides an open door for communication with the youth minister.

Preschool ministry requires a considerable investment of himself by the coach. A consistent coach, though, can expect to receive the highest return on his investment—the assurance that he has helped a little child discover Jesus Christ as his special friend.

Youth Ministry With Preschoolers

Can youth ministry actually happen with an energetic preschooler? *Definitely!* Youth ministry must include preschoolers as *preventive* ministry: A positive attitude about God, church, and self must be built early in a child's life, maximizing potential for positive ministry later when he is faced with so many negative influences.

Effective preschool ministry depends on partnership with the home. Two-way communication between the church ministry and home ministry insures that church teachings will be reinforced. Parent's Night during youth group, letters to parents, and home projects tied to the church are some ways to achieve this partnership. The preschool ministry should also provide enrichment classes for parents, helping them to meet needs of their growing preschooler.

Understanding preschool development and needs enables the youth worker to adequately plan for effective ministry results. The realization that preschool ministry is an important matter, dependent on the youth worker's attitude and commitment, is what makes youth ministry happen!

B. Primary

by Richard H. Hicks

As you read, think about these questions:
—What ideas and methods can the maturing primary youngster comprehend?
—What strategies in carrying out a primary program best suit the characteristics of that age group?

Dekalb General Hospital, a huge 486-bed facility, is among the largest in Georgia. Early one day the pediatrics floor at Dekalb became the scene for personal ministry.

A few weeks before, third-grader Melody had been riding her bicycle and was struck by an oncoming automobile. Fortunately, Melody suffered only a broken hip. She was scheduled for hip surgery at 8:00 a.m. on this morning. I arrived at the hospital to pray with her before surgery. Approaching her room, my footsteps sounded like a giant's, echoing through the dark and quiet corridor. When a kind nurse learned who I was calling on, she quickly explained, "Melody needs you."

As I opened Melody's door, all was quiet and she was alone. "Good morning, Melody," I enthusiastically greeted.

No response.

"How are you this morning, Melody?"

Almost in tears, Melody whispered, "I'm scared."

Immediately questions raced through my mind. "How do I comfort this little girl? Does she really understand God is here with her?"

During the next few moments, exciting ministry happened. We talked about how much God loved Melody. It's all right to be scared, I said, but God is with us—protecting us. He has given wisdom to Melody's doctor. Melody's loving parents arrived just in time for a fantastic prayer circle. Today this same youngster is once again involved in school and church activities.

My experience with Melody prompted a personal investigation into effective youth ministry for primary-age children. "What is the main objective of a congregation's youth program for children?" I asked myself. "Are we equipping primaries to handle life situations—beyond youth group on Sunday?"

Today's child is bombarded by countless influences communicating good and bad value messages. A good value is an important guiding principle for quality life experience.

Picture Sam, a typical second-grade youngster. During a typical week, Sam is exposed to many different kinds of influences, including school, toys, television, family, friends, and church. Sam is constantly bombarded. Though just a youngster in second grade, Sam is involved with life. He doesn't face many "adult" pressures, but he must be able to begin building his value system.

When Sam attends youth group, will he personally be motivated to discover that Jesus Christ must be the living foundation for the life of a second-grader?

The various media capitalize on the fact that Sam is "just a kid." Ministry must also accept this reality, and capitalize on the fact that primary children's attitudes are easily molded. Value systems can be established early in life.

Primary Learning Development

Early Primary Children

The early primary child, according to Piaget, is categorized by the preoperational stage, which usually includes children up to seven years of age. During this stage, primary children make all judgments based on outside appearances. Early primaries find it difficult to focus on more than one main idea at one time.

Implications for primary ministry: 1. Primaries need help distinguishing between television fantasy and Biblical reality. The coach should *emphasize* when a story is from God. He might say, "This really happened and we find out about it in God's Word—our Bible." When a fictitious story is told illustrating a point, it should be identified as such.

2. The child recognizes his youth coach as a model every-

where he sees him. This viewpoint substantiates the vital importance of a coach's personal example. Coaching children is a personal ministry that exists beyond the hours on Sunday.

Later Primary Children

Piaget's third stage of mental development, the concrete-operational, includes children from approximately age seven to twelve. In this stage, the child thinks concretely. He can now conclude that an object can have more than one characteristic. He is also now able to think in a more complex way.

Implications for primary ministry: 1. Phrases like "Let Jesus come into your heart" are abstract. Avoid using symbolic words or phrases with younger children.

Visuals can be good tools to illustrate words like "sheepfold" that primaries are not familiar with. A visual helps them understand by giving them a concrete object to keep in mind.

2. Primaries can begin understanding the trinity, but not fully, because it is an abstraction. However, the child can see Jesus as his friend through the concrete representation the coach provides.

3. As a child develops his personal relationship with Jesus Christ, he should experience Him in three ways. First, Jesus is his friend. Second, He can become the child's Savior. The child recognizes he has sinned, can name specific sins he has committed, and explain how his behavior might be different after becoming a Christian. As a child matures spiritually, Jesus becomes his Lord. However, in counseling children, we should consider their mental developmental stage. A characteristic of Piaget's fourth stage—formal operations—is that a child can understand abstract concepts. His complete understanding of God's plan for personal salvation will later provide a more legitimate commitment to the Lord.

4. Give the child opportunities to use his developing mental processes. Give him a hypothetical situation and let him arrive at a conclusion about the appropriate action. For example, "Harry and Wally are playing soccer. Bill wants to play, too, but Harry says 'No!' What should Wally do?"

Age Characteristics of Primaries

Besides mental development, several other aspects of maturing are notable.

Physical. "Active" is the key word. This limitless energy must be channeled properly. Children this age are developing reading and writing skills through small muscle coordination. Challenge these skills with varied learning experiences such as Bible games, creative writing, and art activities.

Social. A primary-age child needs training in building relationships. A coach can play a vital role in interactions of the child with adults other than his parents. Coaches can also broaden his peer relationships through planned activities.

Cliques can form with primaries, causing some left-out children to stop attending youth group. All activities should promote social interaction among all children in a group.

Many children will want to become Christians because their best friends did. A coach should be sensitive to this peer pressure, but also encourage each child to make decisions on his own at the proper maturity level.

Emotional. Early primaries are experiencing a transition time. They are no longer babies or preschoolers but are "in school." Many primaries are sensitive about their reading ability. A coach can foster emotional development by teaching children that they are loved, accepted, and important.

Strategy for Ministry

The following suggestions merit consideration as a ministry strategy is planned.

1. Combine ministry efforts with the Sunday-morning program. Avoid competition between "youth hour" and Bible school. Outreach is much easier with concentrated teamwork from the Sunday morning and evening staffs.

2. Incentive programs are beneficial to the individual child's growth. But a direct tie to the home is *fantastic!* Concepts presented at church must be reinforced at home.

3. Church programs must model strong personal relationships for the home. Youth group must provide activities that stimulate positive family life at home. Regular "Parents' Nights" are essential, involving families working together through various creative activities that build family relationships.

4. Variety and excitement are the keys to successful youth meetings for primaries.

Like the preschool ministry, a church's ministry to primaries must be viewed as an important investment. Equipped youth coaches can produce results in the lives of children, who will gradually take an active part in the church—producing a functioning, growing family.

C. Juniors

by Richard H. Hicks

As you read, think about these questions:
—How can you plan and provide a life-related, ongoing experience ministry to this age group?
—What formal teaching activities should be part of a fourth- through sixth-grade curriculum?

Juniors are special little people. They can be the bright spot in your ministry. Several characteristics of juniors influence how you must minister to them.

Juniors are hero-worshipers. They will put significant adults such as youth leaders in places of high honor.

Juniors are developing their self-esteem and personal worth; they look hopefully to the people they respect for approval. When ministering to juniors, setting a Christlike example is a crucial priority. They are at the age when they are beginning to question the inconsistencies in the lives of Christians. They need a Christlike model to emulate.

Along with an example, he needs unconditional love for the development of his self-esteem. Juniors, like all of us, need acceptance for what they actually are, from the adults around them and from their peers.

When we minister to juniors, we need to keep in mind the total child: his physical, intellectual, social, emotional, and spiritual personhood. As we come to understand him, we will be better equipped to fill his needs and his desire to know Jesus.

Teaching Is Ministry

Teaching is often divided into two parts: formal or classroom teaching, and informal teaching. Both divisions include many techniques that facilitate learning.

Informal: Life-Related Teaching

While the informal ministry is casual, specific ministries still need to be developed. Some of those ministries may be evening children's hour, Bible raps, camps, special outings, and home teaching sessions. Each of these activities has a role in informal education.

Children's hour: Planning meetings can be fun and creative as you determine the specific needs of your juniors. Brainstorming is a useful technique, and the first step in a planned meeting. No suggestion is outrageous during a planning session. The second step is the elimination of unrelated or impractical activities. The third step is to set behavioral objectives, which are the *attitudes* that you want to teach. Then begin to build lessons around these objectives.

Suppose, for example, during a brainstorming session the need for teaching the kids that "lying is wrong" is suggested and chosen as a concept to be taught. The next step is to develop a lesson on that concept. When doing this, remember these three components: a) devotion, b) activity, c) title. The devotion can be centered around the concept that Satan is the "father of lies." The activity can be playing the game, "Liar's Club" (based on the television show). Title: "Is That True?"

Many methods will convey the point. One is to lie to the kids about the winner's prize. State that it will be money, but let it be play money. If refreshments are offered, describe them extravagantly, then serve crackers and water. (Warning! Your juniors will turn into a mad mob!) Now they will be ready to hear about the attitudes that are developed when they lie to others. The children are thus being ministered to on the level of real life situations.

Bible raps; midweek meetings: These ministries bring Bible concepts to the children's lives in an informal, conversational setting.

One way to develop this kind of program is to use the epistles. Most children's curricula tend to overlook the practical aspects of these books.

Special outings: The advantage of having special outings with your juniors is to allow them to see you in different situations. Outings can really help build counselor-junior relationships. Have variety in your outings. Plan some fellowship outings doing things such as skating, cookouts, or trips to the beach. You could also work together doing something special for senior citizens or some kind of improvement project around the church. Evangelistic outings can be set up so that the kids can bring their non-Christian friends. The last kind of outings are just for the fun of it. Amusement parks are great for these.

Camps: Two kinds of camps are offered to the junior. The most available is summer camp, which is usually a week long. Winter camp consists of a weekend of activities.

The relationships developed at camp could not be developed at any other time. Living with juniors for a week is an unforgettable experience for the counselor and camper. You are guaranteed to learn almost all there is to know about your kids. Camp can be a vital part of a junior's spiritual growth, where many life-changing decisions are made.

Home teaching: The words "home teaching" may communicate many different ideas. Home teaching can mean leading a child to Christ, or it can mean inviting the child to spend time with you in your living environment.

Evangelistic home teaching exists where the opportunity has arisen to lead a junior to Christ. The parents should be present at these appointments to give the teacher the opportunity of sharing with them, and to include them in this special event. If they are Christians, the sharing may involve understanding the child's home life and the parental influences. If the parents are not Christians, it may lead to an opportunity to witness to them also.

The kind of teaching that happens when you invite your juniors to *your* home is a real life-to-life experience. The more you can share yourself with your juniors, the better. They will begin to see you as a real person who lives his Christian life away from the church. Most kids believe that their teachers stay at the church, like the pencil sharpener. The more honest you can be with your kids, the better the relationship.

Formal: Classroom Teaching

Some say that good teaching comes naturally, but good formal teaching techniques are learned. There is hope for us all.

Juniors learn by doing. They need to experience the subjects that they are learning about. The two most known forms of formal teaching are Bible school and children's church.

Bible school: In most Bible-school curricula, the basic teaching technique is the Bible learning activity. These are projects that involve the child in the learning process. Their purpose is to achieve the lesson objectives. Some of these Biblical activities are making posters or mobiles, painting, role-playing, working with puppets, and singing. These all play an important part in helping the junior develop his imagination and creative abilities. These suggestions can also reinforce the lesson aims. Other activities such as discussion, buzz groups, lectures, and the use of the overhead projector, can be used to stimulate thinking. The junior will obtain more information if he is an active part of the learning process.

One way of staffing your Bible school is with teaching teams. Team teachers plan together for a common goal with one class. A team of adults can often generate more creative teaching. Team teaching gives the teachers a sense of belonging, that they are not alone in their awesome task. It gives the child the opportunity of relating with more than one adult. Team teaching allows for more than one Bible learning activity to be conducted at a time, giving the junior a choice. Juniors are able to choose and should be allowed to make choices. A choice of activities often eliminates the "I don't want to" syndrome.

The most frequent mistake in teaching juniors is the lack of emphasis on personal application. The personal application must accompany the visual activity. If the child does not see how this specific activity meets his needs, then the effort is fruitless. Along with personal application comes a greater likelihood of changing attitudes. When personal application is being used, your children will be less likely to become Pharisees who have Biblical knowledge, but do not live the life.

Children's church: Juniors can become a vital part of the children's worship program, and can take on its responsibilities. This section proposes a philosophy of children's church, stated in goals and objectives.

1. Children's church should prepare a child for the adult church service. We therefore need to model children's church after the adult service, yet remain at the level of the child's understanding.

2. It should equip children to begin to use their gifts and talents. For example:

a. By the third grade the child will become aware of the gifts and talents he has been given.

b. By fourth grade the child will come to an understanding of those blessings.

c. The fifth-grade child will begin using his gifts and talents, doing such things as offering and communion meditations.

d. The sixth-grade child will be competent enough in his gifts and talents to his lead peers in a worshipful experience.

3. Children's church must provide opportunities and education for making a meaningful public decision for Christ. This can be accomplished through home teaching, worship, and class instruction.

4. It will help children develop a sense of responsibility towards the family of God through meaningful prayer and sharing time, expressions of love, and mutual encouragement.

5. It will help children develop an appetite for Bible teaching through Bible-based concepts and meaningful sermons.

6. It will develop children's ministry opportunities to the elderly, younger children, parents, and peers.

Conclusion

Teaching is ministry! It is more than the hours spent with kids on Sundays. Juniors may never remember the lessons you taught them, but they will remember who you were.

An effective ministry does not just happen. It is developed. As you allow God to work through you, He will bless your efforts.

D. Junior High

by Wayne Rice

As you read, think about these questions:
—How does the junior high student change in mind and body during
  puberty?
—How are learning and counseling related to the youngster's physical
  experiences?
—What recommendations and methods will help youth workers cope
  with the intense emotions of early adolescence?

This chapter is about adolescents who are between twelve
and fourteen years old. They are referred to as "junior highers"
primarily because of the educational institutions they attend—
junior high schools. Although society had identified these
years as a specific life stage, these young people do not have a
name that is distinctly theirs. Every designation for them refers
to the next stage in life, as if the present one is something to get
over with as quickly as possible: "Junior Highers" (not quite
high schoolers), and "Early Adolescents" (not quite adolescents) are examples. Such titles suggest that this is one of the
most overlooked age groups. The church tends to overlook
them as well.

Yet the early adolescent years are among the most important
in life. Dr. Urie Brofenbrenner of Cornell University recently
testified before the U.S. Congress that the most critical years, in
terms of human development, are the junior high school years.[1]

So why, then, is it such a neglected age group? Perhaps the
most obvious reason is that the vast majority of adults either
dislike or fear junior high kids. The group is often stereotyped
as rowdy, restless, silly, moody, loud, vulgar, disrespectful,
and, worst of all, unpredictable. These characteristics make

working with junior highers a rather unpleasant thing to do at times, and most sane people tend to avoid unpleasant things.

But for the person who catches the vision for junior high ministry, the rewards are great. The junior high years are a time of questioning, decision-making, building meaningful relationships with others, and most of all, a time of tremendous growth in virtually every area of life. A once-in-a-lifetime metamorphosis is going on in their lives, and the junior high worker can play a significant role in it.

Certain characteristics that make junior highers different from other people occur in four areas: physical, mental, social, and emotional. As we acknowledge the most common characteristics of junior highers, we will also deal with a few of their implications.

We will be making a lot of generalizations, which is a dangerous thing to do when talking about people. Everyone is different from everyone else, and it is wise to avoid putting people into little boxes. You must not look at your junior high group as a "group." Instead, you must see them as John, Tim, Mary Lou, and so on. Your group is a collection of persons who are all different and who have different needs at different times.

Nevertheless, some things can be said about junior high kids in general that are accurate in most cases.

Physical Development in Early Adolescents

The most important physical characteristic of junior highers is that they are going through puberty, an enormous change. It only happens once in a person's lifetime; the child is transformed into an adult. Boys and girls do most of their physical development into men and women while they are in junior high school.

The average age for menarche, when a girl has her first menstrual period, is 12.9 years. The female adolescent growth spurt actually begins much earlier, at around 9.6 years. Its peak velocity is at about age 11.8. Comparable milestones, however, occur almost two years later for boys.[2] This is why girls are usually bigger and more developed than boys during early adolescence. The boys don't catch up with the girls physically until around age fifteen.

While these ages are fairly accurate, they cannot be viewed as absolutes. It is normal, for instance, for two boys the same age to be two years apart in physical development.

Regardless of the age, the children are in the process of becoming adults. In our culture, this fact is hardly acknowledged, but in many ancient and contemporary primitive cultures, as soon as a boy or girl manifests the physical signs of adulthood, they take on adult roles immediately. They take part in definite rites or ceremonies to make the passage from childhood to adulthood quick, clear, and sure.

A New Awareness of the Body

With the onset of puberty comes a newly acquired awareness of the body. Junior highers are commonly concerned about how they look and how they measure up to peers. They are, in their own secret fears, growing too rapidly, too slowly, or too unevenly. And for many, these fears are justified. Physical growth can be uneven and unpredictable during early adolescence.

Most junior highers worry a great deal about how they are going to turn out. It is a hidden fear, affecting their lives in ways they are not even aware of at the time. The slow developer, for example, may (for reasons he cannot even understand) feel out of place and compensate by becoming either withdrawn or boisterous.

The junior higher's social life is affected dramatically by this physical development. To illustrate this, consider a five-year-old boy: He will play and become the best of friends with any other child, regardless of size, color, looks, sex, or whatever. But as he grows older and enters puberty, this innocence fades. He becomes more selective in his associations. Suddenly there emerges a popular group and an unpopular group.

Usually one's popularity or unpopularity involves physical characteristics, such as looks or development. Boys who are athletic, tall, and handsome tend to be popular. Girls who are pretty are likely to be popular. If you are ugly (or merely plain), short, fat, or skinny, you may be doomed to join the undistinguished "out" crowd, a fate worse than death. Junior highers thus place a great deal of emphasis on physical characteristics as a matter of survival.

What's Happening to Them

The junior higher's body undergoes changes during puberty that are accompanied by an equal number of puzzling new experiences—some exciting, some embarrassing, and others just plain awful. It's hard to many early adolescents to understand or adjust to these events. What makes it even worse is that few people talk about them, and those who do are often misinformed.

For girls, the more noticeable changes are an accelerated increase in height and weight, a widening of the hips, and the appearance of breasts. Girls now become softer, rounder, and very concerned about their figures. They hope they will be attractive to members of the opposite sex.

This can be a very frustrating time for girls who insist upon comparing themselves to the models they see in fashion magazines. Breasts, especially, have become a preoccupation in our society, becoming almost synonymous with sex appeal. It is thus not surprising that small-chested girls fear that boys will never like them. Girls become anxious, too, if one breast grows faster than the other (as they sometimes do) or even if their breasts are growing too large too soon. Most girls could benefit from some assurance at this point that sex appeal is rarely dependent on any particular part of the anatomy.

During junior high school girls also experience their first period, which can be a real shock if they aren't prepared for it. Embarrassing accidents occur at the worst times. Girls often worry that there is something wrong with them. Menstruation for junior high girls, as it is for older women, is frequently accompanied by abdominal pains, lack of energy, and occasional irritability. Also, it takes a frustrating while before most girls develop a regular twenty-eight-day cycle. Hopefully, someone is able to assure them that all this is normal.

Junior high boys don't develop as early as the girls do, which makes it awkward for them to relate to girl peers. They may still be trying to impress girls with their skateboards, while the girls are more interested in boys with driver's licenses.

When boys do experience the onset of puberty, they grow at a rapid and uneven pace. It is not uncommon for boys to grow as much as six inches in one year, yet the arms, legs, and trunk may grow disproportionately, resulting in awkwardness. Just when a boy is becoming coordinated, puberty strikes and his forward progress may be impaired. Appetites increase dramatically at this age, as well. The voice usually changes, too, which provides more embarrassment at choir practice.

Another sign of approaching manhood is the emergence of pubic hair, similar in significance to breasts for girls. Until you grow a crop of genital pubic hair, your manhood remains in doubt. As a junior high camp director, I have noticed boys who had hardly changed their underwear the entire camp week for fear of ridicule.

Boys also encounter new sexual urges and feelings during puberty. These can be a source of needless worry and guilt. Wet dreams, masturbation, and ill-timed erections are common signs of a developing sexuality. Junior high boys, curious about the opposite sex, usually seek out magazines like *Playboy* to satisfy that curiosity.

Helping Them to Understand It All

I recently surveyed junior highers, asking, "Where do you get your information about sex?" Most answered "School," but it is hard to know whether they meant health classes or friends. The second and third most common answers were "friends" and "parents." Other typical responses were: "TV," "Books," "Porno magazines," "Movies," "Wherever I can get it," or "Nobody gives me a straight answer." Although all 700 junior highers surveyed were members of church youth groups, only three kids indicated that they had received any sex information from their church youth leaders.

I am not suggesting that churches conduct sex education classes, but it would seem appropriate for junior high workers to help kids feel free to talk about sex in church. God created sex in the first place, so junior highers should be able to get information from a Christian point of view. They are already getting answers from every other point of view. God is not trying to make life miserable for junior high kids. They need to know that the changes taking place in their bodies are normal, not something to be ashamed of or afraid of.

Social Development in Early Adolescents

A marked increase in social awareness and social maturity parallels the many physical changes of adolescence. Peer relationships become very important. When younger, junior highers only needed playmates, but now they need more meaningful friendships. Friends are people who can be trusted, who listen, and who understand feelings.[3] Loneliness becomes so commonplace that junior highers will go to great lengths to make friends and keep them.

The Drive for Independence

It is a primary task of early adolescence to break ties with the family and authority figures and begin forming an independent identity.

Junior highers are possessed with a drive toward independence. They want to make their own choices and commitments. Kids become highly critical of their parents, and consider them and their values to be hopelessly old-fashioned.

This disenchanted attitude naturally accounts for many of the problems between parents and their early adolescent children. Many parents are caught completely off guard by this. Just when their children are finally learning to be good, obedient boys and girls, they become junior highers and appear to take a giant step backward in behavior. Adolescent behavior *progresses* via the detour of regression.

The Bridge Toward Independence: The Peer Group

The primary goal for the early adolescent is the impossible: full independence. The gap between the security of home and parents and this sought-after independence is far too great to permit a simple transition. Junior highers want to be treated like adults and to think for themselves, but they lack the confidence to take on the related responsibilities. They need a middle ground to prepare them for independence.

This is the function of the peer group. It is the bridge that links dependence with independence. For a junior higher to find his identity as an individual, he must lose it as part of the crowd. What the crowd thinks or does, he emulates. This herd instinct accounts for the many fads so characteristic of the junior high years. as well as the inevitability of cliques and associations that they may seem destructive. But this conformity is, ironically, essential to the junior highers' quest of the security and confidence needed for adulthood.

By conforming to the peer group, the junior higher is subconsciously trying to find out whether or not he is liked and accepted as a person away from the home. It is only natural that parents offer acceptance and love, but now something more is needed. The early adolescent wants to know if he is equally O.K. "out there" in the real world. Once he feels secure as part of the group, then he is more likely to have confidence to experiment with being "different"—and discover his own identity. The peer group thus becomes the bridge to independence.

The important thing for adults to understand is that this conformity is not all bad. It is true that junior highers are very susceptible people who can choose the wrong kinds of friends, but the alternatives to conformity are usually worse. Better 'a little bad influence than no friends at all. Many adults are maladjusted psychologically because they were never able to fit in as adolescents. It is hardly ever helpful to junior highers for parents or youth workers to overreact to this conformity, which must be considered an important part of adolescent development. In the church, sometimes Scripture verses such as "Be ye not conformed . . ." are quoted as a way of telling kids that they should not be like other kids, or that they should only have "approved" friends. It is not likely that Romans 12:2 was intended to be interpreted or used in that way.

Allow Them to Choose Their Own Peer Group Commitments

One of the great fears of parents is that their young adolescents will become part of the "wrong crowd." Frequently, their fears are justified. Junior highers may choose friends who do not hold Christian values. Young people who smoke, drink, use drugs, and worse, are the majority on many junior high school campuses.

But we cannot choose their friends for them. We can and should offer guidance, but it is usually destructive in the long run to overtly criticize the friends our junior highers select. To do so is to attack their judgment. When some dangers seem inherent in a particular relationship, then it should certainly be discussed. Antisocial behavior, though, is not necessarily contagious.

It's helpful to remember that as young adolescents most of us made some poor choices of friends, and somehow we pulled through.

Mental Development in Early Adolescents

Early adolescence is a time of transition from childhood to adulthood, in more ways than one. Physically, the body changes so that it can function as an adult. Socially, the junior higher's drive toward independence makes possible survival in the adult world. And while these definitive shifts are taking place, the young adolescent is in a period of equally exciting and disturbing intellectual change.

During the junior-high years, most young people begin to develop structural thought changes leading to adult under-standing. The brain shifts gears and a whole new world emerges, much more complex, yet wonderfully exciting. Prior to the age of eleven or twelve, a child's understanding of reality is largely tied to what he or she can experience. But a qualita-tive change occurs coinciding with the onset of puberty. The junior higher develops the ability to reason more logically, to think abstractly, and to move from one abstraction to another. He can keep a lot of "ifs" in his head at one time and yet come up with an answer. These are all things he was unable to do when he thought as a child.

Piaget's Theories of Cognitive Development

Most of the research in the field of cognitive (mental) de-velopment has been done by the highly respected Swiss psychologist, Jean Piaget. He has made brilliant observations of the thought processes of children. He notes that intelligence does not increase at a steady rate, but in spurts. Therefore, the conventional IQ score often is inaccurate because people shift from one "stage" of thinking to a higher "stage" at different ages. Where the child reasons on the basis of objects ("concrete operations"), during early adolescence the young person be-gins to reason on the basis of symbols and principals ("formal operations").

Children between the ages of five and twelve are in the con-crete operations period. They learn to observe, count, organize, memorize, and reorganize concrete objects and information without losing the distinction between the real and the imagi-nary. They can figure things out for themselves and solve prob-lems.

Most people enter the formal operations stage between age eleven or twelve and age fourteen or fifteen. When a person reaches this stage, he or she is able for the first time to deal with abstractions, to reason about the future, to understand and con-struct complex systems of thought, to formulate philosophies, and to struggle with contradictions. A young person who has reached the stage of formal operations can become extremely bored when forced to memorize facts or to accept everything that is taught without questioning. It is not sufficient merely to fill the heads of young adolescents with knowledge. They need to put it into practice and to "learn about their learning."

The Questioning of the Early Adolescent

Also at this age, kids begin to question much of what they have been taught. Young adolescents now find it necessary to reaffirm the learning they acquired from their parents, teachers, and peers. They are quick to spot inconsistencies and contradictions that they were able to reconcile earlier without any problem.

For example, they have been told that sex (for them) is wrong, yet they find pleasure through sexual experiences. Is pleasure therefore wrong? They have been told that God answers prayer, yet sometimes they pray and nothing happens. Why? Left alone, the adolescent grows more and more skeptical, assuming that all religious truth is nothing more than wishful thinking. These major conflicts pivot on the fact that old assumptions are challenged by new perceptions resulting from the transition from concrete to formal operations.

These differences only add weight to the importance of building informed relationships with individual kids. The junior high worker should be aware of kids who are having difficulty understanding certain concepts or who show an apparent lack of interest or seem bored. It is necessary to be willing to listen, to encourage their questions, and to share their struggles.

The Junior Higher and Adolescent Relapse

It would seem logical that with newly acquired mental capabilities, junior highers would be anxious to excel academically, but the opposite is often true. For most young people, the quality of schoolwork goes down drastically during the adolescent years, and this is true in Christian education as well. This time is often referred to as "adolescent relapse."

The reason for this relapse is the emergence of the major distractions such as sudden physical growth, sexual development, the readjustment of relationships with adults and peers, and the surge toward independence. To expect a smooth academic performance when such turmoil is going on is optimistic.

Motivation and the Junior Higher

Another question common among junior high workers is, "How can I motivate junior highers to become more interested in spiritual things, the church, or the youth group?" Some workers resort to force, not only in the physical sense but also emotionally. For example, kids are made to feel guilty for not performing up to prescribed standards. Bribery is also sometimes used: Prizes and gimmickry serve as temporary motivation. More often than not the long-range effects of such approaches are more negative than positive. A few positive incentive ideas follow:

1. If it is, in fact, other urgencies that distract junior highers from concentrating on academic, intellectual, or spiritual things, try to make these things part of the curriculum. In other words, make it relevant. If the subject matter being studied has no practical application, it may be a complete waste of time.

2. Variety is important. Active, growing minds become bored easily.

3. Involve kids in the learning process. Use as many activity-centered learning experiences as you can.

4. Create a warm, friendly atmosphere in which learning can take place.

5. Keep it personal. If each person knows that he is special and cared for, he is motivated not to disappoint you.

Emotional Development in Early Adolescents

By adult standards, junior highers are unpredictably emotional. They have been known to giggle uncontrollably during the first part of a youth meeting and then become despondent during the second half, for no apparent reason. It is possible to have, within a group of fifteen junior highers, some who are boisterous and loud and others who are quiet and shy. Still others in the group might be afraid, or self-critical, or confident, or angry; the list could go on and on. Emotionally, the junior higher experiences myriad peaks and valleys. Junior highers are on a kind of emotional roller coaster ride until they begin to settle down into a pattern, usually at around age fifteen or sixteen.

Unfortunately, we tend to think of emotions as strange forces that arise from the depths to place a person at their mercy. Much of the emotional life of junior highers is actually calm and constructive. A person can be quite emotional without flying into a rage or otherwise showing it. Emotions are always present, no matter what behavior we are displaying at the moment.

Emotional development is closely related to development in other areas of life. Emotions are not foreign intrusions. They reflect what is going on in general in one's life.

It is practically impossible to make any predictions about how a person is going to integrate his emotions and his behavior, since each person responds differently to circumstances. Some early adolescents seem to be sitting on an emotional powder keg, while others take almost everything in stride.

The emotions of early adolescents are intense. There is no middle ground, no halfway mark. People, events, and things are either one extreme or the other. A thing is either superior beyond compare or so inferior as to be worthless. Many events and problems take on an importance out of all proportion to their actual significance. When a junior higher is happy, he is very often ecstatic. When in love, it is greater love than anyone could possibly understand. He fails to cope with his feelings realistically. He tends to surrender to them.

The emotional development of junior highers causes much distress and frustration for parents and teachers, because a junior higher's emotions are often translated into action. They don't hide their emotions well, even when they try to.

Trial-and-Error Personality Development

Emotional unpredictability helps set junior highers apart from other age groups. They may be pleasant one day and terrors the next. The junior higher who is talkative and open one moment could suddenly clam up altogether.

These strange shifts in behavior are not limited to individuals; they are also found in groups. The dynamics in a group of junior highers can change from one week to the next.

Adolescent psychology offers a reasonable explanation for this bizarre behavior. In the process of adolescent development, junior highers are essentially "trying on" different personalities for size. They will express a variety of emotions and temperaments to discover the range of reactions they get from others, especially peers. If the reaction is favorable, the behavior may be repeated; if it is not, the behavior may be discontinued. The personality, like the body and the mind, is being shaped during the junior high years, and it is probably in its most unstable period. A junior higher may try all sorts of personalities—the class clown, the tough guy, the brain, the teacher's pet, the quiet type, the spoiled brat, the flirt—before his or her own distinctive personality traits begin to emerge.

Have Patience, Don't Panic

This erratic behavior pattern generates anxiety for people who work with this age group. It is not an easy task to adapt to the weekly emotional ups and downs of junior highers. It requires a considerable amount of patience, particularly when the behavior of the group is more negative than positive. If you lose your temper, or overreact in a negative way, it rarely accomplishes much. There is nothing wrong with being firm and strict, but the kids need to see maturity and consistency in their adult leaders. Have patience, make as few demands on them as possible, and just wait it out.

Don't Play on Their Emotions

Because of the intensity of their emotions, early adolescents are highly susceptible to emotional appeals. They are fascinated by things that trigger a deep emotional response, such as frenzied rock-and-roll music or heart-rending love songs. Junior highers may also be emotionally lured into drugs or mysticism.

The temptation for the junior high worker is to take full advantage of this susceptibility to produce desired results in the church. You can get junior highers to do almost anything if you get to their emotions. But like emotions themselves, these responses are usually very shallow and temporary. Emotions are not only intense at this age, but they are also transient.

This is not to say that emotions are wrong. They will enter into the picture whenever a young person responds to the gospel, but it is not fair to play on those emotions. Invitations to accept Christ as Savior and to dedicate one's life to Christ should be presented without emotional pressure that may lead only to surface commitments.

Assure Them That Faith Is Not Dependent on Feelings

One of the great mistakes of the Jesus Movement of the late 60's and early 70's was the use of phrases like "Get high on Jesus," which implied that being high is a side effect of a commitment to Christ.

Obviously, this kind of theology leads to problems. Our faith in Christ is never dependent on our emotional condition. Christians have the assurance that the Lord is with us always—even when we are in despair or feeling guilty or afraid. Of course, He is with us when we are ecstatic, but not *because* we are. God is constant. We change. Junior highers, especially, need to know that their faith is not dependent on how they feel. They need to know that Christ is always there and understands them.

---

[1]Dr. Urie Bronfenbrenner, Transcript, *Options in Education, Program #92, Portrait of American Adolescence*. National Public Radio, Washington D.C., 1977, p. 15.

[2]Gilman D. Grave, *The Control of the Onset of Puberty*. New York: John Urley & Sons, 1974, p. xxiii.

[3]Joan Lipsitz, *Growing Up Forgotten*. Lexington, Massachusetts: Lexington Books, 1977, p. 122.

Much of the material in this chapter is reprinted from or is a condensation of material from the book *Junior High Ministry* by Wayne Rice (Grand Rapids, Michigan: Zondervan, 1978). Used by permission.

E. Senior High

by Randy Kirk

As you read, think about these questions:
—What inner and outer pressures are exerted on the senior high youngster?
—How can a ministry build on the strengths and needs of this age group?

The "Average Teenager" is a myth. No such creature exists. No one teen follows an exact given pattern; all are individuals. Teens are more aware of differences among *themselves* than with other segments of society. This individualism makes some painfully aware of their shortcomings and sensitive to any areas in others that might be different from the norm.

Any ministry to high school youth makes a serious mistake when it takes away a teen's individuality. Although he may be hiding in the security of a crowd, he is an individual and has worth as such. "Because he is sixteen, he ought to feel . . ." is a faulty assumption.

Pressures

Any adult who might want to return to that "easy, free life of an adolescent" either has a faulty memory or has not kept in touch with the pressures teens face today. Theirs is truly a "pressure cooker" existence. Physical adjustments, emotional upheaval, pressure from parents and peers, as well as struggles with life's crucial questions team up against today's teen.

Physical
Physically, high school youth are rapidly closing in on

adulthood. Most females have already attained most of their height before reaching high school. Now the males catch and surpass their female classmates. But with that rapid growth spurt comes problems. The awkward self-consciousness about one's physical self is especially acute in those who might mature either extremely early or extremely late.

Sexual characteristics are predominant among the physical changes of adolescents, but other problems may occur resulting from physical changes. The once-smooth complexion suddenly goes haywire. Energy spurts, followed by the need for extended rest, are typical of adolescents.

A ministry has little control over all these problems, but they certainly have a profound effect on any teen ministry. The minister needs to know about these factors and be concerned for their effect on the teen's self-esteem.

Social

Until the middle of adolescence, parents have served as the ultimate authority figures. Pleasing one's parents has been a primary concern. Now, with the high school years, comes freedom and a shift in relationships. The teen's peer group takes on a growing significance. His peers have more influence on him than at any other stage in life. With this shift, a tension is created. The teen is torn between parental approval and friends' acceptance.

Another evidence of adolescence is a shift in the peer group itself. Gradually it includes members of the opposite sex. Along with this need to be accepted by the opposite sex comes the pressure of sexual desires. Add to that pressure the boundaries placed on the expression of these desires, and the trauma of dating for the high school teenager has been defined.

Emotional

Another step in the process of adolescence is the confrontation with the question, "Who am I?" (Or better, "Who am I in relation to... ?") Meaningful existence is based on a purpose for living. In high school, many struggle to discover a purpose. Society demands that immediately following high school, or even sometimes while yet in high school, one set a course for the rest of his life. That course includes vocational choices primarily, but other choices are also involved.

It is frustrating not to understand oneself, and worse yet, not to like oneself. Yet that is the plight of many high school teen-agers.

Teens struggle with self doubts and feelings of inferiority and loneliness. They start to become aware that with the freedom of adulthood comes new responsibility. The struggle for acceptance by peers and adults also breeds these feelings of inadequacy. The cure for this worry lies in their being loved, accepted, and trusted.

Mental

Today's teens have been exposed to more knowledge than any previous generation. That exposure makes them more informed in some areas than their parents—adding to the existing tension. They have also learned the rudiments of logic, and demand a reason why things are as they are.

Teens are primarily concerned with the present moment. Neither the past nor the future hold much interest or significance. History is not as vital as personal experience, and the future is distant and unsure, leaving the present as the only reality. Thus the emphasis on pleasure and adventure. At this point, drugs, sexual experiments, astrology, and the gamut of current moral issues enter the scene.

This concern with the existential *now* has also given the modern teen a different understanding of commitment. Commitment is in regard to effort, not time. Often a commitment made today is just that, a commitment for today.

Spiritual

Spiritually, middle adolescence is often a period of unrest. Some teens respond by avoiding any confrontation with organized religion. Others desire spiritual understanding, but the unrest persists. A part of that unrest stems from idealism: teens become aware of the faults of organized religion and church members. Second, most high school youth feel doctrinally unsure of themselves and uncomfortable with Bible study. But at this point, studies of the Word as it relates to everyday living are most vital.

A misunderstanding of fundamental doctrines has given many teens needless guilt. For example, a senior high church camp survey showed that most kids understand facing temptation as having sinned. Many adolescents also have a faulty concept of the grace of God.

Keys to Ministering With High-School Youth

Individualize. Each teen is worthy of the time and energy necessary to make him whole. It is important to spend time in one-to-one relationships as well as group activities.

Be a model. Models play an integral role in an adolescent who is forming his identity. A good model is consistent in his Christian life; teens despise hypocrisy.

Keep it simple. One cannot assume that a teen understands the moral and doctrinal implications of a word, lesson, or Scripture passage. His silence may be a mark of ignorance, not consent. A leader must be careful with the use of a term peculiar to organized religion. It may have no meaning to adolescents, or worse yet, a misunderstood meaning.

Express love. Many teens grow up in settings where little love is displayed. Love is a learned action. Where can it better be taught than within the body of Christ? One can teach, for example, that touch need not have sexual connotations. Often the church speaks of love, but teens need to see love in action.

Understand discipline. Discipline, to be effective, must stem from love. A part of the adolescent process is learning to accept responsibility. Just as unjustified guilt should be alleviated, deserved guilt need not be minimized. Discipline serves as a means of handling guilt.

Expose them to new experiences. The high schooler's sense of adventure can be a valuable asset. A ministry that includes fresh exciting experiences can find these to be valuable teaching tools.

Offer opportunities to serve. Strommen concludes his book *Five Cries of Youth* with the statement, "They need activities which give them a sense of purpose; that is *mission*." This sense of mission can be a particular answer to many adolescent needs: burning energy, building self-esteem, and determining identity.

CHAPTER

11

Activities for Ministry and Growth

A. Camping and Retreats

by David Wheeler

As you read, think about these questions:
—What are the reasons for including a camp or retreat in a program?
—What goals should the experience accomplish, and what activities make those goals feasible?
—Which projects and activities are most appropriate for various times in the day, weekend, or week?

Christian camping and retreats are similar in purpose. Even the planning and execution are closely related. All that I write concerning retreats is usually applicable and useful in the area of Christian camping as well. The words "camp" and "retreat" are almost interchangeable.

Organizing a Camp or Retreat

Purpose
In war, a "retreat" is a temporary withdrawal from battle for

nourishment, strength, strategy, and perspective. Retreats serve the same purpose in the "battle" of the Christian life.

The Bible contains many examples of "retreats." Paul apparently had an extended retreat in Arabia before beginning his work.[1] Jesus himself undertook a forty-day "wilderness challenge" before beginning His ministry. Jesus learned to retreat even in the midst of great activity. We read of Him spending the night on a hilltop in prayer. When His disciples returned from an exhausting trip, He told them to "Come away by yourselves to a lonely place, and rest a while."[2] What a description of the purpose of a camp or retreat! Penetration into the world will be very shallow unless it is preceded by a retreat for preparation. We have nothing to say until God first speaks to us.

Gene Getz says that three experiences are vital to live a balanced, mature Christian life: knowledge, relating to others, and witnessing. The camping setting can effectively provide these experiences.

The knowledge experience is provided through the concentrated study at a retreat. If a young person comes to church activities three hours per week, from ages three to eighteen, his time spent in Christian education will equal the hours spent in the first and second grades of school! He enters the adult world with a second-grade level Christian education. Much effective supplementary teaching can be done in a retreat setting.

The relational experience is beyond compare. In a week of camp, or on a retreat, we are given a unique chance to model "Christlikeness." It is difficult to build strong relationships in a forty-five minute Sunday-school class or youth meeting. Kids need "live" models, and the only way for us to really "see" one another is by spending extended periods of time with one another. We are able to see others responding to pressure situations. It helps us to see our youth when they are not wearing their "Christian masks." It is also good for them to discover that we adults are not perfect, but that we try to practice what we have been preaching.

Retreats are also great times for incorporating new kids into the body of Christ, and strengthening their relationships with other members.

The witnessing experience is enhanced through times of retreat. Youth receive practical experience in ministering to one another, and become motivated to rejoin the battle for their friends' lives.

Place

In the typical church camp situation, "where" is not a major decision. Camp is held at the regional Christian campground. However, many of our camps are beginning to host weeks that are held away from the camp facility. These "trip camps" or "wilderness camps" are gaining wide acceptance.

If you are planning a retreat, or if you are in an area that does not have an established campground, the "where" becomes a big issue. The location must be decided upon first. The date of your retreat, the type of program, and much more all hinge on the facility chosen.

Choose a variety of locations. Don't always return to the same place. Cabins, commercial campgrounds, colleges (especially Bible colleges in the summer), and the church basement can all make ideal settings. Explore your area and find out what is available.

Be flexible and creative as you choose. Choose a facility that will enhance the type of program you are planning. Since rain or bad weather may mess up your schedule, be sure your indoor facilities will be adequate.

At a church campground, the fees have been decided by the directors. But if you are planning a retreat, the cost factor is up to you. Many elements come into play when you discuss the finances. Will you be doing your own cooking, or will it be done for you at the camp facility? Are you bringing in outside speakers or groups? Are you renting films? Is it necessary for you to charter transportation?

Once you have determined what the total cost of the retreat will be, you must decide how much to charge each young person to register. Are you going to try to meet all expenses through money collected in registrations, or is the church budget going to help meet some expenses? Sometimes it is necessary for the church budget to assist. Otherwise, the cost of the retreat would be so high as to prohibit some youth from attending.

Time

In established Christian camps, "when" is usually decided for you by the directors. You may have some input to the process.

The dates for a retreat, however, are at your discretion. Check the church and school activity calendars for conflicts. You don't want to plan a retreat on graduation weekend! If you plan a retreat that involves a game night, players, cheerleaders and band members may not be available. It helps to arrange for late transportation to the retreat.

Retreats don't always have to be Friday through Sunday. They can be shorter, longer, or even held during the week. Extended wilderness camping experiences may last up to three weeks.

It is a good idea to graduate a retreat program, from primary through college age. In this way, as the youth grow older, the retreat opportunities grow with them. The smaller youth have shorter and fewer retreats, while the older youth have longer and more frequent ones.

Early in your planning, you need to start registering the youth for the retreat. Give them a deadline for registrations and stick to it. Collect the registration money in advance; doing this helps commit them to attending.

Who Should Attend

Who should be present on the retreat? The youth are most important. Local church camps are usually open to youth from all over the area, while a retreat is usually limited to youth from your congregation and their friends. It helps to call personally on kids you want to attend the retreat.

Encourage your youth to bring friends. A camp or retreat is a nonthreatening situation, and it is the most effective time to have a visitor with your group.

Your youth coaches, or camp faculty, also get high priority. Contact them early, so they may arrange their schedules. Try not to overburden them. Give them as much time as possible to be with the youth. Make sure they understand that personal ministry is the purpose of their free time.

Give a special invitation to the senior minister of the church, and any other appropriate staff members. Don't take it for granted that they will automatically feel invited.

Your cook is also a key person. Usually one or two older people in the church not only cook well, but also are great public relations people for the youth department. When you recruit a cook, let that job be their sole responsibility. Don't expect busy youth coaches to do the cooking!

You may need to invite a qualified nurse, the Sunday-school teachers of the attending youth, and a couple of elders or deacons and their wives as observers. There may be some Bible-college students available who could assist.

If you bring in special people such as speakers or singers, make sure that they know their responsibilities clearly and early. Sometimes, churches go together and pool their resources in order to bring in outside personnel. Such joint retreats call for even more planning. An effective retreat, however, is possible using your own people and resources.

Planning a Retreat

You will have to do a lot of planning. For a week of camp, preparation may involve several meetings over the course of a year. These meetings would involve the dean and two or three key faculty members. The final meeting would come a few weeks before the week of camp, and include every faculty person. At this meeting, the entire schedule is blocked out in detail, so everyone is well acquainted with it. Even the smallest details of the schedule must be worked out. These include classes and teachers, worship services, meals, singing and song leaders, recreation, and sleeping arrangements.

For a retreat, you go through a condensed version of the same planning schedule. Early in the planning, decide what the main function of the event will be: teaching, training, inspiration, just fun, or a combination of these? Let some youth have a part in the planning. Camp is for the kids, and we adults often forget what it was like when we were there. When that happens, we end up planning the camp or retreat to suit ourselves, not the youth.

Components of a Successful Retreat

Making New Friends

A few weeks before the camp or retreat, it helps to get a "core group" of kids meeting to pray for a successful experience. Talk over the individual needs of the youth who are registered and discuss ways of ministering to them. When the retreat finally starts, this "core group" really sets the pace for the others.

To have a strong camp or retreat, it is imperative that the youth know one another. Schedule the early part of the camp/retreat with a lot of community-building icebreakers. (The IDEA BOOKS series from Youth Specialties is probably the best resource for activity ideas.)

Some people don't see the need for this "crazy stuff" at a church function, but the maxim is still true: "The family that plays together, prays together." Youth today have almost forgotten how to build deep interpersonal relationships. These relationships have to start with a comfortable introduction. That is the function of icebreakers. Choose activities that fit your personality and the "personality" of the camp.

Some icebreaking ideas include relays, water relays, water balloon fights, and shaving cream fights. These things may sound silly or frivolous, but they work! Strangers can quickly be transformed into a close knit group of laughing friends, with some careful planning and creative play.

Allow plenty of time for these games. If you are doing something fairly physical, participation should be optional, never forced. Glasses and jewelry should be removed. With younger age groups, more control will be necessary—sometimes they don't know when to quit! When you're through, clean up your mess. Finally, see that the craziness decreases during the weekend or week of camp, when the focus should be growing more serious.

All in a "Family"

The "family" concept has been a big plus to many camp and retreat programs. All the youth present are assigned to a "family." Several youth are "adopted" by each couple on the staff, and the kids assume that couple's last name. Groups much larger than twelve people lose the family feeling.

Each family eats meals together, participates in recreation together, has post-lunch devotions together, and holds a nightly prayer circle. Some powerful ministry has taken place in these smaller family groups.

Classes

The possibilities for education at a retreat are staggering! A curriculum published by a Christian company can easily be adapted to fit the schedule. A thirteen-week course of study can be fit into a weekend retreat or spread out over a week of camp. (More learning takes place when the lessons are concentrated into a few days, rather than spread out over weeks or months.)

Retreats and camps are the most convenient times for topical studies, on such subjects as death and dying or the Christian's response to television. The extended time periods allow for

more creative teaching opportunities. These are also exceptional times for expository Bible studies, especially on some of
the shorter books, such as James. The entire book can be
covered in the time available, and a variety of techniques can
be used to convey the message.

Offer a wide variety of classes, with a balance of topical
studies and Bible studies. An offering of classes for a week of
camp, for example, might include a study of love, sex and
marriage; a class on sharing the "good news" with a friend; a
class on how to study the Bible; and a class on the book of
Romans. Try to meet the needs of the youth who will be attending. Having youth on the planning committee will help you
discover their needs. Choose teachers who know the subject,
and can teach it effectively.

Classes will naturally be a big part of your schedule. If possible, give the youth some choice as to which class they will
attend. Electives are getting a good reception wherever they are
offered. If you offer electives, don't limit the class size. Let
everyone who is interested in a certain class attend.

Do not make the class periods too short. Don't allow the
schedule to get crowded and rushed during the teaching times.

Use as many creative approaches to the teaching as possible.
Role plays, simulation games, films, and other methods help
communicate the message more effectively. The classes should
be participation-oriented, not lecture.

Meals

Meals are often ignored as an important opportunity for positive input to the curriculum. There is more to them than just
planning the menu.

As mentioned earlier, the families (or teams) eat together.
They have their own table, and the "parents" have brought
table decorations to make the atmosphere more homey. After
lunch, each family has a devotional time, or they work through
a Serendipity placemat to improve their communication and
relationships.

Lunch is probably the most active meal. The youth are too
sleepy at breakfast to do much, and they are too dressed up and
more serious at supper. So, spend a lot of enjoyable activity
time at lunch.

If you find that your evening schedule will be running late,
consider a brunch. Instead of an early, full breakfast, let the

kids sleep later and then fix their own breakfasts of fruit, cereal, pastry, and juice. Then, have a heavier lunch. It doesn't cost any more, and the kids appreciate the extra rest.

Speaking of mornings, try to make them as creative and lively as possible. If you do morning exercises, do something different each day. We have had obstacle courses, Jack La Lanne on video cassette, and visitors teaching "foreign" exercises, such as the Mexican hat dance!

A special morning might start by serving the kids breakfast in bed. Let them sleep a little later, while the faculty gets up, prepares it, and serves it as a big surprise.

The Camp as Service to God

Over the years, we seem to have lost the idea of Christian *service* camps. The awareness and abilities of your youth may be sharpened by your use of missionaries and by ministry projects.

The missionary may come in many "forms." He or she may be a Bible-college professor, a campus minister, a "home" missionary, or a "foreign" missionary. Give him a place of honor. Make sure that he has ample opportunity to share his ministry with the youth.

Ministry projects help the youth see that serving Jesus involves more than just the Big Four: preaching, teaching, singing, and playing the piano. They discover that *all* of our gifts and talents are usable.

One successful project has been a camp concert. This can even be done during a short retreat. The youth work on a musical that can also involve drama, puppets, and a multimedia presentation. This takes a lot of preparation and work, but it is worth it! The youth are thrilled that God could use them to do something like this. (One precaution is necessary. Work to prevent the program from becoming an "ego trip" for the youth. Keep Jesus at the center.)

Other ministry projects can be varied, such as helping out with physical labor at a local children's home, or work at the camp facility itself, making needed improvements. Community service projects, such as cleaning up parks and roadsides, or presenting a concert in a shopping mall, are other possibilities.

Recreation

I discourage heavy recreational competition, because in a

typical retreat, youth of all levels of athletic ability are present. As the competition becomes heated, self-esteem and relationships can be shattered.

To replace the more common forms of recreation (volleyball, softball, etc.), I suggest the New Games format. This recreation is non-threatening and non-competitive. The motto is: "Play Hard, Play Fair, Nobody Hurt." New Games are just as much fun as traditional games, if not more so. New Gamebooks can be ordered through any bookstore.

In a typical afternoon, you might have two or three hours of recreation. The first half may be structured, with families (or teams) playing against each other. The second half should be free for rest, talk, and unstructured recreation. Only those who are interested and feel they have the abilities should play—no one is forced to participate.

Outside Opportunities

Don't be afraid to leave the facility for certain recreation, such as hiking, canoeing, or rafting. Just make sure you have experienced and capable people leading, and get special permission from parents, if necessary.

Examine the scenic attractions in the area surrounding your camp, and take advantage of any special aspects, such as mountaintop worship services, dramatizing Jesus preaching the Sermon on the Mount. There have been lakeside services with dramatization of Jesus and His disciples coming in from the boats and preaching to the crowds.

If you intend to leave the camp facility for certain activities, make all arrangements in advance. Check with the camp about insurance. Transportation can be arranged by using church buses. Be sure to have adequate adult supervision.

Music

Music also has an important place in a camp/retreat program. Use the youth as much as possible. Let them know in advance that they are welcome to bring solos, group numbers, and instruments. They can provide special music for any of the camp services.

It is a good idea to have some exciting Christian music playing during the meal times, before main sessions, and at other available times. We should constantly expose our kids to Christian music. They need to know that there is an alternative to a constant diet of "rock." Tell them where they can obtain this Christian music.

Outside groups can add a lot to your camp. College music groups are often invited. Their expenses are not high, and the college appreciates the chance to recruit. No matter which group you invite, make sure they understand that you want them more than their music. Their personalities and participation can be either a blessing or a curse to the program.

You might decide that you have enough talent among your own group of youth, and that outside people are not necessary. Or you may have a group come in for just one night and give a concert. In all of your music, remember to keep it Christ-centered, not performer-centered.

Schedule Hints

Schedules are good—even necessary—but remember: "The schedule was made for man, not man for the schedule." You need not stick rigidly to the schedule at all times and at all costs. It is merely a guideline. If a certain session is going well and getting a good response, let it continue and make some schedule changes. Allow enough free time to act as "buffer zones" to absorb the impact of any last-minute schedule changes.

Try to make every day's schedule different. It is a good idea to plan and print a new schedule for each day of the camp. The youth start getting excited each morning as they find the new schedule by their breakfast plates. They know that today is not going to be the "same old thing." You may make simple inter-polations of activities, or schedule drastically different ones; wilderness camping one day, service projects the next.

Always plan for bad weather. It may not materialize, but if it does, you will be glad you were prepared. Have alternate schedules and activities ready when you arrive. "It rains on the just and the unjust," and it also rains on the prepared and the unprepared.

Evening Programs

The evening section of the schedule is a separate entity. Evenings could be called God's "prime time," when the youth are ready to calm down and think more seriously. Mentally, emotionally, and physically, evening should be the best part of your day at the retreat camp.

Do not be hesitant to run your evening program late: the only condition is that you allow the youth time to get adequate sleep. Most American youth are used to late hours, and if you send them to bed too early, the staff will spend a lot of frustrating time trying to get them settled. So, why not use that time more fruitfully? Plan a full evening, so that the young people are ready for bed when the time comes.

The makeup of your evening schedule offers a wide range of possibilities. Films, a concert, and games provide a needed break in the evening. But do not allow lightheartedness to become the core.

The pacesetter for the evening is usually the vesper, or preaching, service. Find the most effective communicator and inspirational speaker possible, and work with him to set the tempo for the evenings.

Campfires can become the most creative parts of your retreats. They are perfect for candlelight prayer walks, multimedia presentations, or dramatic skits. Don't just throw the campfire program together after arriving at camp. Plan each one carefully in advance. You may offer a "linger longer" campfire, with two or three key faculty members, for youth who have special needs that they want to discuss.

If you use the family concept, after the campfire is a perfect time for the families to get together, discuss the day, talk about tomorrow, pray together, and say "good night, John-Boy!"

Evening activities are almost unlimited. Why not have a coffee house instead of the usual talent night? It is still a talent night, but with soft lights, candles on the tables and light refreshments. Homemade ice cream socials, Christmas in July, Halloween in August—all these and many more ideas have evolved into powerful evening programs. Only your creativity limits the potential!

Final Details

Make sure that you have adequate insurance.

Appoint an official photographer who knows the special activities you want photographed. These slides will be valuable when recruiting youth for the next time. It helps to make available to the faculty a list of all the non-Christian youth present. The faculty then knows the ones who may need some special attention.

It often helps to send a letter to the youth a few weeks before the camp, giving them any needed information. Keep rules at a minimum—common sense covers a lot of area.

Spoil your faculty. Let them know how very special they are, both to you and to the youth.

Take time before the end of the retreat to prepare the youth for "coming down off the mountain." It is sometimes a shock to re-enter the "real" world. Constantly keep the awareness before the youth that they will be leaving this place. Keep prodding them to decide what is going to be different when they return to their families, jobs, churches, and schools.

Make love your only motivation for Christian camping or retreating. Love for the Lord and love for kids are not just "important"—they are vital. On a retreat or during a week of camp, you might be with those young people for a greater amount of time than you will be with them the rest of the year. Ephesians 5:6 says we should make the best of our time. Don't just show them a good program; show them Jesus, in all His love, glory, and power!

---

[1] Galatians 1:17
[2] Mark 6:31

B. Social Activities

by Andy Hansen

As you read, think about these questions:
—How do social events serve Christ's purpose in youth ministry?
—What specific steps must be considered to insure a successful social?
—What are some workable ideas that could become a beginning base for planning local events?

In the beginnings of youth work, socials were overused. Attendances were large, yet no depth was attained. Soon, the youth crowds became restless and bored with the constant diet of superficial fun, and their numbers dwindled. Ministers, elders, parents, and youth became frustrated with the lack of meaningful results. As a reaction, the pattern began to shift to in-depth Bible study. Again after a few weeks the results were the same—youth started to drop out.

In both cases, our problem was not with the majority of youth themselves, but with *our conception* of the needs of youth!

In many ways our youth ministries have come full circle. We have tried numerous ideas but have come to a deeper, more meaningful, and more productive balance. Hopefully, this is true with our concept of socials in youth work.

Now our ministries are developing a more balanced program to meet the needs of our young—socials for physical and social needs, Bible study for spiritual growth and maturity, and productive ways of service for fulfillment and purpose.

Purpose of Socials

We have two main reasons for providing quality socials in our youth work. One is to develop friendship and fellowship among the youth. The second is to draw new youngsters into our church functions.

Youth within the church desperately need to build themselves into a support group that is not only enjoyable, but concerned and uplifting. Before this can take place, however, the youth must first begin to enjoy being together and relaxing with one another. In most cases, our youth are divided among numerous public schools and classrooms. They sit together in Sunday school and youth meetings, but rarely do they let down and really relate in these settings. Hence, the real need for socials with a purpose!

A trained youth coach also realizes the importance of building his own personal relationships with the youth. If half of youth work is teaching, the other half is providing a model image the youth can share their lives with and thereby gain a vision of committed Christianity. Socials can be a means of 1) building kids' relationships and 2) giving the adult coaches and youth a means of interaction.

To a non-Christian youth, the church often means lectures on rules and regulations and a lot of boredom. They will not come near any place that even smells like a church building or Bible study, no matter how sincerely their friends implore them.

Socials provide a non-threatening atmosphere that will allow youth to invite such friends and experience good results. If the youth experiences a positive environment at the social, slowly he will begin to trust and like the youth and the church. However, if a new youth finds the social to be poorly organized and dull, or if he encounters no warmth or friendship, we have lost a chance to build a bridge to his salvation.

Our youth cannot be forced to mingle, but if they are challenged and taught, they will! Ask the youth to pray for the social's success. Ask them to invite certain youth and strive to be their friends. Teach them that a young person might eventually become a Christian only if he finds a group of people who care about him. After a social, get your core youth together and discuss the results. Those core youth must be committed to the real purpose in order to have a dynamic social.

Organization of Socials

Nothing is more disastrous than a poorly organized, dead social. The "blahs" hang heavy after such an experience!

Planning

Gather a small group of coaches and two or three youth and brainstorm about the projected social. Try to be original. When you plan a roller-skating social for the fifth time in a row, mutiny will strike!

First, think of the *purpose* of the social. Is it to develop your own group, or will it major on bringing in new youth? What financial range are you aiming for? What type of social do you want—simple (mini-golf outing) or complex (area-wide weekend backpacking trip)? Discuss the ideas and expand upon them; assign responsibilities, and begin building enthusiasm.

Once the basic structure of your social has been filled out, your group must set time limits for certain specific actions, planned on a workable schedule.

Promotion

One of the keys to a successful social is the communication and promotion of the event.

Recently a church in our vicinity organized an area rally. The program was excellent: creative events, dynamic music group and speaker. But only twenty or thirty young people showed up, mostly from the sponsoring church. What a disappointment!

Why did this happen? Most of the churches knew nothing of the upcoming event, and those that did had received a one page flyer two weeks before the date—too late for them to schedule the event, secure transportation, and encourage their youth to attend.

Activities must not only be planned well in advance, but also promoted in advance by as many methods as possible. Posters, handout flyers with *place, time,* and *cost* should be handed out or mailed to every prospective youth. Publicity that is humorous, with a few comical drawings, does much to catch the eye. Les Christie has been a forerunner of this concept by using clippings of MAD magazine characters and catchy quips in his publicity. Every youth possible should be phoned and encouraged to attend. Let your creative imagination run wild, but make sure you *get the message out, and get it out early.*

Decorations

Creative decor does not just happen. For those "special"

events such as Halloween or a Fifties Night, decorations greatly influence the flavor and mood of the event. The quality of a well-planned social will impress youth. Good decorations take plenty of time, and they are a good means of involving more of your youth in the preparation.

Drivers

For your own safety and for the church's, a detailed policy should be established as to when youth are allowed to drive to socials. If you are going any distance at all, detailed maps should be supplied for all drivers. Rules and liability should be established and explained with care.

Be flexible. Don't wait until a week before the event and try to arrange for drivers. *Estimate your attendance and have plenty of cars, vans, and buses to cover.*

Food

The stomach greatly affects the success of a social. If full and content, the typical young person is happy and enjoys the activity. If he's empty and growling, a large dark cloud of restlessness hovers over him.

Whether it is something as light as popcorn or as major as a hundred pizzas, plan ahead. Most youth are willing to pay to be guaranteed food.

Be creative. My kids get violently ill at the sight of sloppy joes and spaghetti after seeing it at the tenth straight activity.

Even changing the eating utensils can be fun. Put odd-sized bowls and irregular utensils in a sack for the youth to eat with. When our group did this, the kids talked and laughed almost more about this than the main activity of the social.

Cleanup

Leave responsible people in charge of this area. Rotate the responsibility so everyone gets his turn. Once in a while do extra jobs, such as washing the bus or waxing the hallway floor so that church adults will be happy and peaceful.

Make the Most of It

The long-range goal of a social should be more than just a good event. What has been done to challenge the youth with the message of Christ? What devotions are planned? Some youth may be attending who may never hear the Scriptures again unless we make a personal application that will touch their lives. We need not be apologetic for the devotional period in our social. It should be one of the highlights, not an after-thought. With good preparation, the truth can be shared in such a creative way that it penetrates the conscience of the unchurched youth and begins to bear fruit. Our youth should be trained to be attentive, to show by their actions that this is the most important part of the social. Others will catch the idea. They would be even more impressed if one of their own peers, one of the youth, shared his feelings about Christ. A special guest speaker might relate well to the youth. Be in prayer for this time and opportunity, but do not overkill with a forty-five minute sermon. Challenge them, then let them think on the one or two main points.

After the social, ask your youth what new youth attended. Did they meet any of them? Did they get their names and ad-dresses? Were guests personally invited to come back?

To capitalize on your social, organize a visitation night im-mediately after the activity, and call on youth that visited. En-courage them to come back.

How sad it would be if we expected youth to come to our building and activities, and then failed to notice them and en-courage their return. With planning and commitment, socials can become an outreach ministry, winning young people to Christ.

Methods for Socials

By planning your schedule a year in advance, you can con-trol the content and variety of socials and arrange the timing to best suit your needs.

You will probably be scheduling two types of socials:
1. Frequent simple activities
2. Occasional large-scale, complex activities

Simple Socials

Youth need interaction in a relaxed atmosphere to develop the bonds of friendship. Therefore, our own junior high and senior high youth plan a simple social almost every month. These socials build a supportive group, allow coach/youth in-teraction, and draw small numbers of new youth. Costs for these activities are minimal. Food is brought by the kids them-selves or donated. Devotions are shared by youth within the group. Publicity is usually low-key—phone calls, newsletter, a few posters. Every month a different group of youth assist in the organization of the social, giving almost all the youth an opportunity to carry some of the responsibility.

Examples of such activities are:

—20 mile bike hike to a given destination, campfire with the usual hot dogs and smores, group singing, and a short teaching and testimony session. A bus takes the group back home.

—Winter sledding and tubing, then head back home for hot chocolate and indoor games. Short devotions and small group prayer time.

—Senior high youth sponsor movie night for children, with cartoons, a puppet show, and prayer with children in small groups led by teens. (Don't forget the free popcorn!)

Major Socials

This major type of social involves many youth and adults in service, can draw many new youth, and builds responsibility into your core youth. Cost will be determined by the activity. Food should be plentiful and even better than what your youth would expect. Facilities should be rented in advance, and if possible, reserved totally for your group (gymnasiums, roller rinks or bowling alleys, for example). Devotions should be one of the highlights.

Strive for a high-quality, well-planned social. This will be one of the key factors influencing how new youth will respond to your future activities. You should have much attractive publicity. You also need to make a close estimate of your food needs and reservations for activities. If other churches are involved, communication is vital, since their commitment to publicizing and pushing the social is essential. Youth should constantly be challenged to pray for friends, for the devotional leaders, and for their own involvement.

Examples of such major social activities are:

A camera scavenger hunt. Teams of four or five youth are given a camera and a designated number of pictures they can take. Each group is given a sheet listing possible pictures— each worth a certain amount of points. The object is to accumulate the most points possible. Groups must be back on time, and will be penalized points for every minute late. The fun is in taking the pictures. For instance:

—Ten points for group on ninth hole of golf course; five extra points for every golfer outside of the group on the course (get permission from the golf course).

—Fifteen points for picture of group around dining table in someone's house. Must be in home of total stranger.

After everyone is back at the home destination, serve up the food, announce winners, award prizes. Then have each group share their experiences. Lead into devotions and prayer. Then pass out publicity about the coming year. Get every name, address, and phone number. Later in the week have core youth follow up on visitors and invite them back to other youth group activities.

An all-night New Year's Eve Social for area churches. The evening can consist of group-breaker games, relays, volleyball round robin, Laurel and Hardy films, one serious Christian film, pizzas, and drinks.

Two other points should be considered: one is summer programming, the other is socials for the family.

Summer is a great time for many good socials. Some of your youth will be on vacation, but the majority will be at home withering. Outdoor activities that are inexpensive seem to work best. We run a program throughout the summer that takes place almost every Wednesday afternoon that is dubbed M.A.D. (Mid-Afternoon Diversion). Perhaps you can envision the publicity that could be sent out with that title! Most activities are cheap, and a devotion and prayer time is always included. Bike hikes, picnics, beach, horseback riding, pools, mini golf, visiting a rest home, mowing people's lawns for free, and ball games are among the many possibilities for summer socials.

One of the greatest responsibilities of the church is to support the family unit. Yet the church, with its multiple programs, often tends to divide instead of support the home. We must begin to plan family activities into our long-range goals. Men-and-boys fishing trips, family trips to ball games, and group picnics could prove to be dynamic activities.

Resources

Examine all the possibilities within a reasonable distance of your community, and keep your files filled with such discoveries.

Ask around. Since we youth ministers are notorious for plagiarism, we might as well be cooperative and share our ideas. Occasionally all the associates in our state gather in a common meeting area and brainstorm on socials all day.

Be a hawk for any materials that come within grabbing distance. Some magazines will hold only one good idea, but are well worth it. Be sure to refer to the resource list appended to this text.

Attend clinics that major in youth ministry, such as Ozark Bible College's Youth Workers Seminar and Cincinnati Bible College's Youth Leader Clinic. Success with Youth, Youth Specialities, Serendipity, and Standard Publishing's *Ideashops* can all contribute numerous ideas to your ministry.

Types of Socials

Seasonal

Christmas	Everybody's Birthday
Valentine's Day	Fourth of July

Traveling

Bike Hikes	Baseball Games
Canoeing	Horseback Riding
Amusement Parks	Snowmobiling

Local

Bowling	Ping-Pong Tournament
Golfing	Basketball
Swimming	Roller Skating
Picnics	Park or Zoo
Volleyball	Table Games and Pizza Night
Hayride	Frisbee Football

Ideas for Socials

Progressive or Regressive Dinner
Car Rally (hunt for clues; not a race)
Camera Scavenger Hunt
Bigger and Better (go door to door exchanging items for something bigger and better)
Operation Snow (shovel snow for elderly)
Gorilla Kidnap (Dress one person up as a gorilla, and have him "kidnap" some of the youth to bring to a social sponsored by other kids in the group. Notify parents ahead of time.)

Socials are not and should not become the main method of youth ministry. However, in the right balance (with Bible studies, discipleship, and service projects) socials can be a strong and effective tool for your youth ministry if you will plan in advance and develop responsible adults and youth to assist you. Your youth will unite, your coaches will understand youth and be respected, and new youth will be won to Christ.

C. Teen Choirs

by Gene Shepherd

As you read, think about these questions:
—How can the quality of the performances be balanced with the need for involvement of a wide ability range of youth?
—What is the real ministry of a youth choir?

Three guidelines are essential to creating and maintaining an effective teen choir.

Take Anyone Who Breathes

Since most youth programs are constantly trying to increase their number, this may seem like a ridiculous statement. However, many teen choirs are made up of auditioned or selected youth. You may get the best singers at the moment, but this is not wise in the long run.

First of all, the junior high and high school voice is unpredictable. It can literally become beautiful overnight. Voices lacking potential in October may be soloists next May. Usually that change happens because they have been in a disciplined choir program. Without practice and experience, those voices might never change.

A second reason for using all interested youth is because of the peculiar nature of a teen choir. It can build and unify a group. Often the choir will become a base for evangelistic efforts. Young people may sing even though they do not participate in any other church activity, because they readily identify with music. A properly planned choir program can take that interest and give it new meaning. The end result is youth who come in contact with Christ. When youth are passed over because they lack talent, the choir becomes a clique. It is better to sacrifice a little musical quality then it is to have a superb choir and risk dividing the fellowship of your group.

The final reason for using anyone is because of good singers aren't necessarily the best choir members. Actual performance time is only a small part of the total picture. It takes many hours of disciplined work to put a song or program on the platform. Enthusiasm, dedication, and a concept of purpose are essential elements for a successful rehearsal and performance, Many times, a poor singer will lead the way in interest and discipline and motivate the rest of the choir. This kind of contribution cannot be measured.

Strive for Ministry, Not Performance

Music is powerful enough to teach, motivate, and encourage a listener. It can also warp the performer. The public nature of singing, the "feel" of lights and the applause, can cause people to put their egos ahead of the ministry that music can have. The singer may not even be aware of his own selfish motivation. It is amazing that a function so directed to "others," can be the cause of so much selfishness, strife, and ego problems. The choir director, therefore, must carefully establish the reasons for singing:

1. To praise God
2. To teach
3. To encourage

The role of the singer is that of a servant who is practicing good stewardship of his talent.

The end result is that people will be brought into an obedient relationship to God. Every detail of the choir program must be carefully planned to achieve this goal.

Three things can help you emphasize ministry instead of performance. To anyone who has worked with a high school choir, these suggestions may seem a bit lofty. However, these are targets that can be reached, and must be aimed for.

Maintain a Regular Ministry at Home

Unfortunately, many choirs' major goal is fun trips to other congregations, but the consistency of such a ministry is spasmodic. Young people need to be involved in *regular* service projects. They need to concentrate their performances at home.

A week-to-week responsibility, such as singing every Sunday, emphasizes the continuing needs of the congregation.

This method gives down-to-earth reasons for singing, and it can accomplish great things. The tone of many worship services is set by the choir. The youth can have a valuable leadership role in the spiritual life of that congregation.

Use Only Appropriate Music

Appropriate music is music that accomplishes the goals mentioned. If the song has a beautiful melody or harmony and the words are pointless, don't use it. Nothing impresses the power of ministry in music on your young peoples' minds as the careful selection of appropriate message-oriented songs. For too long, our leaders have been selecting songs that had a good beat, with the emphasis on pleasing the audience. Select instead musical works that inspire people with God's truth. The style, classical, popular, or gospel, is not important. When your young people are concerned about delivering the songs' message, then you are on the right road.

Keep Rehearsals on a Devotional Level

Rehearsal time is important, consuming the vast majority of time. Rehearsals must therefore be carefully planned. Add seriousness to practice with a solid devotional base. Never begin or end practice without time in prayer for the ministry of the group. Constantly mention the goals of singing and point out obvious ways of accomplishing them. Young people must learn that it is a spiritual duty to use their time wisely in rehearsal. Let individual youth lead in giving these devotionals. Their concern will have an effect on the others, especially in discipline and respect for leadership.

Demand Their Potential

Jesus Christ gave up everything for us. When He calls men to Him, He asks that they do the same. We do our youth a great injustice when we let them get by with a mediocre output in any Christian endeavor. If Christ is pleased with a halfhearted attempt at singing in a choir, then He's pleased with a halfhearted attempt at Christian living. One of the most important things we can do is start conveying that message of the need for commitment. The teen choir is a perfect place to begin. If they have the potential to sing a passage, work till they can sing it well. Stretch them to their limit.

Not only will youth begin to realize the extent of their commitment, but the choir itself will benefit. Choirs aren't made of good voices, but hard work. If youth will dedicate themselves to Christ and give 100% to the cause, and if they can work with someone who knows what he's doing, an acceptable choir will result. Success will be achieved because the members will be working up to their potential. Christian witness will come through, loud and strong.

A choir is not the miracle answer to every youth program's need. It can be a tremendous moving force or a terrible problem. The key is the director. Get your goals firmly in mind and let nothing change them. Give 100% to Christ. He will give the increase.

> Take my voice and let me sing
> Always only for my King
> Always only for my King.

D. Drama

by Richard Hargrove

As you read, think about these questions:
—What major factors influence selecting the appropriate dramas and the casts for them?
—What is a workable schedule and rehearsal plan that can bring a good youth drama to fruition?

When I think of teenagers, my thoughts center on energy in abundance, restless desires, inner needs of participation, group interaction, and needs for constructive expression. Are you interested in a medium that can really challenge everyone in your youth group to express a unique talent? Something that can help develop leadership characteristics and start overcoming timidity and disinterest?

One answer is drama, a flexible medium. If your youth group is small, dramas are available involving two or three characters. If you have a very large group, plays that demand casts of thirty to thirty-five people are obtainable. Adding student directors, stage constructors, lighting technicians, ushers, and publicity and program planners will involve sixty to seventy young people.

The "stage" is a tremendous training ground for young church leadership. Not only can a worthwhile message be conveyed through a carefully selected drama; the training of delivering lines or the responsibility for creating costumes can teach lessons of value to the young congregation leaders.

If you involve young people in a drama project, do it justice by planning it well. Nothing is more discouraging to a young person than the fear that they may be embarrassed. Many high schools have excellent drama departments; don't overlook as-

sistance and advice that might be available through the director
of drama at the local school.

Selecting a Play and Cast

The first step in production is to select an appropriate play.
Be realistic about your resources. One excellent resource for
scripts is *Baker's Plays*, 100 Chauncy Street, Boston, Massachusetts, 02111. Read through their catalog and order individual copies of scripts that interest you. Most plays require a
royalty payment and the purchase of a certain number of
scripts before permission is given to present a drama. Don't
omit this important legal requirement.

As you receive scripts and begin to read them, look for stories
that will appeal to young people. Try to picture your own
teenagers dramatizing the personalities of the play. If you are
working on your first production, select one that allows
economy of setting and costuming. Many plays require only a
bare stage with a few carry-on props. As you continue working
in drama, materials and costumes prepared for earlier presentations become valuable resources for the future if carefully
stored.

Larger youth groups will want to hold cast auditions, an
important function in the success of your presentation. It is at
this point that you can really minister to the young people.
Youth groups should seek to develop in young lives the confidence and talent that can eventually be used in the church of
Jesus Christ. Shy, hesitant teenagers can be challenged to gain
confidence as they are assigned minor acting roles. Talented,
outgoing teenagers can use their abilities for the Lord.

Audition time is often surprise time for me. Young people
are filled with abilities that we overlook.

It is thus wise to have several people serve as a selection
committee to help decide on the major cast members. Each
member of the auditioning committee should have an in-depth
understanding of the play.

Scripts should be available several weeks before auditions.
Encourage your youth to select several roles that interest them
and to decide what kind of personalities should be portrayed.
The committee should then select pages of the script that feature the desired personality.

On the day of audition, before the young people arrive, meet with members of the auditioning committee for prayer. Seek the Lord's guidance for the committee. Allow plenty of time for auditions. Announce a part, then ask for volunteers to read it. If you get no response, select a young person to read this part, then fill in with other teenagers reading supplementary parts. You may need to assign parts for several readings, but usually, the young people loosen up and start asking to try out. Be aware of timid teenagers in the room and assign them parts. Look for expressiveness in their voices, faces, and body movements. Jot down your reaction as they read. After all have read, close the session with prayer. Meet in another room for the selection of play cast members.

Organization

Organizing the responsibilities of play production is a very important factor. A director should not try to handle every job by himself. In a large production, assistant directors can help, as well as committees for set design and construction, costume coordination, stage props, makeup, publicity, programs, and ushering.

Thought must be given to a place for presentation, lighting needs, and costuming. It is not necessary to have a curtain to pull at the end of scenes in a play. The same illusion can be obtained merely by dimming lights to signify a change of action. Several good books available from *Baker's Plays* tell how inexpensive, effective stage lighting can be constructed. Slide projectors with a two-inch by two-inch cardboard insert punched with a round hole in the center make excellent spotlights.

Good costumes are essential. Don't do the easy and obvious. A well rehearsed Biblical drama deserves more than bathrobes, towels, and scarves. Watch for sales at local fabric stores, frequently check the remnant rack, and ask for donations for material from church members. After the costumes have been made, provide safe storage for them.

In constructing your first stage set, some expenses will be incurred. But if you build carefully, the finished product can be used over and over again. Let your artistic teenagers plan and dream with you. The end result may be a surprise to all involved.

Rehearsals

As rehearsals begin, plan to make them a memorable and enjoyable experience. Impress on your cast the need for good attendance. Make each rehearsal a matter of prayer and discuss the important teaching ministry of dramas. The first session should be simply a reading. Plan this rehearsal in an informal setting with cokes and potato chips. The next few rehearsals should acquaint the cast with the script and how their assigned characterizations fit in with the entire scope of the play.

Then, block out action in the play. Use folding chairs to serve as couches or tables if the setting is indoors, or as trees and bushes if outside. All stage directions should be given in reference to an actor facing the audience. When you direct, make your stage directions precise. For example, "Tom, move to down stage right [toward the audience and to the actor's right] after you enter the room." Be aware of actors' backs. Lines delivered in the direction of up stage (away from the audience) are usually not heard by an audience. Have your actors turn toward the audience. Make actions natural.

In blocking out, explain what action is to take place, then have participants walk through these actions. You will need to do your homework before practice and plan the movements of each character. Set a date by which lines are to be memorized. The sooner you can work without a script, the sooner hand motions and facial gestures begin to appear.

Plan an adequate number of rehearsals. For a one-act play lasting thirty to forty minutes, allow four to six weeks, meeting three or four times per week.

As the date for your presentation draws near, you will need to bring all the efforts of committees and individuals together. With six rehearsals remaining, all small hand props should be available. With four rehearsals left until performance, *all* sound effects should be included. With three rehearsals remaining, costumes should be worn. Two remaining rehearsals should include all of the above plus lighting. The final night of rehearsal is dress rehearsal, and includes every dramatic aspect.

Does it sound like work? Believe me, it is! But it's worth it. So light the lights, open the curtain, start the music, and give your young people an experience they'll fondly remember for the rest of their lives.

E. Puppet Ministry

by Dan R. Lawson

As you read, think about these questions:
—How can a "child's" medium like puppetry grow into a true component of youth ministry?
—How can a puppet ministry be established and organized?

Puppets are fun! They provide an entertainment method of teaching in the church and a unique means for Christian service. Puppetry is one of the most popular means of self-expression in contemporary society. Puppets are not new, however. The oldest form of puppetry was seen in ancient China in the form of "shadow puppets." As early as 300 B.C., marionettes were used in Greek and Roman cultural centers. Later, glove and sock puppets were the predecessors of hand-held puppets.

The hand puppet is generally constructed to allow the hand to operate inside its head to give mouth movement. The arms of the puppet are manipulated by the remaining hand. Only the portion from the waist up is visible. The puppet is lifted in the air by the puppeteer. The puppet talks, sings, and acts.

The Cast of a Puppet Theater

Puppeteers
A puppet ministry in the church provides a valuable opportunity for youth to serve. Many junior high youth, for example, are hesitant to join a performing group, and puppets allow such youth to hide behind the stage curtain and still provide constructive service.

Ideally, a theater has a minimum of four youth and a maximum of eight. The stage size prohibits greater involvement. If more young people are interested, a graded puppet program could be the answer. Some churches divide their puppet programs further into groups for girls and groups for boys. A graded puppet program should provide a greater challenge for the more advanced ages. A more complex type of puppetry and a wider use of scripts and props might persuade a young person to continue over the years. The best puppet groups start young and gain experience together. Some beginner puppeteers may even be younger than junior-high age.

The development of a distinct personality for a puppet directly relates to the personality of performing individuals. The mannerisms, voice, and habits of the puppeteer are gradually exposed through the puppet's personality as the puppeteer becomes more comfortable and experienced.

While hand puppets can be used to teach from the Bible, there must always be humor in their plays. Strictly serious scripts can turn into mockery because puppets are mere cartoon characters. Exercise caution when using puppets around serious activities. The Lord's Supper is no time for puppets.

The Director

A director is to the puppet theater what the sponsor is to the youth group. A mature Christian leader filled with enthusiasm and creativity makes an excellent coach. In a puppet group made up of young people, the director must not be one of the puppeteers. He must do his coaching during rehearsal times, but then allow the young people the privilege of self-expression in the actual performance. The puppet director is coach, teacher, advisor, minister, and manager—the person in charge. The pitfall of puppets merely being a group for entertainment can best be prevented when the director accepts the puppet theater as a youth ministry. He determines whether the puppet theater is a ministry or simply an art group.

Equipment for a Puppet Ministry

Puppets

Several companies manufacture good equipment. Puppet Productions, Inc. of San Diego, California, puts out some fine professional puppets of soft, lightweight material. Their collection includes cartoon characters, people puppets (Chicanos, Anglos, Afros), animals, and a grandpa and grandma character.

Some puppets can be operated by a single hand. Other, more complex puppets, require two people: one to operate the head and a second to move the human arms of the puppet. At least four puppets are necessary (some theaters collect dozens). One puppet on stage can have impact, but four puppets, or even sixteen puppets at one time, singing, or acting, can be quite impressive.

A good wardrobe, ranging from Bible-times robes to contemporary garb, is helpful. Numerous jackets, hats, hair pieces, and scarves make quick changes possible.

Stage and Props

Necessary equipment includes an attractive two-level stage, constructed to allow rapid setup and portability. A curtain of heavy, non-wrinkle material will easily conceal puppeteers as they perform. The bi-level feature allows the puppeteers to be mobile and uncrowded and adds a dimension to staging.

The play or song will dictate the necessary props. Much can be left to the imagination if only symbolic props are available. A backdrop can also be hung, or a door post can be judiciously placed. Some groups even use rear-screen projection to provide elaborate backdrops.

Sound Equipment

The best stage, props, and puppet collection are worth nothing to players whose scripts cannot be heard. Amplifiers and speakers of good quality make it possible for live scripts to be read through microphones or for prerecorded scripts to be played. Without adequate sound equipment, performances in shopping centers, church auditoriums, or outdoor theaters are not possible. The message must be heard.

Scripts

While creating original puppet scripts can be challenging, sometimes this is too difficult a task. An easier approach is to purchase prerecorded programs from puppet manufacturers. Tapes are available for scripts on Noah, David, Jonah, Daniel, Zaccheus, and the Good Samaritan. For variety, let the puppets sing gospel songs or barbershop music. Exercise caution to insure that the songs have slow wording but quick instrumentation. Some contemporary youth musicals with singing and narration provide good material. Consider the age and attention span of your audience before you perform. Keep the Biblical truth as well as the humor at your audience's level of appreciation.

Lighting

Lighting equipment gives a professional appearance. Two white lights at each side of the stage connected to a dimmer box controlled behind the puppet stage provide good lighting. When the lights go up, the audience gives immediate attention and knows that the puppets are about to perform.

Final Tips on Equipment

1. Have at least one puppet for each puppeteer.

2. Care for all of the theater equipment, and provide adequate storage for tour and home use.

3. Don't be afraid to invest in the puppet ministry. Good equipment may have substantial initial expense, but good puppets, properly cared for, should last ten years.

Rehearsal Sessions

It is best to operate a puppet theater only during the school term. Weekly rehearsal when school is in session brings a good discipline and allows an annual closing time for those youth who lost interest and an annual entering time for joiners.

A regular weekly rehearsal session should last no more than two hours and no less than one hour. If possible, practice where the stage could remain assembled. When practicing, first listen to the script and coordinate puppet lip movements, then block the location of each puppet throughout the play. Practice movement and gestures, considering the personality of the puppet. Finally, rehearse the whole drama at least three times.

Rehearsals are off limits to visitors. They prevent the atmosphere from being relaxed and creative.

Puppet Performances

A puppet theater can achieve some valid purposes. Performances should glorify Christ, not the puppet theater. When

they tell a story or sing a song, the puppeteers discover that
they have talents that can be used in service for Christ and His
church.

Some critical principles should be observed:

1. Puppeteers should not be seen before or after a performance. They should never be introduced. Introductions spoil
the "illusion."

2. Puppets should only be seen while "alive" and performing.

3. Equipment must always be neat, orderly, and out of
sight.

4. Stick to the script. Keep ad-libbing to the bare minimum.

5. Be punctual; start on time and end on time.

6. Never allow the pace of the performance to drag or be
delayed.

7. Consider the audience in advance to determine the appropriate length of performance.

8. Delays between puppet changes, tape changes, or play
changes should be minimized.

The best place to use your puppet theater is in your home
church. Prior to a Sunday-school class lesson, the puppets can
perform the lesson's Bible story. In vacation Bible school, puppets can creatively be involved by telling the daily Bible story
or singing VBS songs.

A puppet program can also be an outstanding tool for Christian outreach. Puppet theaters will find captive audiences at
fairs and carnivals. Shopping centers provide relaxed audiences, but here the performance will have to quickly catch the
eye and provide several opportunities for the people to come
and go at leisure. The success of the *Muppet Show* proves that
television is a medium for puppets also. Local television stations offer excellent opportunities. A puppet theater needs less
equipment to perform on television than anywhere else. Let the
director of the theater serve as an agent in securing as many
performances as the theater can handle in the local church and
community.

One of the best means of motivation for any puppet theater is
the opportunity to take an annual tour. Tours provide an excellent way to see the kingdom of God beyond the home church
front. Orphanages, church camps, retirement centers all provide good touring stops for puppet groups.

Puppetry is an avenue of ministering to youth and through youth. Its popularity is on the rise in the entertainment world, and the church can use puppets as a means of ministry. In order to be heard, a group must be either good or unusual. Puppetry can be both. The time necessary to be good at puppetry may be limited. Nevertheless, a puppet theater can still draw attention because of its uniqueness. The Christian message can be effectively translated through lifeless figures of cloth and color.

APPENDIX

APPENDIX

Section Outline

Resources for Youth Ministry

by Ron Mobley

This resource guide will help you acquaint yourself and your co-laborers with the in-depth, specialized materials available in many areas of youth ministry. This list will not be universally applicable to all ministries, but it does encompass many of the broad categories of current interest and a variety of alternatives and combinations in each category.

Every youth worker should develop his own list of special resources—those books, periodicals, audiovisuals, filing systems, time management procedures, publicity aids, etc., that he finds most beneficial in his area of service. This resource list can serve as a basis for such a personalized list.

Special acknowledgement is due Christ In Youth, Inc., for their contributions to the sections on exceptional children. The vast number of people who fit one or more of these categories, and their parents, need the support and encouragement of the Lord's church.

Minister and Ministry

Adams, Jay E. *The Pastoral Life*. Grand Rapids, MI: Baker, 1974.
Bell, A. Donald. *How to Get Along With People in the Church*. Grand Rapids, MI: Zondervan, 1976.

Holck, Manfred. *Making It On a Pastor's Pay*. Nashville: Abingdon, 1974.

Johnson, James. *The Nine to Five Complex*. Grand Rapids, MI: Zondervan, 1971.

Jowett, John Henry. *The Preacher: His Life and Work*. Grand Rapids, MI: Baker, 1968.

Judy, Marvin T. *The Multiple Staff Ministry*. Nashville: Abingdon, 1969.

McDonough, Reginald M. *Working With Volunteer Leaders in the Church*. Nashville: Broadman, 1976.

Oates, Wayne E. *The Minister's Own Mental Health*. Great Neck, NY: Channel Press, 1961.

Robertson, A. T. *The Glory of the Ministry*. Grand Rapids, MI: Baker, 1969.

Smith, Wilbur. *The Minister in His Study*. Chicago: Moody Press, 1973.

Southard, Samuel. *Pastoral Authority in Personal Relationships*. Nashville: Abingdon, 1969.

Stone, Sam E. *The Christian Minister*. Cincinnati: Standard Publishing, 1980.

Weed, Michael R. (ed.) *The Minister and His Work*. Austin, TX: Sweet Publishing, 1970.

The Church and Church Growth

Benjamin, Paul. *The Growing Congregation*. Cincinnati: Standard Publishing, 1972.

_____. *The Equipping Ministry*. Cincinnati: Standard Publishing, 1978.

Getz, Gene A. *Sharpening the Focus of the Church*. Chicago: Moody Press, 1976.

Glen, J. Stanley. *Justification by Success: The Invisible Captivity of the Church*. Richmond, VA: John Knox Press, 1979.

McGavran, Donald A. *How Churches Grow*. New York: Friendship Press, 1965.

Montgomery, John Warwick. *Damned Through the Church*. Minneapolis: Bethany Fellowship, 1970.

Richards, Larry. *A New Face for the Church*. Grand Rapids, MI: Zondervan, 1970.

Schaeffer, Francis A. *The Church at the End of the Twentieth Century*. Downers Grove, IL: InterVarsity Press, 1970.

Schuller, Robert H. *Your Church Has Real Possibilities*. Glendale, CA: Regal, 1975.

Shaller, Lyle. *The Local Church Looks to the Future*: Nashville: Abingdon, 1968.

Snyder, Howard A. *The Community of the King*. Downers Grove, IL: InterVarsity Press, 1977.

_____. *The Problem of Wineskins*. Downers Grove, IL: InterVarsity Press, 1975.

Stedman, Ray. *Body Life*. Glendale, CA: Regal, 1972.

Trueblood, Elton *The Company of the Committed*. New York: Harper and Row, 1961.

Wagner, C. Peter. *Your Church Can Grow*. Glendale, CA: Regal, 1976.

Yamamori, Tetsunao and Lawson, E. LeRoy. *Introducing Church Growth*. Cincinnati: Standard Publishing, 1975.

Counseling

Adams, Jay E. *The Christian Counselor's Casebook*. Grand Rapids, MI: Baker, 1974.

_____. *The Christian Counselor's Manual*. Grand Rapids, MI: Baker, 1974.

_____. *Competent to Counsel*. Grand Rapids, MI: Baker, 1977.

Bechtle, Mike. *Counselor's Guidebook* ("The Complete Camp Counselor's Training Kit") Tempe, AZ: Success With Youth, 1978.

Berne, Eric. *Games People Play*. New York: Grove Press, 1964.

_____. *What Do You Say After You Say Hello?* New York: Bantam, 1975.

Collins, Gary. *Effective Counseling*. Carol Stream, IL: Creation House, 1972.

_____. *How to Be a People Helper*. Santa Ana, CA: Vision House Publishers, 1976.

Crabb, Lawrence J. *Basic Principles of Biblical Counseling*. Grand Rapids, MI: Zondervan, 1975.

Frellick, Frances I. *Helping Youth In Conflict*. Philadelphia: Fortress, 1968.

Hamilton, James D. *The Ministry of Pastoral Counseling*. Grand Rapids, MI: Baker, 1972.

Harris, Thomas A. *I'm OK—You're OK*. New York: Harper and Row, 1969.

Hiltner, Seward. *Pastoral Counseling*. Nashville: Abingdon, 1969.

Mackay, Foy. *Creative Counseling for Christian Camp*. Wheaton, IL: Scripture Press.

Morris, J. Kenneth. *Marriage Counseling—A Manual for Ministers.* Englewood Cliffs, NJ: Prentice-Hall, 1955.

_____. *Premarital Counseling—A Manual for Ministers.* Englewood Cliffs, NJ: Prentice-Hall, 1955.

Narramore, Clyde M. *Counseling Youth.* Grand Rapids, MI: Zondervan, 1966.

_____. *The Psychology of Counseling.* Grand Rapids, MI: Zondervan, 1960.

Oates, Wayne E. *An Introduction to Pastoral Counseling.* Nashville: Broadman, 1959.

_____. *Pre-Marital Pastoral Care and Counseling.* Nashville: Broadman, 1958.

Oglesby, William B., Jr. *Referral in Pastoral Counseling.* Nashville: Abingdon, 1968.

Rassieur, Charles L. *The Problem Clergyman Don't Talk About.* Philadelphia: Westminster Press, 1976.

Stone, Howard W. *Crisis Counseling.* Philadelphia: Fortress, 1976.

Switzer, David. *The Dynamics of Grief.* Nashville: Abingdon, 1970.

Westberg, Granger. *Good Grief.* Philadelphia: Fortress, 1962.

Wright, Norman. *Help! . . . I'm a Camp Counselor.* Glendale, CA: Regal, 1969.

Discipleship, Leadership, Bible Study

Alexander, John W. *Managing Our Work* (revised edition). Downers Grove, IL: InterVarsity press, 1975.

Eims, Leroy. *Be the Leader You Were Meant to Be.* Wheaton, IL: Victor Books, 1975.

_____. *The Lost Art of Disciple Making.* Grand Rapids, MI: Zondervan, 1978.

Emswiler, Tom N. *Love Is a Magic Penny.* Nashville: Abingdon, 1977.

Engstrom, Ted W. *The Making of a Christian Leader.* Grand Rapids, MI: Zondervan, 1976.

Ezell, Mancil. *Youth in Bible Study.* Nashville: Convention Press, 1970.

Henrichsen, Walter A. *Disciples Are Made—Not Born.* Wheaton, IL: Victor Books, 1974.

Hocking, David L. *Be a Leader People Follow.* Glendale, CA: Regal, 1979.

Kuhne, Gary W. *The Dynamics of Personal Follow Up.* Grand Rapids, MI: Zondervan, 1976.

Peterson, Eugene H. *More Creative Bible Studies for Youth.* Tempe, AZ: Success With Youth, 1976.

Peterson, Gladys, J. *Hark! Hark! the Quark.* Elgin, IL: (*I Am His* Club) David C. Cook, 1971.

Pratney, Winkie. *Youth Aflame I* and *Youth Aflame II.* Santa Rosa, CA: Communication Foundation, 1970.

_____. *Doorways to Discipleship.* Minneapolis: Bethany Fellowship, 1977.

Richards, Lawrence O. *Creative Bible Study.* Grand Rapids, MI: Zondervan, 1979.

Schaeffer, Francis A. *How Should We Then Live?* Old Tappan, NJ: Revell, 1976.

Smith, Bob. *When All Else Fails . . . Read the Directions.* Waco, TX: Word Books, 1975.

Snyder, Howard A. *The Community of the King.* Downers Grove, IL: InterVarsity Press, 1977.

_____. *The Problem of Wineskins.* Downers Grove, IL: InterVarsity Press, 1975.

Stedman, Ray C. *Body Life.* Glendale, CA: Regal, 1979.

Wilson, Carl. *With Christ in the School of Disciple Building.* Grand Rapids, MI: Zondervan, 1976.

Yohn, Rick. *Now That I'm a Disciple.* Irvine, CA: Harvest House Publishers, 1976.

Ziglar, Zig. *See You at the Top.* Gretna, LA: Pelican Publishing Co., 1975.

The Occult, Angels, and the Devil

Bayly, Joseph. *What About Horoscopes?* Elgin, IL: David C. Cook, 1970.

Graham, Billy. *Angels.* Minneapolis: WorldWide Publications (and Pocket Books, New York), 1976.

Koch, Kurt E. *Christian Counseling and Occultism.* Grand Rapids, MI: Kregel, 1972.

Lindsell, Harold. *The World, the Flesh, and the Devil.* Washington, DC: Baker.

Lindsey, Hal (with C. C. Carlson). *Satan Is Alive and Well on Planet Earth.* Grand Rapids, MI: Zondervan, 1974.

Lovett, C. S. *Dealing With the Devil.* Baldwin Park, CA: Personal Christianity, 1967.

Home and Family

Child-Rearing:
Brandt, Dr. Henry and Landrum, Phil. *I Want to Enjoy My Children.*
  Minneapolis: Bethany Fellowship, 1975.
Dads Only (magazine). P.O. Box 20594, San Diego, CA, 92120.
Dobson, James. *Dare to Discipline.* Wheaton, IL: Tyndale, 1970.
_____. *Hide Or Seek.* Old Tappan, NJ: Revell, 1974.
_____. *The Strong Willed Child.* Old Tappan, NJ: Revell, 1977.
Haystead, Wesley. *You Can't Begin Too Soon.* Glendale, CA: Regal,
  1974.
Murray, Andrew. *How to Raise Your Children for Christ.* Minneapolis:
  Bethany Fellowship, 1975.
Narramore, Bruce. *A Guide to Child Rearing.* Grand Rapids, MI: Zon-
  dervan, 1972.
_____. *Help! I'm a Parent.* Grand Rapids, MI: Zondervan, 1972.

Finance:
Holck, Manfred. *Making It on a Pastor's Pay.* Nashville: Abingdon,
  1974.
Kilgore, James. *Getting More Family Out of Your Dollar.* Irvine, CA:
  Harvest House Publishers.
MacGregor, Malcolm, and Baldwin, Stanley C. *Your Money Matters.*
  Minneapolis: Bethany Fellowship, 1971.
Young, Amy Ross. *It Only Hurts Between Paydays.* Denver: Accent
  Books, 1975.

Marriage and Family:
Anderson, Wayne J. *Design For Family Living.* Minneapolis: T. S.
  Denison & Company, 1964.
Beardsley, Lou. *A Family Love Story.* Irvine, CA: Harvest House Pub-
  lishers.
Christensen, Larry. *The Christian Family.* Minneapolis: Bethany Fel-
  lowship, 1970.
Dads Only (magazine). P.O. Box 20594, San Diego, CA, 92120.
Family Life Today (magazine). Gospel Light, Box 180, Glendale, CA,
  91209.
Garrison, Marjorie J. *Happy Families Are Homemade.* Elgin, IL: David
  C. Cook, 1976.
Getz, Gene A. *The Measure of a Family.* Glendale, CA: Regal, 1977.
_____. *The Measure of a Man.* Glendale, CA: Regal, 1974.
_____. *The Measure of a Woman.* Glendale, CA: Regal, 1977.

Granberg, Lars. . . . For Adults Only. Grand Rapids, MI: Zondervan, 1973.

Hardisty, Margaret. Forever My Love. Irvine, CA: Harvest House, 1975.

Hendricks, Howard G. Heaven Help the Home! Wheaton, IL: Victor Books, 1974.

Kilgore, James. Being a Man in a Woman's World. Irvine, CA: Harvest House Publishers.

LaHaye, Tim. How to Be Happy Though Married. Irvine, CA: Tyndale House.

LaHaye, Tim and Beverly. Spirit-Controlled Family Living. Old Tappan, NJ: Revell, 1978.

Rickerson, Wayne E. Good Times for Your Family. Glendale, CA: Regal, 1976.

Samuel, Dorothy. Fun and Games in Marriage. Waco, TX: Word Books, 1976.

Staton, Knofel. Home Can Be a Happy Place. Cincinnati: Standard Publishing, 1975.

Today's Christian Parent (magazine). 8121 Hamilton Ave., Cincinnati, OH, 45231.

Williams, H. Page. Do Yourself a Favor; Love Your Wife. Plainfield, NJ: Logos, 1973.

Sex Education:

LaHaye, Tim and Beverly. The Act of Marriage. Grand Rapids, MI: Zondervan, 1976.

Mace, David R. Whom God Hath Joined (revised edition). Philadelphia: Westminster Press, 1973.

Miles, Herbert J. Sexual Understanding Before Marriage. Grand Rapids, MI: Zondervan, 1972.

Miles, Herbert J. Sexual Happiness in Marriage. Grand Rapids, MI: Zondervan, 1967.

Schweizer, Edsel. The Christian Parent Teaches About Sex. Minneapolis: Augsburg Publishing House, 1966.

Shedd, Charlie W. The Stork Is Dead. Waco, TX: Word Books, 1976.

Willke, Dr. and Mrs. J. C. The Wonder of Sex, How to Teach Children. Cincinnati: Hayes Publishing Co., 1964.

Witt, Elmer N. Life Can Be Sexual. St. Louis: Concordia, 1967.

General Resources for Youth Workers

Aultman, Donald S. Guiding Youth. Cleveland, TN: Pathway Press, 1977.

_____. *Idea Catalog for Youth Sponsors*. Lincoln, IL: Lincoln Christian College Press.

Benson, Dennis. *The Now Generation*. Richmond, VA: John Knox Press, 1969.

Bueltmann, A. J. *Teen-Agers Need Parents*. St. Louis: Concordia.

Church Recreation Magazine, Sunday School Board (Southern Baptist Convention), 127 Ninth Avenue North, Nashville, TN 37203.

Dobson, James. *Dare to Discipline*. Wheaton, IL: Tyndale, 1970.

Frellick, Francis I. *Helping Youth in Conflict*. Philadelphia: Fortress, 1968.

Habel, Norman C. *For Mature Adults Only*. Philadelphia: Fortress, 1969.

Harrell, John and Mary. *Communicating the Gospel Today*, Box 9006, Berkeley, CA, 94709.

Hechinger, Grace and Fred. *Teen-Age Tyranny*. New York: Morrow, 1963.

Hoglund, Gunnas, and Virginia Grabill. *Youth Leader's Handbook*. Grand Rapids, MI: Wheaton Miracle Books (Zondervan), 1950.

Hunt, Gladys. *Listen to Me*. Downers Grove, IL: InterVarsity Press.

Idea Books. Youth Specialties, 861 Sixth Avenue., San Diego, CA, 92101.

International Society of Christian Endeavor (Youth and Jr. C.E. Meetings), 1221 Broad Street, Columbus, OH 43216.

Irving, Roy G. and Zuck, Roy B. (eds.) *Youth and the Church*. Chicago: Moody Press, 1968.

Jones, G. William. *Sunday Night at the Movies*. Richmond, VA: John Knox Press.

KEY to Christian Education (magazine). 8121 Hamilton Ave., Cincinnati, OH, 45231.

Leavitt, Guy P. (revised by Eleanor Daniel). *Teach With Success*. Cincinnati: Standard Publishing, 1979.

Little, Sara. *Youth, World, and Church*. Raymond, VA: John Knox Press, 1968.

Mackay, Foy. *Creative Counseling for Christian Camp*. Wheaton, IL: Scripture Press.

Mallett, Harold. *When Not to Obey Your Parents*. Grand Rapids, MI: Zondervan.

Parent Brochures (eight in series). Tempe, AZ: Success With Youth, P.O. Box 27028.

Reemer, H. H. and Radler, D. H. *The American Teenager*. New York: Bobbs-Merrill Co., 1957.

Regal Paperback Series, Glendale, CA: Gospel Light Publications.

Richards, Larry. *Youth Ministry.* Grand Rapids, MI: Zondervan, 1972.

Seger, Doria Louis. *Young People's Programs.* Wheaton, IL: Scripture Press.

Specialized Christian Services, 1525 Cherry Road, Springfield, IL, 62704.

Strommen, Merton. *Profiles of Church Youth.* St. Louis: Concordia, 1963.

Teach. Gospel Light Publications, Box 1591, Glendale, CA, 91209.

Ten Basic Steps Toward Christian Maturity, Campus Crusade for Christ, Arrowhead Springs, San Bernardino, CA, 92404.

Toni, Henry N. *Ventures in Youth Work.* Philadelphia: The Christian Education Press of 1957.

Towns, Elmer. *Successful Youth Work.* Glendale, CA: Gospel Light Publications, 1966. (Re-released as *Successful Biblical Youth Work.* Nashville: Impact Books)

_____. *Teaching Teens.* Grand Rapids, MI: Baker.

Troup, Dick. *Resources for Youth Mini-Camps.* Tempe, AZ: Success With Youth, 1974.

Understanding the Pupil and *Ways to Help Them Learn.* (International Center for Learning [ICL] graded/age-group training books.) Glendale, CA: Gospel Light Publications, 1972.

Walsh, Chad. *Campus Gods on Trial* (revised edition). New York: Macmillan, 1962.

Yaxley, Grace. *Sparkling Youth Meetings.* Chicago: Moody Press.

"Youth Leaders Handbooks" Specialized Christian Services, 1525 Cherry, Springfield, IL 62704.

Zuck, Roy B. *How to Be a Youth Sponsor.* Wheaton, IL: Scripture Press, 1960.

Zuck, Roy B. and Getz, Gene. *Christian Youth, An In-Depth Study.* Chicago: Moody Press.

Training Sponsors and Coaches
(Including Conventions and Clinics)

Alexander, John W., *Managing Our Work* (revised edition). Downers Grove, IL: InterVarsity Press, 1975.

"Christ in Youth" Adult Training Seminars, % C.I.Y., P.O. Box 2170, Tulsa, OK 74101.

C.B.S. "Youth Leaders Clinic," (*annually* in August) Cincinnati Bible Seminary, 2700 Glenway Ave., Cincinnati, OH 45204 (Mss. available).

Coop, Tim. "Will the Real Youth Sponsor Please Stand Up." Minister, Church of Christ, Corona, CA.

Engstrom, Ted W. and MacKenzie, Alex. *Managing Your Time.* Grand Rapids, MI: Zondervan, 1968.

Fraley, Doug. "Youth Sponsors Training Course." Boulevard Christian Church, Tulsa, OK.

"Ideashops," % Standard Publishing Co., 8121 Hamilton Ave., Cincinnati, OH 45231.

Institute in Basic Youth Conflicts, % Campus Teams (Bill Gothard, Director), Box 1, Oak Brook, IL 60521. (In large cities throughout the U.S.)

International Center for Learning (ICL), Gospel Light, Box 1650, Glendale, CA 91209.

National Youth Ministers & Leaders Convention *(annually* in January), Ozark Bible College, 1111 N. Main Street, Joplin, MO 64801. (Mss. available).

National Youth Workers Convention, % Youth Specialties, 861 Sixth Ave., San Diego, CA 92101.

Nido R. Quebin & Associates, Inc., Box 5367, High Point, NC 27262.

Roadcup, David. "Developing Youth Sponsors, I & II," % Cincinnati Bible Seminary, 2700 Glenway Ave., Cincinnati, OH 45204.

Richards, Lawrence O. *You and Youth.* Chicago: Moody Press, 1973.

Richards, Lawrence O. (ed.) "Youth Education Service," (two complete series of tapes and workbooks for workers with teens and pre-teens). Success With Youth, Inc., Tempe, AZ, 1972.

"Serendipity Workshops" and "Festivals of Hope," Serendipity House, Box 354, Scottsdale, PA 15683.

"Upgrade" (church training program) Sunday School Board (Southern Baptist Convention), 127 Ninth Avenue North, Nashville, TN 37203.

"Why Sunday School Is Not Enough" and "Summer Harvest," Success With Youth, Box 27028, Tempe, AZ 85281.

"Youth Workers Survival Kit," Youth Specialties, 861 Sixth Ave., San Diego, CA 92101.

Preschool

Aldridge, Betty, Downs, Kathy, and Grewell, Joy M. *Teaching Toddlers.* Cincinnati: Standard Publishing, 1978.

Anderson, Robert H., and Shane, Harold G. (eds.) *As the Twig Is Bent: Readings in Early Childhood Education.* Boston: Houghton-Mifflin. 1971.

Baker, Katherine Read, and Fane, Xenia F. *Understanding and Guiding Young Children* (third edition). Englewood Cliffs, NJ: Prentice-Hall, 1975.

Barbour, Mary E. *You Can Teach 2's and 3's*. Wheaton, IL: Victor Books, 1974.

Barnette, J. N. *The Cradle Roll Department Can Build Your Church*. Nashville: Sunday School Board (Southern Baptist Convention), 127 Ninth Avenue North, 37203.

Barry, James C., and Treadway, Charles F. *Kindergarten Resource Book*. Nashville: Broadman, 1965.

Better Homes and Gardens Baby Book. Des Moines: Meredith, 1951.

Beyer, Evelyn. *Teaching Young Children*. New York: Irvington, 1969.

Brubaker, J. Omar and Clark, Robert E. *Understanding People*. Wheaton, IL: Evangelical Teacher Training Association, 1972.

Chamberlain, Eugene, Harty, Robert A., Adams, Saxe. *Pre-schoolers at Church*. Nashville: Convention Press, 1969.

Children. U.S. Children's Bureau, Superintendent of Documents, U.S. Government Printing Office, Washington, D.C. 20025.

Christianson, Helen M. *The Nursery School*. Boston: Houghton-Mifflin, 1961.

Chukovsky, Kornei. *From Two to Five*. Berkeley, CA: University of California, 1963.

Cory, Bernice T. *Cradle Roll Manual*. Wheaton, IL: Scripture Press, 1967.

_____. *The Pastor and His Cradle Roll Department*. Christian Education Monographs, Pastors' Series, No. 21, Glen Ellyn, IL: Scripture Press, 1967.

_____. *The Pastor and His Interest in Preschoolers*. Christian Education Monographs, Pastors' Series, No. 8, Glen Ellyn, IL: Scripture Press, 1966.

Dixon, Dorothy A. *Growth in Love*. West Mystic, CT: Twenty-Third Publications, 1972.

Doan, Eleanor L. *It's Never Too Early*. Glendale, CA: Gospel Light Publications, 1967.

Dodson, Fitzhugh. *How to Parent*. New York: New American Library, 1973.

Fritz, Dorothy B. *Child and the Christian Faith*. Richmond, VA: John Knox Press, 1964.

Gardner, Elizabeth C. *The 2's at Church*. Philadelphia: Judson, 1953.

Gesell, Arnold, and Ileg, Francis L. *Infant and Child in the Culture of Today* (revised edition). New York: Harper and Row, 1974.

Gilliland, Anne Hitchcock. *Understanding Preschoolers*. Nashville: Convention Press, 1969.

Harrell, Donna, and Haystead, Wesley, *Creative Bible Learning*. Glendale, CA: Gospel Light, 1978.

Hartley, Ruth E., Frank, Lawrence K., and Goldenson, Robert M. *Understanding Children's Play*. New York: Columbia, 1952.

Hearn, Florence Conner. *Guiding Preschoolers*. Nashville: Convention Press, 1969.

Heaton, Ada Beth. *The 3's at Church*. Philadelphia: Judson Press, 1953.

Hildebrand, Verna. *Introduction to Early Childhood Education* (second edition). New York: Macmillan, 1976.

Hymes, James L. *The Child Under Six*. Englewood Cliffs, NJ: Prentice-Hall, 1963.

Jahsmann, Allan H. *The Church Teaching Her Young*. St. Louis: Concordia, 1967.

Jenkins, Gladys Gardner, and Shacter, Helen S. *These Are Your Children* (fourth edition). Chicago: Scott Foresman, 1975.

Kaluger, George and Kolson, Clifford, J. "The Speaking Religious Vocabulary of Kindergarten Children." *Religious Education 58* (July-August 1963): 387-89.

Leach, Joan, and St. Louis, Patricia. *Caring for Babies*. Cincinnati: Standard Publishing, 1978.

LeBar, Mary E. *You Make the Difference for Fours and Fives*. Wheaton, IL: Victor Books, 1974.

_____. *Patty Goes to Nursery Class*. Wheaton, IL: Scripture Press, 1969.

Llewellyn, Russ. "A Man in Every Preschool Department," *Teach* 12 (Spring 1971).

McDaniel, Elsiebeth and Richards, Lawrence O. *You and Preschoolers*. Chicago: Moody Press, 1975.

Murphy, Lois B. *Personality in Your Children*. New York: Basic Books, 1960.

Nicholson, Dorothy. *Toward Effective Teaching*. Anderson, IN: Warner, 1970.

Pitcher, Evelyn G., and Prelinger, Ernst. *Children Tell Stories*. New York: International Universities, 1969.

Read, Katherine H. *The Nursery School* (sixth edition). Philadelphia: Saunders, 1976.

Rosenberg, Edward D., and Warner, Silas L. *A Doctor Discusses the Pre-School Child's Learning Process*. Chicago: Budlong, 1967.

Rowen, Dolores. *Ways to Help Them Learn: Early Childhood Education, Birth to Five Years*. Glendale, CA: Regal Books, 1972.

Royal, Claudia. *Teaching Your Child About God*. Westwood, NJ: Revell, 1960.

Salisbury, Helen Wright. *The Church Nursery School and the Bible Stories for the Very Young*. Los Angeles: Cowman, 1955.

Schoolland, Marian M. *Leading Little Ones to God*. Grand Rapids, MI: Eerdmans, 1962.

Skaugset, Arlene and Short, Loretta. *Help! I've Got Problems*. Cincinnati: Standard Publishing, 1978.

Smart, Mollie Stevens, and Smart, Russell C. *Preschool Children: Development and Relationships* (second edition). New York: Macmillan, 1978.

Smiley, Palma. *Handbook for Cradle Rolls and Toddler Teachers*. Elgin, IL: David C. Cook, 1969.

Strang, Ruth M. *An Introduction to Child Study* (fourth edition). New York: Macmillan, 1959.

Tested Ideas for Nursery-Kindergarten Teachers. Elgin, IL: David C. Cook, 1964.

Tester, Sylvia. *How to Teach Kindergarten Children*. Elgin, IL: David C. Cook, 1963.

The Young Child. National Association for the Education of Young Children. 1834 Connecticut Ave., Washington, D.C. 20009.

Thompson, Jean A., Klein, Sara G., and Gardner, Elizabeth C. *Before They Are Three*. Philadelphia; Westminster Press, 1954.

Toby, Katherine. *When We Teach Kindergarten Children*. Philadelphia: Westminster Press.

Today's Child. Edward Publications, Inc., School Lane, Roosevelt, NJ 08555.

Todd, Vivian E., and Heffernan, Helen. *The Years Before School* (third edition). New York: Macmillan, 1977.

Welch, Meryl. *Cradle Roll Handbook*. Des Plaines, IL: Regular Baptist, 1970.

Woodward, Carol. *Ways to Teach 3's to 5's*. Philadelphia: Lutheran Church, 1965.

Young, Lois H. *Teaching Kindergarten Children*. Valley Forge, PA: Judson Press, 1959.

Your Child ... From Birth to Twelve. New York: Metropolitan Life, 1966.

Zimmerman, Eleanor. *Bible and Doctrine for 3's to 5's*. Philadelphia: Lutheran Church, 1963.

Primaries

Baker, Dolores, and Rives, Elsie. *Teaching the Bible to Primaries.* Nashville: Convention Press, 1964.

Bolton, Barbara. *Ways to Help Them Learn: Children Grades 1 to 6.* Glendale, CA: Regal, 1972.

Biggs, Dorothy Corkille. *Your Child's Self-Esteem.* New York: Doubleday, 1970.

Brubaker, J. Omar, and Clark, Robert E. *Understanding People.* Wheaton, IL: Evangelical Teacher Training Association, 1972.

Chamberlain, Eugene, and Fulbright, Robert D. *Children's Sunday School Work.* Nashville: Convention Press, 1969.

Cohen, Dorothy. *The Learning Child.* New York: Pantheon Books, 1972.

Dobson, James. *Dare to Discipline.* Wheaton, IL: Tyndale, 1970.

_____. *Hide or Seek.* Old Tappan, NJ: Revell, 1974.

Dreikurs, Rudolf. *Coping With Children's Misbehavior.* New York: Hawthorne Books, Inc., 1973.

Dunn, Rita, and Dunn, Kenneth. *Practical Approaches to Individualizing Instruction.* West Nyack, NY: Parker Publishing, 1972.

Fulbright, Robert G. *New Dimensions in Teaching Children.* Nashville: Broadman, 1971.

Ginott, Haim. *Between Parent and Child.* New York: Avon, 1973.

_____. *Teacher and Child.* New York: Macmillan, 1972.

Hammond, Phyllis E. *What to Do and Why: Activities for Elementary Groups at Church.* Valley Forge, PA: Judson Press, 1963.

Horne, Herman H. *Teaching Techniques of Jesus.* Grand Rapids, MI: Kregel Publishers, 1971.

Jenkins, Gladys G., and Shacter, Helen, S. *These are Your Children* (fourth edition). Glenview, IL: Scott Foresman, 1975.

McDaniel, Elsiebeth, and Richards, Lawrence O. *You and Children.* Chicago: Moody Press, 1973.

Narramore, Bruce. *A Guide to Child Bearing.* Grand Rapids, MI: Zondervan, 1972.

_____. *An Ounce of Prevention.* Grand Rapids, MI: Zondervan, 1973.

_____. *Help! I'm a Parent.* Grand Rapids, MI: Zondervan, 1972.

Odor, Ruth. *Help! I've Got Problems!* Cincinnati: Standard Publishing, 1978.

Phillips, Ethel M. *So You Work With Primaries.* Anderson, IN: Warner, 1960.

Rives, Elsie, and Sharp, Margaret. *Guiding Children*. Nashville: Convention Press, 1969.

Smith, Charles T. *Ways to Plan and Organize Your Sunday School: Children, Grades 1 to 6*. Glendale, CA: Regal Books, 1971.

Stith, Marjorie. *Understanding Children*. Nashville: Convention Press, 1969.

Tobey, Kathrene M. *Learning and Teaching Through the Senses*. Philadelphia: Westminster Press, 1970.

Juniors

Gangel, Kenneth O. *The Family First*. Winona Lake, IN: BMH Books.

Getz, Gene A. "What Juniors Think About Honesty." *Teach* 12 (Fall 1970). pp. 4, 5.

Jersild, Arthur. *Child Psychology* (seventh edition). Englewood Cliffs, NJ: Prentice-Hall, 1975.

McDaniel, Elsiebeth and Richards, Lawrence O. *You and Children*. Chicago: Moody Press, 1973.

Narramore, Clyde M. *How to Understand and Influence Children*. Grand Rapids, MI: Zondervan, 1957.

Odor, Ruth. *Help! I've Got Problems!* Cincinnati: Standard Publishing, 1978.

Ramier, Phyllis, and Iverson, Gary. "A Teacher's Case Book: Juniors." *Teach* 13 (Spring 1972), p. 39.

Soderholm, Marjorie. *Explaining Salvation to Children* (Seventh edition). Minneapolis: Free Church Publications, 1968.

_____. *The Junior: A Handbook for the Sunday School Teacher*. Reprint. Grand Rapids, MI: Baker, 1968.

_____. *Salvation, Then What*. Minneapolis: Free Church Publications, 1968.

_____. "Teaching Junior Children," in *An Introduction to Evangelical Christian Education*. (J. Edward Hakes, ed.) Chicago: Moody Press, 1964.

Taylor, Kenneth N. *Almost Twelve*. Wheaton, IL: Tyndale, 1968.

Wonderly, Gustavia M. *Training Children*. Lincoln, NE: Back to the Bible Broadcast, Box 65801, Lincoln, NE 82808.

Zuck, Roy B., and Clark, Robert E. *Childhood Education in the Church*. Chicago: Moody Press, 1975.

Adolescents

Aultman, Donald. *Building Youth*. Cleveland, TN: Pathway Press, 1965.

_____. *Guiding Youth*. Cleveland, TN: Pathway Press, 1965.

Benson, Dennis. *The Now Generation*. Richmond, VA: John Knox Press, 1969.

Briscoe, Stuart. *Where Was the Church When the Youth Exploded?* Grand Rapids, MI: Zondervan, 1972.

Bueltmann, A. J. *Teen-Agers Need Parents*. St. Louis: Concordia, 1957.

Duval, Evelyn Mills. *Today's Teen-Agers*. New York: Association Press, 1966.

Ginott, Dr. Haim G. *Between Parent and Teen-ager*. New York: Macmillan, 1969.

Graham, Billy. *Talks to Teenagers*. Grand Rapids, MI: Zondervan, 1958.

Hechinger, Grace and Fred. *Teenage Tyranny*. New York: Morrow, 1963.

Johnson, Mel. *Tips for Teens*. Chicago: Moody Press, 1973.

Joiner, Verna. *What Teens Say*. Anderson, IN: Warner Press, 1965.

Kesler, Jay. *Let's Succeed With Our Teenagers*. Nashville: Broadman, 1965.

Koonce, J. Vernon. *Understanding Your Teenagers*. Elgin, IL: David C. Cook.

McPhee, Norma. *Discussion Programs for Junior Highs*. Grand Rapids, MI: Zondervan, 1974.

Mobley, Ron. *Help! I've Got Problems!* Cincinnati: Standard Publishing, 1979.

Reemer, H. H., and Radler, D. H. *The American Teenager*. New York: Bobbs-Merrill Co., 1967.

Richards, Lawrence O. *You and Youth*. Chicago: Moody Press, 1973.

_____. *Youth Ministry*. Grand Rapids, MI: Zondervan, 1972.

Roberts, Dorothy M. *How to Work With Teen-Age Groups*. New York: Associated Press.

Snyder, Ross. *Young People and Their Culture*. New York: Abingdon, 1969.

Towns, Elmer, *Successful Biblical Youth Work*. Glendale, CA: Gospel Light, 1973.

Wilkens, William H. R. *The Youth Years*. Valley Forge, PA: Judson Press, 1967.

Zuck, Roy B., and Getz, Gene. *Christian Youth, An In-Depth Study*. Chicago: Moody Press.

Additional Sources (General)

ACT (Association for Church Teachers), newsletter and magazine, 219 Sandy Bank Road, Media, PA 19063. ($7.00 each for 10 or more; $5.50 for 15 or more; $4.50 for 25 or more. Membership includes both service with discount.)

Brethren House. 6301-29 56th Avenue N., St. Petersburg, FL 33709. (Provides newsletter with creative ideas and resources for learning sources.)

Learning—The Magazine for Creative Teaching. 1255 Portland Pl., Boulder, CO 80302 ($12.00 per year)

NICE (Notes of Interest to Church Educators), Shirley Jennings, 955 Fillmore Ave., Ogden, UT 84404. ($5.00 per year. Lists and describes articles of interest and provides the source. Published monthly except July and August.)

Teacher's Swap Shop. Published monthly for an offering, renew in January. Sacred Literature Ministries, Box 777, Taylors, SC 29687.

Teaching Babies and Toddlers. Nashville, Broadman Films, Color, 45 frames. With record. Rental charge.

Gifted Children

Brunner, Jerome S. The Process of Education. Cambridge, MA: Harvard University, 1960.

Dunn, Lloyd M., et al. (eds.) Exceptional Children in the Schools. New York: Holt, Rinehart, and Winston, 1963.

Fleigler, Louis A. (ed.) Curriculum Planning for the Gifted. Englewood Cliffs, NJ: Prentice-Hall, 1961.

Freehill, Maurice F. Gifted Children: Their Psychology and Education. New York: Macmillan, 1961.

Gowan, John C., and Demos, George D. The Education and Guidance of the Ablest. Springfield, IL: Thomas, 1964.

Hill, Mary Broderick. Enrichment Programs for Intellectually Gifted Pupils. California Project Talent, Publication No. 4, Sacramento, CA: California State Department of Education, 1969.

Hillingsworth, Leta. Children Above 180 IQ. New York: Harcourt, Brace and World, 1942.

Kemp, Charles F. Church: The Gifted and Retarded Pupils. St. Louis: Bethany, 1958.

Martinson, Ruth A. Special Programs for Gifted Pupils. California State Dept. of Education bulletin, Vol. 31, No. 1, January, 1962. Sacramento, CA: California State Department of Education, 1962.

Piaget, Jean. *Language and Thought of the Child* (third edition). New York; Humanities, 1962.

Roebeck, Mildred C. *Acceleration Programs for Intellectually Gifted Pupils.* California Project Talent, Publication No. 3, Sacramento, CA: California State Department of Education, 1968.

Mentally Retarded

Agee, J. Willard. "The Minister Looks at Mental Retardation." *Pastoral Psychology* 13 (September 1962), pp. 12-22.

Bauer, Charles E. *Retarded Children Are People.* Milwaukee: Brice, 1964.

Baumgartner, Bernice. *Helping Every Trainable Mentally Retarded Child.* New York: Teachers College, 1975.

Blodgett, Harriet E. *Mentally Retarded Children: What Parents and Others Should Know.* Minneapolis: University of Minnesota, 1971.

Bogardus, LaDonna. *Christian Education for Retarded Persons* (revised edition). Nashville: Abingdon, 1969.

_____. *Christian Education for Retarded Children and Youth.* Nashville: Abingdon, 1963.

Buck, Pearl S. *The Gifts They Bring.* New York: Day, 1965.

Carlson, Bernice, W., and Ginglend, David R. *Play Activities for the Retarded Child.* Nashville: Abingdon, 1961.

Carpenter, Robert D. *Why Can't I Learn.* Whittier, CA: RDC Pubs., 1972.

Doll, G. L. "Church and the Handicapped Child." *Christianity Today* 9 (February 26, 1965), pp. 15-19.

Egg, Maria. *Educating the Child Who Is Different.* New York: Day, 1968.

_____. *When a Child Is Different.* New York: Day, 1960.

French, Edward L., and Scott, J. Clifford. *Child in the Shadows: A Manual for Parents of Retarded Children.* New York: Lippincott, 1960.

Hahn, Hans R., and Raash, Werner H. *Helping the Retarded Child.* St. Louis: Bethany, 1957.

Kemp, Charles F. *The Church: The Gifted and the Retarded Child.* St. Louis: Bethany, 1957.

Monroe, Doris D. *A Church Ministry to Retarded Persons.* Nashville: Convention Press, 1972.

Organizing Religious Classes for Mentally Retarded Children. Nashville: Convention Press, 1972.

Organizing Religious Classes for Mentally Retarded Children. St. Louis: Lutheran Church (Missouri Synod).

Palmer, Charles E. *The Church and the Exceptional Person.* Nashville: Abingdon, 1961.

Perry, Natalie. *Teaching the Mentally Retarded Person* (second edition). New York: Columbia University, 1974.

Peterson, Sigurd D. *Retarded Children: God's Children.* Philadelphia: Westminster Press, 1960.

Pierson, James. *77 Dynamic Ideas for the Christian Education of the Handicapped.* Cincinnati: Standard Publishing, 1977.

Sieving, Hilmar A. (ed.) *The Exceptional Child and the Christian Community.* River Forest, IL: Lutheran Educational Association, 1960.

Films (black and white):

Mentally Retarded: Trainable. Audio-Visual Center, Indiana University, Bloomington, IN 47401. 29 minutes.

New Experience for Mentally Retarded Children. Film Production Service. Virginia Department of Education, Richmond, VA, 23216. 31 minutes.

Lesson Materials:

Abingdon Press. 201 Eighth Ave., S., Nashville, TN 37202.

Concordia Publishing House. 3558 S. Jefferson Ave., St. Louis, MO 63118.

John Knox Press. 341 Ponce De Leon Ave., N.E., Rm. 416, Atlanta, GA 30308

Milwaukee County Association for Retarded Children. 1426 West State St., Milwaukee, WI 53233.

Shepherds, Inc. P.O. Box 1261, Union Grove, WI 53182.

Sunday School Board. Southern Baptist Convention. 127 Ninth Ave., N., Nashville, TN 37203.

Other Sources:

Association for Childhood Education International. 3615 Wisconsin Avenue, N.E., Washington, D.C. 20016.

Canadian Association for Retarded Children. 4700 Keele St., Downsview, Ontario.

Child Study Association of America. 9 E. 89th St., New York, NY 10028.

National Association for Retarded Children, 910 17th St., N.W., Washington, D.C. 20006.

Public Affairs Pamphets. 22 E. 38th St., New York, NY 10016.
U.S. Department of Health, Education, and Welfare. Washington, D.C. 20025.

Visually Limited

Baker, Harry. *Introduction to Exceptional Children.* Detroit: Macmillan, 1950.
Bishop, Virginia E. *Teaching the Visually Limited Child.* Springfield, IL: Thomas, 1978.
Jones, Reginald L. *New Direction in Special Education.* Boston: Allyn and Bacon, 1970.
Kerby, C.E. "Cause of Blindness in Children of School Age." *The Sight-Saving Review* 28 (Spring 1958), pp. 10-21.
Kirk, Samuel A. *Educating Exceptional Children.* Boston: Houghton-Mifflin, 1962.

Speech Handicapped

Johnson, Wendel, Brown, Spencer J., Curtis, James F., Ednery, Clarence, and Keaster, Jacqueline. *Speech Handicapped School Children* (third edition). New York: Harper and Row, 1967.
Palmer, Charles B. *Speech and Hearing Problems.* Springfield, IL: 1961.
"Speech Disorders and Speech Correction." *Journal of Speech and Hearing Disorders.* Vol. 17, Midcentury White House Conference, June 17, 1962.
Travis, Lee Edward. *Handbook for Speech Pathology.* New York: Appleton-Crofts, 1957.
Van Riper, Charles. *Speech Correction-Principles and Methods* (sixth edition) Englewood Cliffs, NJ: Prentice-Hall, 1978.

Deaf

Deaf and Hard of Hearing Institute, 7036 Harrison Ave., Cincinnati, OH 45239
National Association of the Deaf, 814 Thayer Ave., Silver Spring, MD 20910
Bender, Ruth. *The Conquest of Deafness.* Cleveland: Western Reserve University, 1970.

Goodhill, V. *Pathology, Diagnosis, and Therapy of Deafness.* New York: Appleton-Crofts-Century, 1959.

Myklebust, Helmer R. *The Psychology of Deafness* (second edition). New York: Grume and Stratton, 1964.

Emotionally Disturbed

Asquith, Melrose, Barton, Clifford, and Donaher, Robert. "I Have an Emotionally Disturbed Child in My Classroom." *Grade Teacher 85* (April 1968), pp. 77-78, 127.

Hewett, Frank M. *The Emotionally Disturbed Child in the Classroom.* Boston: Allyn and Bacon, 1971.

Haring, Norris G., and Phillips, E. Lakin. *Educating Emotionally Disturbed Children.* New York: McGraw-Hill, 1962.

Behavioral Disorders and Learning Disabilities

Cruickshank, William M., and Johnson, Orville. *Education of Exceptional Children and Youth* (third edition). Englewood Cliffs, NJ: Prentice-Hall, 1975.

Dunn, Lloyd M. *Exceptional Children in the Schools.* Chicago: Holt, Rinehart, and Winston, 1966.

Lerner, Janet W. *Children With Learning Disabilities* (second edition). Boston: Houghton Mifflin, 1976.

McCarthy, James J., and McCarthy, Joan F. *Learning Disabilities.* New York: Allyn and Bacon, 1969.

Myklebust, Helmer R. *Progress in Learning Disabilities.* New York: Allyn and Bacon, 1970.

Patterson, Uretha. "Children With Specific Learning Disabilities." In *Methods of Special Education,* ed. Norris G. Haring and R. L. Shiefelbusch. New York: McGraw-Hill, 1967.

Literature and Program Materials

Campus Crusade for Christ, Arrowhead Springs, San Bernardino, CA 92404

C.E.I. Publishing Company, Box 858, Athens, AL 35611

Christian Board of Publication, Box 179, St. Louis, MO (Disciples)

Christ In Youth, Inc., Box 2170, Tulsa, OK 74101

Christian Workers Service Bureau, Box 413, Redondo Beach, CA
Children's Church, Inc., P.O. Box 773, Corona, CA 91720
Concordia Publishing, 3558 S. Jefferson Ave., St. Louis, MO 63118,
    (Lutheran)
David C. Cook Publishing Co., 850 N. Grove Ave., Elgin, IL 60120
DeHoff Publications, 49 N.W. Broad St., Murfreesboro, TN 37130
Exhorter Publishers, P.O. Box 267, 1102 N. Oak, Hammond, LA 70401
Gaylord Bros., Inc., 155 Gifford, Syracuse, NY
Geneva Press, Philadelphia, PA (Presbyterian)
Gospel Light Publishing Co. (Regal Books), P.O. Box 1591, Glendale,
    CA 91205
Gospel Teachers, Box 4427, Dallas TX 75208
International Society of Christian Endeavor, 1221 E. Broad St., Colum-
    bus, OH 43216
InterVarsity Press, Box F, Downers Grove, IL 60515
Judson Press, Valley Forge, PA 19481
The Navigators, Colorado Springs, CO 80901
Pack-O-Fun, 14 Main Street, Park Ridge, IL 60068
Peak Publications, Colorado Springs, CO
Nido R. Qubein & Association, Inc., Box 5367, High Point, NC 27262
Scripture Press Publications (Selective Series) 1825 College Ave.,
    Wheaton, IL 60187
Scripture Union, 38 Garrett Road, Upper Darby, PA 19082
Seabury Press, 815 Second Ave., New York, NY 10017 (Episcopalian)
Serendipity House (Lyman Coleman), Box 7661, Colorado Springs, CO
    80933
Specialized Christian Service, 1525 Cherry, Springfield, IL 62705
Standard Publishing, 8121 Hamilton Ave., Cincinnati, OH 45231
Story-O-Graphs, Box 145M, Pasadena, CA 91102
Success With Youth, Inc., P.O. Box 27028, Tempe, AZ 85281
Sunday School Board, 127 Ninth Avenue N., Nashville, TN 37203
Sweet Publishing Company, Box 4055, Austin, TX 78765
Westminister Press (Senior High Youth Kit), Witherspoon Bldg.,
    Philadelphia, PA 19107
Word, Inc., 4800 W. Waco Dr., Waco, TX 76710
Youth Specialties (Ideas Books), 861 Sixth Ave., San Diego, CA 92101

Graded Worship/Children's Church

Alley, Steve and Cora. *Creative Dramatics for Children's Church* (two
    books). Cincinnati: Standard Publishing, 1979. Mss. and tapes also
    available from Children's Church, P.O. Box 773, Corona, CA 91720.

Daniel, Eleanor. % Midwest Christian College, Oklahoma City, OK

Doan, Eleanor L. *How to Plan and Conduct a Junior Church*. Grand Rapids, MI: Zondervan, 1954.

Gorman, Julia. *Churchtime for Juniors*. Wheaton, IL: David C. Cook, 1967.

Mobley, Ron. "Graded Worship" (Outline of options), % First Christian Church, 450 N.E. 51st St., Boca Raton, FL 33431

Richards, Lawrence O. *The Pastor and Children's Church*. Christian Education Monographs, Pastors' Series #2, Glen Ellyn, IL: Scripture Press, 1973.

Sullivan, Jessie P. *Children's Church Handbook*. Grand Rapids, MI Baker, 1970.

(See the "Literature and Program Materials" section for addresses of publishing companies, many of which handle graded worship materials.)

Vacation Bible School

Burnett, Sibley. *Better Vacation Bible Schools*. Nashville: Convention Press, 1957.

Getz, Gene A. *The Vacation Bible School in the Local Church*. Chicago: Moody Press, 1962.

Richards, Lawrence O. *The Pastor and His Vacation Bible School*. Christian Education Monographs, Pastor's Series #4, Glen Ellyn, IL: Scripture Press, 1966.

VBS—New Patterns for Growth: Nineteen Ways to Teach More Bible and Reach More People This Summer. Glendale, CA: Gospel Light, 1967.

(See "Literature and Program Materials" section for addresses of publishers, many of whom publish VBS material.)

Magazines for Youth and Youth Leaders

Campus Life, Youth for Christ International, Box 149, Wheaton, IL 60187 (For college bound: "Campus Life Guide to Colleges and Universities")

Change Magazine, 59 E. 54th Street, New York, NY 10022

Christ In Youth News, Box 2170, Tulsa, OK, 74101

The Christian Athlete, Fellowship of Christian Athletes, 812 Traders National Bank Bldg., Kansas City, MO 64106

The Christian Reader, Box 80, Wheaton, IL 60187

Christian Teen-Ager, R. B. Sweet Co., Inc., Box 4055, Austin, TX 78751

Christian Youth Today, Kansas City Baptist Temple, 2715 Swope Parkway, Kansas City, MO 64130

Collegiate Challenge & Athletes In Action, Arrowhead Springs, San Bernardino, CA 92403

Dads Only, P.O. Box 20594, San Diego, CA 92120

Face to Face, The Methodist Publishing House, 201 Eighth Avenue S., Nashville, TN 37203

Family Life Today, Gospel Light, P.O. Box 180, Glendale, CA 91209

Focus On Youth, Young Life, 720 W. Monument Street, Colorado Springs, CO 80901

GROUP Magazine (for youth groups), Box 481, Loveland, CO 80537

Have A Good Day, Tyndale, 336 Gundersen Drive, Wheaton, IL 60187

HIS Magazine, 5206 Main St., Downers Grove, IL 60515

Hollywood Free Paper, Box 1891, Hollywood, CA 90028

Mission (non-instrumental), P.O. Box 2822, Abilene, TX 79604

Living Water, Christian Evangelizers Association, Joplin, MO 64801

Motive (Methodist), P.O. Box 871, Nashville, TN 37202

RADAR (for third- through sixth-grade children), Standard Publishing, 8121 Hamilton Ave., Cincinnati, OH 45231

Straight (for teens), Standard Publishing, 8121 Hamilton Ave., Cincinnati, OH 45231

Sojourner, 1029 Vermont Avenue N.W., Washington, D.C. 20005

Sources and Resources, Youth Specialties, 861 Sixth Avenue, Suite 411, San Diego, CA 92101

Spirit and *Inter-Action Magazine*, Concordia, 3558 S. Jefferson Avenue, St. Louis, MO 63118

Tempo (National Council of Churches), P.O. Box 81, Madison Square Station, New York, NY 10010

20th Century Christian, 2809 Granny White Pike, Nashville, TN 37204

Vision, Christian Board of Publication, Box 179, St. Louis, MO 63166

Vista, British Youth for Christ, St. Mark's Church, Kennington Park Road, London, S.W. 11

The Wittenberg Door (for youth ministers), 861 Sixth Avenue, San Diego, CA 92107

Yokefellows International (Society of Friends), 230 College Avenue, Richmond, IN 47374

Youth, 1505 Race Street, Philadelphia, PA 19113

Youth Illustrated, Scripture Press, 1825 College Avenue, Wheaton, IL 60187

Youth Letter, 1716 Spruce St., Philadelphia, PA 19103

Camps and Retreats

Bechtle, Mike. *Counselor's Guidebook*. Success With Youth, Tempe, AZ, 1978.

Church *Recreation*. Dept. of Church Recreation, Southern Baptist Convention, 127 Ninth Avenue N., Nashville, TN 37203.

Christian Camping, International, Box 400, Somonauk, IL 60552.

Cowle, Irving M. *Day of Camping*. Minneapolis: Burgess Publishing Co.

Mackay, Foy. *Creative Counseling for Christian Camp*. Wheaton, IL: Scripture Press.

Nelson, Virgil and Lynn. *Retreat Handbook*. Valley Forge, PA: Judson Press, 1976.

Wright, Norman A. *Help! I'm a Camp Counselor*. Glendale, CA: Regal, 1969.

Crafts

(See special sections in religious and secular bookstores.)

American Handicrafts (Locations in major cities . . . for arts and crafts.)

Craft Shops, "Snoop Shops," Ceramic Shops, etc.

Creative Craft Ideas. Cincinnati: Standard Publishing.

Doan, Eleanor. *157 Handcrafts* and *261 Handcrafts and Fun*. Grand Rapids, MI: Zondervan.

51 Paper Craft Projects. Cincinnati: Standard Publishing.

Magnus Craft Materials, Inc. 109 Lafayette St., New York, NY 10013.

Pack-O-Fun (the only scrap-craft magazine). 14 Main Street, Park Ridge, IL 60068.

Rainbow Crafts, Inc., Cincinnati, OH 45212

Reese, Loretta E. *54 Crafts With Easy Patterns*. Cincinnati: Standard Publishing.

Self, Margaret M. (ed.) *Now What Can We Do?* Glendale, CA: Regal.

Magic

Miller, Jule L. *Spiritual Applications for Tarbell I*. MAGISSIONS, Gospel Services, Inc., Houston, TX.

Tarbell, Dr. Harlan. *Tarbell Course in Magic, Vol. I*. New York: Louis Tanner, Publisher, 1540 Broadway 10036.

Recreation and Socials

American Association for Health, Physical Education and Recreation, 1201 Sixteenth St., N.W., Washington, D.C. 20036.

Church Recreation Magazine. (For crafts, camping, retreats, sports, games, puppetry, drama, socials, etc.) Southern Baptist Convention, 127 Ninth Avenue N., Nashville, TN 37203.

Clark, Naomi. Party Time Game Book. Waco, TX: Word.

Games for Children. Cincinnati: Standard Publishing, 1967.

Howard, Vernon. Fun Games for Boys and Girls. Grand Rapids, MI: Zondervan, 1974.

Ideas Books. (For crowd-breakers, retreats, socials, skits, jokes, games, puppetry, drama, socials, etc.) Youth Specialties, 861 Sixth Ave., San Diego, CA 92101.

KEY to Christian Education (magazine). 8121 Hamilton Ave., Cincinnati, OH 45231.

Wackerbarth, Marjorie and Graham, Lillian S. Successful Parties and How to Give Them. Grand Rapids, MI: Baker, 1974.

Yukic, Thomas. Fundamentals of Recreation. New York: Harper and Row, 1970.

Evangelism, Shepherding Aids

American Bible Society, 1865 Broadway, New York, NY 10023

American Tract Society, Oradell, NJ 07649

Argus Communications, 3505 N. Ashland, Chicago, IL 60657

Bible Tracts, Inc., Box 508, Waterloo, IA 50704

Bradfield Tract Service, Henderson, TN 38340

Campus Crusade for Christ, Arrowhead Springs, San Bernardino, CA 92403

Christ In Youth (C.I.Y.) (Christian Church/Church of Christ) P.O. Box 2170, Tulsa, OK 74101

Christian Publications, Inc., Third & Reily, Harrisburg, PA 17105

Christian Workers Foundation, 20 N. Wacker, Chicago, IL 60606

Christian Stewardship Unified, Box 5636, Indianapolis, IN 46206 Promotion (Disciples)

Cokesbury Press (Abingdon) (Regional Service Center) (Methodist), 201 Eighth Ave., S., Nashville, TN 37202

College Press Tracts (Christian Church/Church of Christ), Box 1132, Joplin, MO 64801

Concordia House Publishers (Lutheran), Box 201, St. Louis, MO 63166

Cornerstone, 3201 Fourth Ave., S., Birmingham, AL 35222
Current, Inc., Box 2020, Colorado Springs, CO 80901
Don Gossett, Box 640, Cloverdale, BC, Canada
Equipping Christians International (Christian Church/Church of Christ), P.O. Box 294, Englewood, OH 45322
Faith, Prayer, & Tract League, 934 11th St. N.W., Grand Rapids, MI 49504
General Board of Evangelism, 1980 Grand, Nashville, TN 37203
Good News Publishers, 9825 W. Roosevelt, Westchester, IL 60153
Gospel Tract Center, P.O. Box 5135, Johannesburg, Republic of South Africa
Great Commission Publications, 7401 Old York, Philadelphia, PA 19126
Herald Press, 616 Walnut Ave., Scottsdale, PA 15683
InterVarsity Press, Box F, Downers Grove, IL 60515
Life Messengers, Box 1967, Seattle, WA 98111
Lutheran Colportage SVS., Inc., 2101 Chicago, Minneapolis, MN 55440
Norman Vincent Peale, Foundation for Christian Living, Pawling, NY 12564
Open-Church Foundation, 58 Middle Street, Gloucester, MA 01930
Peak Publications, Box 1210, Colorado Springs, CO 80901
Perry Cotham Tracts, P.O. Box 786, Big Spring, TX 79720
Personal Christianity (C. S. Lovett), 14952 E. Pacific, Baldwin Park, CA 91706
Positive Attitude Posters, The Economic Press, Inc., 12 Daniel Road, Fairfield, NJ 07006
Robert W. Burns, 1730 Barnesdale Way, Atlanta, GA 30309
San Dalton Tracts, 1331 W. Evans, Denver, CO 80223
Sar Shalom Publications, 236 W. 72nd St., New York, NY 10023
Silver Publishing Society, 623 Pittsburgh Life Bldg., Pittsburgh, PA 15222
Standard Publishing, 8121 Hamilton Ave., Cincinnati, OH 45231
Star Bible Publications, P.O. Box 13125, Ft. Worth, TX 76118
Sunday School Board, Southern Baptist Convention, 127 Ninth Ave. N., Nashville, TN 37203
Tidings, 1908 Grand, Nashville, TN 37203
Tracts, Inc., P.O. Box 6002, Mobile, AL 36606
Tyndale House Publishers, 33 Gundersen Dr., Wheaton, IL 60187
Westminster Press, Witherspoon Bldg., Philadelphia, PA 19107

Media/Audiovisuals

Audio Visual Idea Book for Churches. Minneapolis: Augsburg Publishing House.

Barnhouse, Donald Grey. *Teaching the Word of Truth*. Grand Rapids, MI: Eerdmans, 1958.

Brian, James W; Lewis, Richard B., and Harcleroad, Fred F. *Audio Visual Instruction: Media and Methods*. New York: McGraw-Hill, 1969.

Getz, Gene A. *Audiovisual Media in Christian Education* (revised edition). Chicago: Moody Press, 1972.

Kuhns, William, and Stanley, Robert. *Exploring the Film*. Dayton, OH: Pflaum-Standard, 1969.

Roper, David. *Teaching With a Visual Punch*. Cincinnati: Standard Publishing, 1973.

Wiman, Raymond V. *Instructional Materials*. Worthington, OH: Jones Press, 1972.

Projected Visuals and Supplies

Ken Anderson Films, Box 618, Winona Lake, IN 46590 (through distributors)

Argus Communications, 7440 Natchez Avenue, Niles, IL 60448

Association Films, Inc., 866 Third Ave., New York, NY 10022

Association of Media Educators in Religion, Audio-Visual Center, University of Iowa, Iowa City, IA 52242

Audio-Brandon Films, 2512 Program Drive, Dallas, TX 75229

Audio Visual Res. Guide, 475 Riverside, New York, NY 10027

Audio Visual Services, Kent State University, Kent, OH 44240

Augsburg Films, Dept. 57 E. Main, Columbus, OH 43215 (through distribution also)

Baptist Film Centers, 317 Guthrie Street, Louisville, KY 40202 (Also Charlotte, NC, Atlanta, GA, Jackson, MS, Arlington, TN)

Cathedral Films, Box 4029, West Lake Village, CA 91359 (through distributors also)

Christian Cinema Inc., 277 Keswick, Glenside, PA 19038

Concordia Audio Visual Media, 3558 S. Jefferson Avenue, St. Louis, MO 63118 (through distributors also)

Contemporary Films, 267 West 25th Street, New York, NY 10001

Department of Audio Visual Service, 222 S. Downey, Indianapolis, IN 46207

Family Films, 14662 Lanark St., Panorama City, CA 91402 (outlets in major cities)

Films, Inc., 1144 Wilmette Ave., Wilmette, IL 60091

Gospel Films Dist., Box 8240, Orlando, FL 32806 (outlets in major cities)

Gospel Service, Box 12303, Houston, TX 77017

Ideal Pictures Co., 55 N.E. 13th Street, Miami, FL 33132

Kairos, Box 24056, Minneapolis, MN 55424

Levy's Film Service, Pullan Avenue, Cincinnati, OH 45223

Lincoln Christian College AV Dept., Box 178, Lincoln, IL 62656 (Movies, filmstrips, etc.)

Mark IV Pictures, Gateway Films, Heartland Productions (through distributors only)

Mass Media Ministries, 1720 Chocteau Avenue, St. Louis, MO 63103

McGraw-Hill Films, 327 West 41st Street, New York, NY 10036

Modern Talking Film Services (Includes Con. Bell Film Library) #9 Garfield Place, Cincinnati, OH 45202 (outlets in major cities)

Moody Press, Film Department, 150 W. Chicago Avenue, Chicago, IL 60610

Mottas Films, 1318 Ohio Avenue, Canton, OH 44705

Outreach Films, Box 1608, Burbank, CA 91507

Pyramid Films, Box 1048, Santa Monica, CA 90406

Rainbow Film Library (religious and secular), 1301 Main Street, P.O. Box 4155, Sarasota, FL 33578

Roa's Films (religious and secular), 1696 N. Astor Street, Milwaukee, WI 63202

Sermon & Pictures, P.O. Box 15499, Atlanta, GA 30333

Society for Visual Education, 1345 Diversey Parkway, Chicago, IL 60614

Spire Audio Visual Co., 24 N.W. 36th Street, Miami, FL 33127

Star Bible Publishing, Box 1325, Ft. Worth, TX 76118

St. Clement's Film Association, 423 W. 465th Street, New York, NY 10036

Swank Motion Pictures, 201 S. Jefferson, St. Louis, MO 63166 (regional outlet)

Twyman Films, 329 Salem, Dayton, OH 45401

Universal/16 (Universal City Studios), 205 Walton Street N.W., Atlanta, GA 30303 (regional outlet)

Visual Evangels Publishers, Arnold Carl Westphal, 1401 Ohio, Michigan City, IN 46360

Word & Work, 2518 Portland, Louisville, KY 40202

Major university film libraries and public libraries are excellent sources for A.V. materials, including movies, projectors, rentals, etc. (at low cost and occasionally *free!*)

Drama

Baker's Plays (listings), 100 Chauncy Street, Boston, MA 02111
Barton, Lucy. *Costuming the Biblical Play.* Boston: Walkter H. Baker Co.
Brown, Jeanette Perkins. *The Storyteller in Religious Education.* Philadelphia: United Church Press, 1951.
Contemporary Drama Service, Box 68, Downers Grove, IL 60515.
Dolman, John, Jr., and Knaub, Richard K. *The Art of Play Production* (third edition). New York: Harper and Row, 1973.
Loomis, Amy. *Drama Workshops in the Church.* New York: Council Press.
Miller, Sara Walton. *Acting Out the Truth* (and many other skits and plays). Nashville: Broadman, 1961.
Perry, Wilma D. and Perry, Earl. *Puppets Go to Church.* Grand Rapids, MI: Baker, 1976.
Plays for the Church. New York: Council Press.
Using Drama in the Church. St. Louis: Bethany Press.
"A Bibliography of Plays Suitable for Production by College Students and Young Adult Groups" by Barbara Johnson, American Baptist Board, Valley Forge, PA 19481.

Music

Sample, Mabel W. *Leading Children's Choirs.* Nashville: Broadman, 1966.
_____. *Music Making With Older Children.* Nashville: Convention Press, 1972.
Stillwell, Martha, Scroggins, Roy, Williams, Ruth, and Robinson, V. Kenneth. *Music Making With Younger Children.* Nashville: Convention Press, 1970.

Publishers:
John T. Benson, 136 Fourth Avenue N., Nashville, TN 37219
Broadman Press, 127 Ninth Avenue N., Nashville, TN 37234
Lillenas Publishing Co., Kansas City, MO 64141
Singspiration (Zondervan), 1415 Lake Dr. S.E., Grand Rapids, MI 49506

Willis Music, 7th and Race, Cincinnati, OH 45202

Word Music, P.O. Box 1790, 4800 W. Waco Drive, Waco, TX 76703
(also Lexicon, Rodeheaver, Canaanland, Sacred Songs)

Puppetry

Biinyon, Helen. *Puppetry Today*. New York: Watson Guptil Publications, Inc., 1966.

Cummings, Richard. *One Hundred and One Hand Puppets*. New York: David McKay Book Co., 1962.

Perry, Wilma P. and Perry, Earl. *Puppets Go to Church*. Grand Rapids, MI: Baker, 1976.

Puppet Pals. 100 Belhave Drive, Los Gatos, CA 95030.

Worrell, Estelle Ansley. *Be a Puppeteer: The Lively Puppet Book*. New York: McGraw-Hill, 1969.

Publicity Aids

Atlas Corp., 908 W. Hallandale Blvd., Hallandale, FL 33009

Amsterdam Company, Amsterdam, NY 12010

Bill-A-Pak, 2900 Aldrich Ave., S., Minneapolis, MN 55408

Church Extension Service, P.O. Box 552, Golden, CO 80401

CLD Industries Inc., (National Creative Sales), 435 North Ave., New Rochelle, NY 10802

Crown National Bureau, 424 N. 3rd Street, Burlington, IA 52601

Arthur Davenport Associates, P.O. Box 18545, 13 N.W. 41st Street, Oklahoma City, OK 73118

Evangelical Enterprises Society, Box 600, Beaverlodge, Alberta (Canada)

House of Ideas, 10212 Georgibelle, Suite 400, Houston, TX 77043

Jeffco Industries, Inc., 205 Hallock, Middlesex, NY 08346

Ministry of Ideas, P.O. Box 24666, Dallas, TX, 75224

One Way Products, P.O. Box 1177, Joplin, MO 64801

Promotions With Results, P.O. Box 37252, Cincinnati, OH 45237

The Stationary House, Inc., Box 1393, Hagerstown, MD 21740

Transparent Industrial Envelopes, Inc., N. Washington St., Brownsville, TN 38012

20th Century Plastics, P.O. 15715, Philadelphia, PA 19103

U.S. Pencil & Stationary Co. (USCO), 21 Henderson Drive, West Caldwell, NJ 07006

V.I.P. Suppliers, 5006 Vineland Ave., N. Hollywood, CA 91601 (School Supplier. Reduced/School/Institutional prices for all supplies. Pens, pencils, markers, glue, overhead projection supplies, crayons, scissors, tape of all kinds, first aid kits for church and bus, etc.)

Westenberg, Robert W., 565 River Bluff Road, Elgin, IL 60120

Index

Scripture Index